Dreamweaver Developer's Instant Troubleshooter

Rachel Andrew

Gareth Downes-Powell

Nancy Gill

Kevin Marshall

Drew McLellan

Apress™

Dreamweaver Developer's Instant Troubleshooter

ISBN 978-1-59059-233-5   ISBN 978-1-4302-0806-8 (eBook)
DOI 10.1007/978-1-4302-0806-8

Trademarked names may appear in this book. Rather than use a trademark symbol with every occurrence of a trademarked name, we use the names only in an editorial fashion and to the benefit of the trademark owner, with no intention of infringement of the trademark.

The Dreamweaver MX logo is a trademark of Macromedia, Inc. and is used with permission.

Credits

About the Authors

Solve Dreamweaver's most frequent problems with the help of renowned professionals.

Rachel Andrew

Rachel Andrew runs her own web solutions company in the UK, *edgeofmyseat.com*, the company web site also being home to various "web standards"-focused articles and Dreamweaver extensions. Rachel is a member of the Web Standards Project on the Dreamweaver Task Force, and hopes to encourage best practices in the support and use of W3C Standards in Dreamweaver.

When not writing code, or writing about writing code, Rachel spends time with her daughter, tries to encourage people to use Debian GNU/Linux, studies with the Open University, and enjoys a nice pint of beer.

Thanks must go to everyone at glasshaus for making the process of working on this book enjoyable; to Drew McLellan for his constant love and support; and to my daughter Bethany, who thinks that all mummies are permanently attached to a computer.
Thank you.

Gareth Downes-Powell

Gareth has been working in the computer industry for the last 12 years, primarily building and repairing PCs, and writing custom database applications. He branched out onto the Internet 6 years ago, and started creating web sites and applications. This is now his main area of expertise, and he specializes in writing custom PHP sites and applications, utilizing MySQL back-end databases.

Gareth is a partner in Buzz inet, *http://www.buzzinet.co.uk*, an Internet company specializing in business solutions, and offering professional web design and hosting services. Through his work he uses a wide range of Macromedia products, from Dreamweaver MX through to Flash MX and Director for custom Internet and multimedia applications.

Recently he started *http://www.dreamweavermxsupport.com/* as a way of providing support for the whole Macromedia Dreamweaver MX community, and he regularly adds new tutorials and guides to this rapidly expanding site, as well as extensions such as the PHP Login Suite for Dreamweaver MX.

Gareth enjoys keeping up with the latest developments, and he has been providing support to many users to help them use Dreamweaver MX with PHP. He actively promotes Linux servers running PHP and the MySQL Database System, and has now cowritten a number of books, and has contributed articles to a number of magazines on a freelance basis.

Thanks to all the staff at glasshaus for their help in creating this book.

Nancy Gill

Nancy Gill is the owner of Web Wish Productions, a web design business she founded in 1996 after being turned on to the Internet at a seminar designed to get customers interested in a mass mall. Web Wish Productions targets mostly small- to mid-sized businesses and has worked with companies in every field from agriculture to entertainment and media. Currently, about 90% of the company's business consists of data-driven sites.

After hand-coding in Notepad for nearly 3 years, Nancy discovered Macromedia and Dreamweaver in 1999 and never looked back. She became involved in the Macromedia forums in late 2000 and has been a member of Team Macromedia since December of 2001. Nancy has also participated in a number of beta programs for Macromedia over the past year and is excited about the new MX line of products.

Kevin Marshall

Kevin Marshall lives in Perth, Scotland. He is a senior programmer with WebXeL.com Ltd and is also IT manager with Spectraglass Ltd; both companies are based in Perth, Scotland. He has been involved in computer programming since 1990, web-based programming using ASP since 1997, and has been building ASP.NET applications since ASP.NET Beta 2 was released in 2001.

He has been an avid Dreamweaver user since version 1 was launched and with the release of MX has moved into developing extensions. WebXeL.com Ltd launched a new web site in November 2002 dedicated to the development of free and commercial Dreamweaver MX extensions for ASP.NET. The site can be found at *http://www.webxel-dw.co.uk*.

Kevin is also a regular contributor to the Macromedia newsgroups, providing advice and assistance to other Dreamweaver users.

I would like to thank my wife, Abby, and my parents, Elliott and Patricia, for their continued support. I would also like to thank Lawrence McNamara of WebXel.com Ltd.

Drew McLellan

Drew McLellan has been involved in web design and development since 1996. Starting originally as a hand-coder, Drew quickly saw the great productivity benefits that could be brought by a Visual Editor with the arrival of Dreamweaver 1.2. Since then, Drew has been pushing the boundaries of Dreamweaver through its solid HTML-based methodology and powerful extensible architecture.

With literally tens of thousands of his Dreamweaver Extensions in use around the globe, Drew has established a firm seating within the center of the online Dreamweaver community and can be found on a daily basis teaching and aiding fellow developers in Macromedia's news forums. Drew's online tutorials from his DreamweaverFever.com web site are recognized as one of the more valuable Dreamweaver resources available, due to their clear and nonassuming use of language.

Drew also helps out at the Web Standards Project *(http://www.webstandards.org/)* as a Dreamweaver expert, focusing on the issues surrounding web standards in Macromedia's flagship HTML editor.

As a Team Macromedia volunteer, Drew is a committed Dreamweaver user and enjoys nothing more than being able to share his knowledge and experience of the product with fellow developers. Drew has a wide knowledge of both web design and development, and is currently working for a design, marketing, and IT agency in London, UK.

Table of Contents

Introduction   1

Chapter 1: Setting Up Site Definitions   5

Before You Start 6

Basic Site Definition..6

Basic HTML Site..7

Dynamic Site 8

Advanced Site Definition 11

Local Info 11

Remote Info 11

Testing Server..12

Cloaking 13

Design Notes 13

Site Map Layout 14

File View Columns 14

Contribute 15

The Edit Sites Window **15**

Bringing It All Together 15

Top Questions..**16**

Summary **18**

Chapter 2: Databases and Connections   **21**

Understanding Databases **21**

Choosing a Database...**22**

Microsoft Access 22

SQL Server..23

Oracle 23

PostgreSQL 24

Other Databases 24

Designing Your Database..**25**

An Example Database 25

Creating the Connection **27**

ASP...27

ASP.NET 30

ColdFusion 31

Getting Data from the Database **32**

Frequently Asked Questions..**34**

Summary **35**

Chapter 3: Setting Up IIS for HTML, ASP, or PHP   **37**

Installing and Setting Up IIS **37**

Checking the Installation 39

Administering a Basic Web Site 40

Checking That Web Pages Are Being Served Correctly 42

Troubleshooting IIS Install Problems 44

Installing PHP for IIS **45**

Downloading PHP 45

Installing PHP 46

Adding PHP to IIS 48

Testing PHP Pages...52

Installing PHP Extensions 53

Troubleshooting PHP 54

Summary **56**

Chapter 4: Apache and Windows   **59**

Apache...**59**

Which Version of Apache? 60

Security..60

Downloading Apache 61

Installing Apache 61

Apache's Configuration Files 65

Checking the Apache Installation 68

Troubleshooting Guide 69

Apache Modules...70

Installing PHP with Apache on Windows...**70**

Downloading PHP 70

Installing PHP 71

Configuring Apache for PHP 72

Configuring PHP..73

Restarting Apache 75

Testing Apache and PHP 76

Troubleshooting a PHP Installation...77

PHP Extensions 77

Summary **78**

Chapter 5: Apache and PHP Setup on Linux   **81**

Linux **82**

Recommended Software **82**

Telnet 83

Samba 84

Firewall 85

The Apache Web Server **85**

Downloading Apache 85

Installing Apache 86

Configuring Apache 91

Controlling the Apache Server 93

Testing Apache 94

Troubleshooting the Apache Installation...95

Apache Modules..96

Installing PHP into Apache **96**

Downloading PHP 96

Extracting the PHP File 97

Compiling PHP and Configuring Apache 99

Configuring Apache 100

Configuring PHP..102

Restarting Apache 104

Testing Apache and PHP 105

Troubleshooting the PHP Installation 106

Summary **107**

Chapter 6: MySQL Setup   109

Installing MySQL on Windows 110
Downloading MySQL 110
Installing MySQL 110
Starting the MySQL Server 112

Installing MySQL on Linux 113
Downloading MySQL 113
Installing MySQL 114
Starting and Stopping the MySQL Server 116
MySQL File Locations 117

MySQL Server Setup and Configuration 118
Setting the MySQL Root Password 119
Working with MySQL 119
Working with Users...122

Frequently Asked Questions..130
Summary 138

Chapter 7: CSS   141

Why Use CSS for Text Styling Instead of <font> Tags? 141
Separating Document Structure from Presentation 141

CSS Tools in Dreamweaver MX..146
Preferences 146
The CSS Styles Panel 147
The Properties Inspector 148

Frequently Asked Questions..148
Summary 161

Chapter 8: Templates 163

How Templates Work 163
Locked Regions 163
Editable Regions 164
Advantages and Disadvantages of Templates 164

Creating a Basic Template Page 164
Adding Template Features 165
Editable Regions 166

Creating a Template for Dynamic Pages 174

Frequently Asked Questions...175

Summary 177

Chapter 9: Web Standards 179

Who Sets the Standards? 179

Does It Take Longer to Work with the Standards? 180

Why Should I Work with the Standards? 180
Future-Proofing...180
Accessibility 181
Ease of Debugging...181
Working As a Team 182

Creating Standards-Compliant Documents in Dreamweaver MX 182
HTML or XHTML? 182
What Is a DOCTYPE? 186

How Can I Convert an HTML Document to XHTML? 191

How Can I Check That My Document Is Standards-Compliant? 192
Validating Within Dreamweaver 192
Validating At the W3C Web Site..193

Validating Dynamic Pages 194

Structured Markup 194

Frequently Asked Questions...197

Summary 199

Chapter 10: Creating Flexible Layouts   **201**

Sizing Up the Problem 201

The Trouble with Resolution 202

Why Should the Layout Stretch? 204

Considerations 205

Building a Stretchable Page 209

Styling the Banner 211

Styling the Navigation...211

Styling the Content 212

Frequently Asked Questions...213

Summary 214

Chapter 11: Top PHP Questions   **217**

Why Don't Session Variables Work? 217

How Do I Check That Session Variables Are Working? 218

When Do I Have to Use session_start? 220

How Do I Upload a File Through the Browser? 220

Displaying an Uploaded Image..222

How Do I Get a List of Files in a Directory? 222

E-mail...223

How Do I Send an E-mail As HTML?..223

How Do I Send a Newsletter with PHP? 224

How Do I Stop a Script After Timing Out When Sending Many E-mails? 225

Date and Time Problems 226

How Do I Read the Date or Time from the Server? 226

How Do I Convert a Date to and from MySQL Format? 226

How Do I Find the Length of Time Between Two Dates? 228

How Do I Find a Date, x Days/Months/Years in the Past or Future? 228

Common PHP Errors 229

Parse Errors 229

Undefined Index or Variable 230

Headers Already Sent Errors 231

How Do I Force a File to Download Rather Than Open? 232

How Do I Find the Dimensions of an Image? 233

How Do I Create a Random Password? 234

Summary 235

Chapter 12: Top ASP Questions   **237**

How Do I Connect to a Database Without a DSN? 237

So What's a Connection String? 238

How Do I Modify My Connection? 239

How Do I Preserve Line Breaks from a Textarea? 240

Can I Prevent Offensive Language from Being Displayed? 241

How Can I Remember a Visitor's Name? 242

How Do I Create Tables with Striped Rows? 244

How Do I Group Data by Its Headings? 246

Sorting the Data 246

How Do I E-mail the Results of My Form?..**248**

Setting Up the Form 249

Creating the E-mail...250

Summary **252**

Chapter 13: Top ASP.NET Questions   **255**

How Do I Install the .NET Framework? **255**

What Version Should I Install? 256

What Are the System Requirements? 256

How Can I Fix a Broken .NET Framework Installation?...........................257

What Does the Error "Access is Denied 'some.dll'" Mean? 257

What Is a Server Control? **258**

What's the Difference Between Web Controls and HTML Controls? 259

What Is a User Control?...260

Why Does Dreamweaver MX Sometimes Fail to Render Server Controls? 260

How Do I Edit a Server Control's Tag After It Has Been Inserted? 261

What Is Code-Behind? **263**

Compiled Assemblies 263

Direct Link to the Code-Behind File 263

Naming Your Code-Behind File 263

What's web.config? **264**

How Do I Make My Site Use Its Own bin Folder? **264**

Can I Use Dreamweaver MX and Visual Studio .NET Together? **266**

What Process Do I Use? 267

What Are PostBack and ViewState?...**268**

Why Must Some Server Controls Be Placed Within a Form? 269

Events? A Page's Life Cycle? What's That About?.....................................270

The Life Cycle of a Page 270

Events..271

When Do I Use <%# %> Instead of <%= %>? 272

**Why Does the Selected Item of a DropDownList or ListBox
Get Lost on a PostBack?**...273

How Can I Insert an Item into a Data-Bound DropDownList or ListBox? 275

How Do I Programmatically Select an Item in a DropDownList or ListBox? 276

What's the Difference Between an MM:DataSet and a True DataSet? 278

Summary 279

Index   **281**

Introduction

Dreamweaver MX is a complex tool. With its new features for building web sites with server-side scripting, standards-compliant code, advanced template features, and Cascading Style Sheets, it can hold many traps for the unwary. Sometimes you'll end up with problems you just can't find answers for.

This book is here to help you find those answers. Rather than focusing on the basics of the interface, this book deals with the problems encountered with the more complex parts of the program. So whether you're having difficulty setting up IIS to test your PHP pages or you have a flexible layout quandary that you just can't get your head around, this is the book for you.

Each chapter focuses on a particular area of Dreamweaver MX development, looking at the common problems and providing solutions. It's written by people who are members of Team Macromedia or use Dreamweaver every day, so they know which problems come up regularly and, more important, how to solve them.

Who Is This Book For?

This book is for the experienced Dreamweaver user who has come up against problems when experimenting with the new features available in MX. If you know everything about client-side development and HTML, but not much about PHP, ASP, and ASP.NET, then this book will help you set up a development environment. If you're mystified by templates, CSS, and web standards, then this book will enlighten you.

What's Inside?

Each chapter focuses on a particular problem area:

- **Chapter 1** looks at site definitions and the important steps to follow when creating them.

- **Chapter 2** covers databases and the problems you may encounter with them in ASP, ASP.NET, and ColdFusion.

- **Chapter 3** teaches you how to set up Microsoft Internet Information Services (IIS) on your own PC, so that you can test ASP or PHP pages on your own machine.

- **Chapter 4** looks at installing Apache, a free open source web server, on Windows and configuring PHP to work with it.

- **Chapter 5** details how to install Apache on the Linux OS as a test machine for PHP.

- **Chapter 6** shows you how to install MySQL and covers typical problems you may have when connecting to the database with Dreamweaver MX.

- **Chapter 7** introduces the CSS tools in Dreamweaver and suggests solutions to problems like Netscape 4 compatibility and styling forms.

- **Chapter 8** details the new template features in Dreamweaver MX.

- **Chapter 9** is about web standards, why you should use them, and how to do so in Dreamweaver MX.

- **Chapter 10** shows you how to build flexible layouts with CSS—pages that stretch to fill a browser window.

- **Chapter 11** focuses on the most common PHP development problems, from sending e-mail to uploading files.

- **Chapter 12** helps you with some common ASP problems, including DSN-less connections and cookies.

- **Chapter 13** is full of advice for the ASP.NET user, including server controls, code-behind, and the page life cycle.

What Do You Need to Begin?

A copy of Dreamweaver MX is essential for all chapters. Some chapters may require you to download installation files from the Web, so a fast Internet connection would be helpful.

Support/Feedback

If you spot an error, please let us know about it by submitting it on this book's page at *http://www.apress.com*.

Web Support

You'll want to go and visit our web site, at *http://www.apress.com*. It features a freely downloadable compressed version of the full code for this book, in both .sit and .zip formats, for Mac and Windows users. You can also find details of all our other published books, author interviews, and more.

1

In this Chapter

- Site Definition in Dreamweaver MX
- Cloaking, design notes, and the site map

Author: Nancy Gill

Setting Up Site Definitions

The vital first step in starting a new web site with Dreamweaver MX is setting up the site definition. This will determine where the program looks for local files, remote files, and testing server files. It gives the program the information it needs to put all those files together as an orderly web site. If this information is wrong, the ability of Dreamweaver MX to function is crippled, and you won't be able to complete the dynamic connections and functionality you need to be successful.

With the advent of Dreamweaver MX, users have a choice when setting up site definitions. What users of Dreamweaver 4 and UltraDev 4 saw as the *Site Definition* window is now the *Advanced* tab of the *Site Definition* window in Dreamweaver MX. It looks much the same as in the older versions with the exception of expanded features such as cloaking and the new Contribute features introduced in the 6.1 updater (for more information on this, see *http://www.macromedia.com/ software/dreamweaver/special/updater/*).

New in Dreamweaver MX, however, is the basic *Site Definition* window for novice users. The wizard-like interface found in that window is much like what users of Microsoft products have grown accustomed to. Simple questions are asked and the answers to those questions form the site definition. In this chapter, we will take a look first at the Basic Window and then move through the tabs of the Advanced window to see how it fits together to provide the vital information needed by Dreamweaver MX. Think of the site definition as the glue that holds the files and folders together to organize them into a functioning web site.

Think of the site definition as the glue that holds the files and folders together to organize them into a functioning web site

Before You Start

When starting a new web site, it's best to set aside a little time to plan and organize your site before you even begin to design. Start by creating a folder on the computer within which to store your files. This folder will hold the folders of the local site. You have probably been given an array of files, pictures, and other media and data from which to work. We like to keep those separate from the working site so we create a subfolder in the local site folder that called `Documents`. Into that folder, we place all the information received from the client, including e-mail correspondence, Word documents, and images. That way, everything received is kept separately from the working copies and can be reaccessed in its original form, if needed.

The second subfolder we create is called `Design` and is used for the artistic design of the site before any documents are actually created in Dreamweaver MX. There are various ways of creating the look you want, but for us, every site starts in an art program with layers, such as Fireworks MX. Layers allow you to move design elements around freely until the right look is achieved. All Fireworks and similar files are saved in this folder, which will also not be a part of the online web site. When we have the look we want, we can quickly create slices, buttons, and other elements in Fireworks and export the document to Dreamweaver MX. Then we're ready to build the site.

Basic Site Definition

The first step is to access the *Site* window. This can be done via the menu bar by selecting *Site > New Site* or from the *Files* panel at the side of the screen by accessing the *Site* tab, clicking the *Site* button, and selecting *New Site* from the drop-down list. In the *Site Definition* dialog box there are two choices, *Basic* or *Advanced*. Let's select the *Basic* tab for now.

This option will ask you, one question at a time, for the information the program needs to complete the site definition. The first screen asks you to supply a name for your site. Fill in that text box and click *Next*.

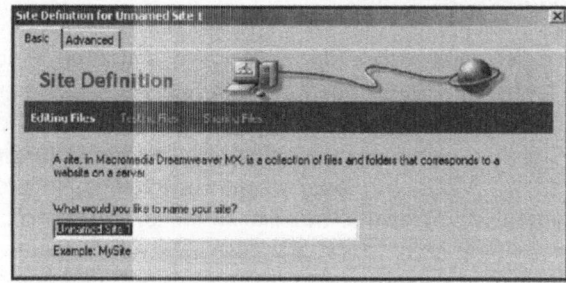

The next screen asks if you want to use a dynamic server technology or not. This will determine whether your site will be static (using HTML only) or dynamic (using ASP, PHP, ASP.NET, etc.). For this example, assume that you're making an HTML site so answer *no* to this question. We'll cover dynamic sites in a moment.

Basic HTML Site

In the next screen, you're asked a few questions about when you would like to publish the site. Those options are a little confusing, so let's look at them one at a time. If you edit local copies on your machine, then upload to the server when ready, you'll be able to work with the files where they sit and publish them to the Web all at one time. This is recommended for a static site, because static pages can be viewed using only a browser, so no special server is needed on the machine, making it easy to see how the pages will look even without publishing.

 Those options are a little confusing, so let's look at them one at a time.

The second choice, to edit directly on the server using a local network connection, isn't as efficient because you are still viewing the pages locally, but you have to go through the process of local FTP, and that is just not necessary with a static site.

The third option, to edit directly on the server using FTP or RDS, is the least recommended option because you would have to transfer each page via FTP before editing and you would have to retrieve each page from the server just to view it, which is very time consuming.

Under these options, there's a box asking you where on your computer you wish to store your files. In most cases, this will already be filled in with the folder you chose at the beginning. If it is different, simply click on the little folder to the right of the box, navigate to the correct folder, and click *Next*.

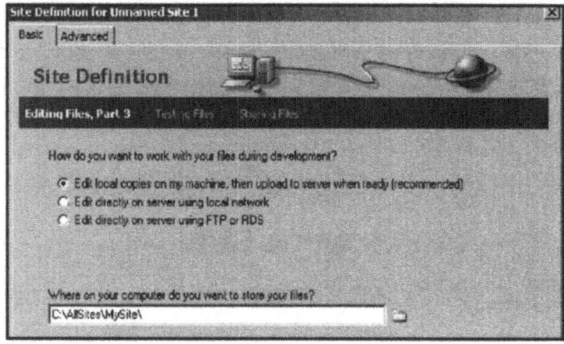

The next screen asks how you wish to connect to the server. You have a choice of *None*, *FTP*, *Local Network*, *SourceSafe Database*, or *WebDAV*. Each choice presents a short series of other questions depending on the answer to the first question.

With a static site, it is possible to view local files without FTP involvement at all, so you could select *None* here. However, then you would need to change to FTP at transfer time, so it's easiest to just set up that information now so it's ready when you are. Select *FTP*.

First in the drop-down list of questions is the FTP address. This varies depending on the server, but it's usually something like *ftp.yoursite.com*. Some servers are set up so you enter the actual name of the site, *www.yoursite.com* into the FTP address block. Since most hosts provide you with the Internet Protocol (IP) address and that will always work, that is usually the safest address to use. An IP address looks like a series of numbers separated by periods. In the screen shot below, the IP address is *160.241.62.10*.

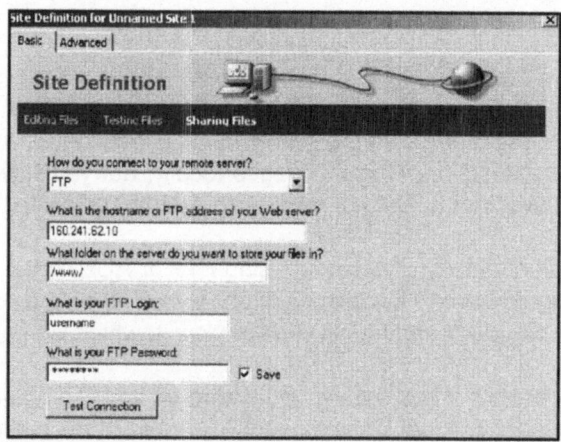

The next box asks where on the server to put your files. This location is called the host directory and this will also vary. Often, this box will be blank because access to the site is at the root of the space. In our case, our files sit in a folder on the server called www.

The last two questions asked are the FTP login or username for the site, and a password. After entering these, you can test the connection by clicking the *Test Connection* button. This will make sure that DMX can connect to the remote files based on the information you provided. If the connection is successful, you are ready to create your static site.

> *During development, it is recommended that you use a local server on your computer because you will be checking frequently in the browser to make sure the code works.*

Dynamic Site

With a dynamic site, you will need a server present for testing. This can be a local server on your computer or it can be a remote server on a host. See Chapters 3, 4, and 5 for information on setting up a server on your computer. During development, it is recommended that you use a local server on your computer because you will be checking frequently in the browser to make sure the code works.

There are several options available for a local server, and these are discussed in detail in later on in this book. Which of these servers you choose will depend in part on the server technology you have chosen for your site. For instance, PHP/MySQL works on both Apache and Internet Information Services (IIS). ColdFusion requires a ColdFusion server, which can be run on top of IIS or on the standalone CFMX server. ASP is usually run on IIS or Personal Web Server (PWS) for local development.

Returning to the *Basic Site Definition* window, you will now answer that first question with *Yes* and create a dynamic site. Selecting *Yes* opens another box that asks which server technology you would like to use. For our purposes, assume *ASP VB Script* and Internet Information Services (IIS) for development.

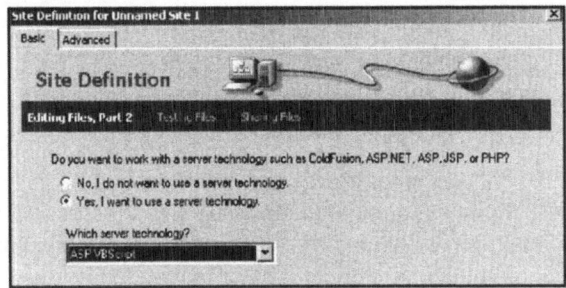

The next screen asks how you wish to work with your files. This just means you specify whether you are working on a local or remote server and when you will serve the files to the server. For our purposes, you will be using a server on your computer, so select first option. At the bottom of the screen it asks where to store the files. Again, this will be filled in if you specified a directory at the beginning. If it's not correct, simply browse to the right folder and click *OK*. Click *Next* to go to the next screen.

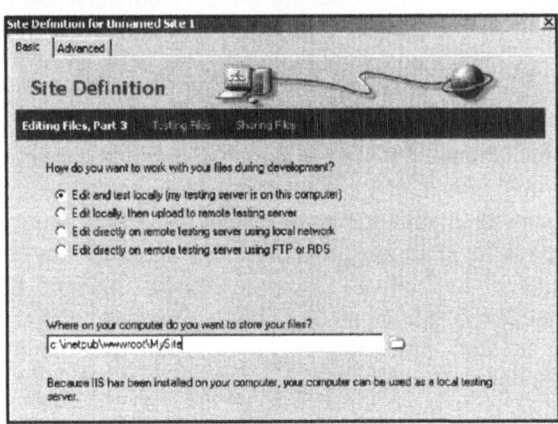

The next screen asks for the Uniform Resource Locator (URL) of the local testing site. You can test the connection by clicking the *Test URL* button and verify that the connection works. This instantly tells you whether the information you entered was correct. If not, you can correct it now. When you are satisfied with your selection, click *Next*.

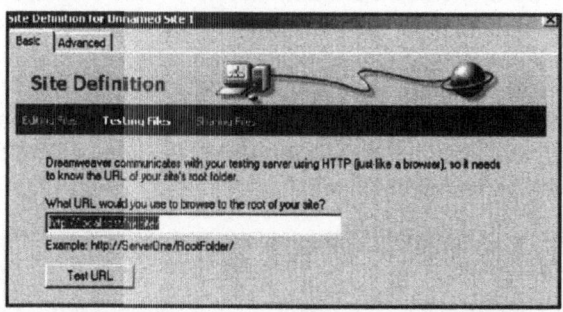

The next question asks if you want to copy it to another location for testing after editing is finished. This will be *Yes* if you are using a local machine and have two copies of the files on your computer (one under `Sites` for local editing and the second in a folder set up for the testing server) or *No* if you're building the site in a folder that the testing server will use. It will also be *Yes* if you are using a remote server for testing purposes.

If you selected *No*, you are presented with a screen that recaps the information you entered and you have the ability to use the *Advanced* tab for other setup options. This is as far as the *Basic* tab will take you, but all the information needed to define the site has been entered.

> *This is as far as the Basic tab will take us, but all the information needed to define the site has been entered.*

If you selected *Yes*, you are asked to specify the location of the testing server. You may use the drop-down box to specify if this is a local/network server, an FTP location, or some other option. You may click the file folder to find a local server location, or you can type in the URL of the remote server. Click *Next*. You are then asked if you want to enable check in and check out. This is a useful feature if there is a team of people working on the same web site (if you are working alone on the site, you will not need this option). Two people cannot access the same file at the same time if check in and check out is enabled, thus preventing someone else on the team from overwriting your changes. It also gives you name of the person who has the file checked out so you can easily contact that team member if you need to. Clicking *Next* now gives you a recap of the information you have entered and tells you that you may use the *Advanced* tab for more options.

Advanced Site Definition

The *Advanced* tab of the Site Definition window may look familiar if you have previously used either Dreamweaver 4 or UltraDev 4. However, it can be confusing to a new user, so it is recommended that novices use the *Basic* tab. Some features are only accessible using the *Advanced* tab, though. Let's step through all of the categories in the list box on the left of this window.

Some features are only accessible using the Advanced *tab.*

Setting Up Site Definitions

Local Info

The first category is *Local Info*. Start by supplying a name of the site. Click the folder next to the second text box and navigate to the local folder for that site. The next item is a check box labeled *Refresh Local File List Automatically* and it is checked by default, which means that additions or changes to the local files will be available without manual action on your part.

The next box is where you tell Dreamweaver where the images will be stored for the site. In this example, we've put them in `C:\AllSites\MySite\images`.

The next section is the HTTP address of your site. In our example, which is a local site on our computer, the address is *http://localhost/MySite*. If we were deploying the site to a remote location, we would put something like *http://www.mysite.com* in this space. That completes this category. Move to the next tab on the *Advanced* window.

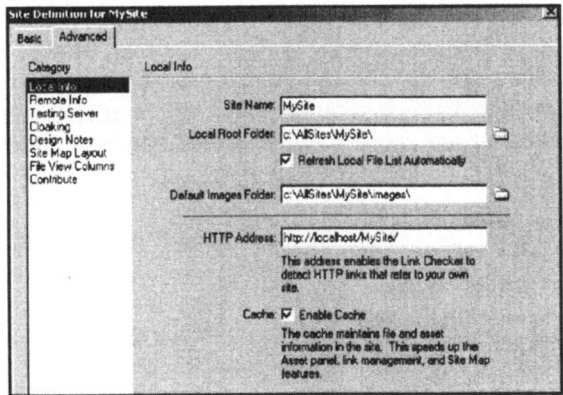

Remote Info

The *Remote Info* options are next. You are asked to specify the kind of remote access you are using. This is the information that will be used to connect to the remote server and will allow you to publish your files. In our case, we are deploying the site on a local computer so we are prompted for the filename and location of that remote folder.

This will vary depending on the server used. For this example, we're using IIS and the default path for that server, `C:\Inetpub\wwwroot\MySite`. If we were using Apache, the remote folder would most likely have been located at `C:\ApacheGroup\Apache\htdocs\MySite`.

If we were deploying the site on a remote server, the host address, host directory, username, and password information would need to be supplied. We can also select the check in and check out facility, as described in the section for the *Basic* window.

This window is crucial to successful deployment of your site on the server, so quickly double-check to make sure it's right. If the remote location is reached over FTP, Dreamweaver provides a test button so the connection can be tested to make sure everything has been entered properly. If the connection doesn't work, find the problem (probably a typo) and get it working before moving to the third category.

> *This window is crucial to successful deployment of your site on the server.*

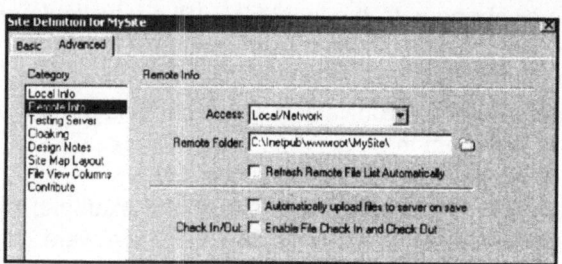

Testing Server

The next category is the *Testing Server*. Here you can specify the server model you are using and the kind of access you are using for the testing server. Notice that the dropdowns that appear after you specify the testing server are already filled in with the information you gave on the first two screens. If that information is the same for the testing server, then your work has been done. If not, you have the opportunity to fill in the correct information here.

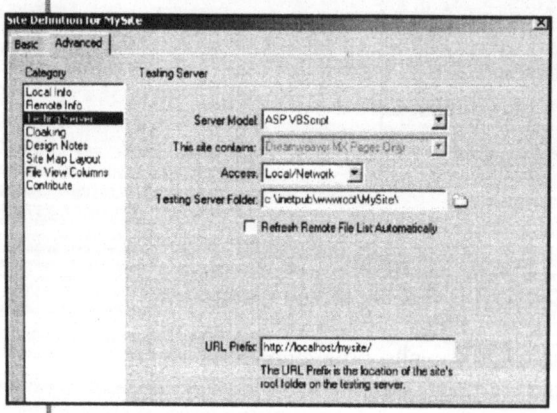

In this example, the information is going to be the same in both categories. However, usually we'll give details of a local testing server in this category, but specify our remote production server in the *Remote Info* category. It's best to get these details correct from the start, although you can go back and change them later.

> *It's best to get these details correct from the start, although you can go back and change them later.*

Cloaking

The next category is for *Cloaking*. This is not available in the *Basic* tab and is a new feature in Dreamweaver MX. Cloaking allows you to designate certain folders or file types that might be stored in the same folder as your web site files, but don't need to be uploaded to the server. You can enable cloaking for your site by checking the *Enable Cloaking* box here.

What file types might you want to cloak? We usually cloak things such as Fireworks, Flash, Photoshop, Word, or other files in the site that are for our use only and not for upload to the server. You can also cloak large multimedia folders so they are not sent to the testing server or to the remote server until the site is ready to go, which can save lots of time.

Cloaking works in two ways. You can cloak entire folders of files such as your Documents folder for client information and communication—you'll never want to send this folder to the server so cloaking it keeps it from accidentally being published. Select *Cloaking* from the *Site* menu or right-click on the folder in the *Site* window to access the cloaking option.

You can also cloak files by file type. Files such as .png for Fireworks format and .psd for Photoshop format aren't usually published to the server, and adding them to the file types on this screen will prevent accidental publishing of these files throughout the site. To add these files, check the option *Cloak Files Ending With* and fill in the file types to cloak. Enter the extensions of the file type starting with a period and put one space after each entry. There are no other characters allowed here. Do not separate entries with a comma.

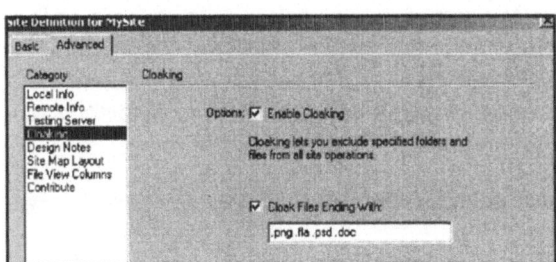

Design Notes

The next category is *Design Notes*. Design Notes let you attach notes to individual files that are shared among team members. Fireworks and Flash also use them for integration with Dreamweaver. This screen allows you to specify whether you will use Design Notes. There is a trade-off involved here that needs to be understood if you are considering leaving this option off. Design Notes take up space, but before you turn off this option, remember that Fireworks and Flash use them for Dreamweaver integration. If you lay out your site in Fireworks, for example, and then import it to Dreamweaver MX, you should leave the Design Notes enabled.

If you are working in a team, you will definitely benefit by leaving Design Notes enabled. Design Notes can be used to communicate what is going on with any page in the site. If someone wants a change or wishes to explain why he made a particular change to his portion of the site, Design Notes are an excellent way to document this communication.

You then get to choose whether or not to upload Design Notes to the server, which is only really useful if you are working as part of a team. If you are alone on a project, you will want to deselect this option, as the Notes take up server space.

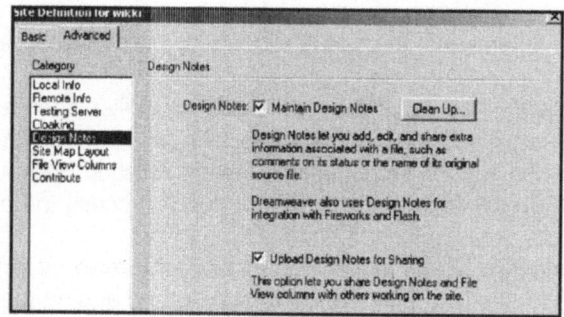

Site Map Layout

The next category is *Site Map Layout*. The Site Map is a graphical representation of the layout of the web site and is a great Dreamweaver MX tool for visualizing the site. It starts with the homepage at the top and gives an easy-to-follow picture of the entire site. The *Site Map Layout* category dialog box governs the display of the site map, and you can elect to show, hide, reorder, or change display options, such as column width. You will soon find what works best for you. You can also select whether or not to show hidden and dependent files and to display filenames or page titles on the site map.

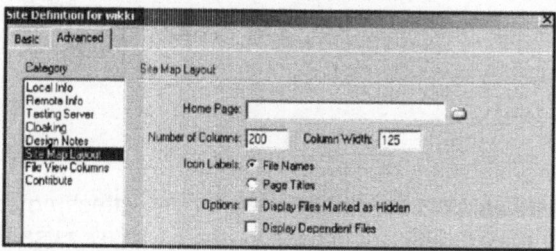

File View Columns

This category allows you to change the order of the columns, add a new column, or delete a column from the File View. The columns themselves represent properties of each file.

Contribute

The last option is available only to users of Dreamweaver MX who have the 6.1 update installed. This option allows integration of Dreamweaver MX with Macromedia Contribute, Macromedia's web page editing software.

The Edit Sites Window

The *Edit Sites* window is accessed from *Site>Edit Site* on the menu bar and displays the names of all the sites you have defined in Dreamweaver MX. From this window, you can choose *New* to create a new site as you did previously, *Edit* to edit an existing site, or *Duplicate* to create another site definition from an existing one. It should be noted here that this does not actually duplicate the files and folders of the site—only the site definition.

Dreamweaver MX also gives you the ability to export and import site definitions. This is for backup purposes—site definitions should be exported to a location other than where Dreamweaver MX resides, in case a reinstall of Dreamweaver MX is needed in the future. If you had located your backup in the same folder as the program, you would lose your backup!

It is strongly suggested that you export new site definitions as soon as you have created them. Though exporting and importing can only be done one definition at a time, it takes only a few moments to reload all of them from the backup location. It's far easier than having to retrieve all your FTP information and start over in the event of a failure. Backups of site definitions are also useful in case you are working in a team. Sending other members your site definitions for them to import into their copies of Dreamweaver MX makes working across multiple locations easy.

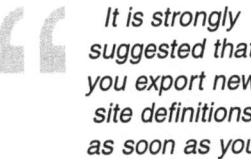

It is strongly suggested that you export new site definitions as soon as you have created them.

Bringing It All Together

Once the site definitions are set up, let's talk about how you're going to work during site development. As new documents are created, they will be saved in the Local Files folder. In the case of a dynamic site, they will be deployed to the testing server and tested throughout the development process.

Publishing to the testing server is done in the same manner as to the remote server. To make the testing server active, expand the *Site* window and click on the *Testing Server* icon at the top left. Once done, files are sent to the testing server when the *Put File(s)* (upward arrow) button in the *Site* window is clicked. Files will continue to be uploaded to this server until you either change it or close the active site. It is important to note that by default Dreamweaver will try to upload files to the remote server, so ensure that the testing server is the active server.

Once the site is finished and tested, you need to switch the active server to the remote server by clicking that server's icon at the top left of the *Site* window, and publish the files by selecting the files or folders to be published and clicking the *Put File(s)* (upward arrow) button. If you need to download files from a remote server, selecting the files in the *Remote* window and clicking the *Get File(s)* (downward arrow) button will download those files to your computer. Should files of the same name already exist, Dreamweaver will ask if they should be overwritten.

Frequently Asked Questions

I'm setting up my site on a local computer and using IIS on my computer as the testing server. The tutorials suggest creating my local files under C:\Sites\nameofsite and my testing server copy is under C:\Inetpub\ wwwroot\nameofsite. Is it necessary for me to have two copies of the files on the same computer?

During the UltraDev period, we would have recommended having two copies because there are so many files that you don't wish to publish, and it was nearly impossible to keep them sorted. Storing our local information in one location and our testing files in the testing server location allowed us to publish to the remote server from the testing server so only the files we wanted to publish were published.

However, Dreamweaver MX gave us cloaking! Therefore, it is now possible to store the main site in Inetpub\wwwroot\nameofsite, develop and test your site, and just cloak private folders before uploading to the final production server.

I set up my remote file destination, but I keep getting an error when I test it that it doesn't map to the root of the site. I double-checked the FTP address and the username and password. What could be wrong?

Often, remote hosts place your files in a secondary folder that you don't realize is there. This folder needs to be specified as the *Host Directory* on the *Remote Info* definition. If you are not sure what that is, try accessing the site through an independent FTP program such as WS_FTP. Upon accessing the site, if you are being let into the root, you will see just a / at the top of the window. If your pages are actually stored on the remote server in a subdirectory such as `/public_html` or `/htdocs`, that is the *Host Directory* that you need to specify.

When I create my dynamic site, no matter what I do, I can't get the testing server to check off in the Site box. I've checked and rechecked my site information and it's all correct. But the testing server won't check off and therefore, I can't proceed with the connection. What do I do?

There are a couple of reasons that this happens. The first thing to check is that the testing server information is correct. Going through that and clicking *OK* will sometimes get the testing server to publish the check mark. If that doesn't work, stop and restart the server. This is particularly true with the ColdFusion standalone or Apache, but it is also sometimes true with IIS. Stopping and starting the web server will often initialize the new site, allowing Dreamweaver to check off the site.

I'm the only developer on the sites I develop, so is there any reason for me to create Design Notes?

If you are the sole developer on the site, you don't need them if you don't use Fireworks or Flash. Using Dreamweaver MX all by itself without a team of developers, there is no benefit for you, and yes, they do take up room on your computer and on the server if you deploy them.

However, if you use Fireworks for laying out your document, or you created graphics with Fireworks that you might wish to edit later, or you have Flash elements on your page that you may edit later, then Design Notes are used by these programs in locating the parent document at edit time. You can, however, enable Design Notes for your use and not deploy them to the server. Then you have the best of both worlds!

Developers who work in groups or in different geographical locations on the same project will find Design Notes on the server helpful for being able to explain why changes are made and for sending workflow comments and notes to each other. Design Notes also need to be enabled if you are working with Contribute users on the site.

I am using cloaking for the first time, and I can't cloak all the files that I want to because they are in different folders. What is the solution?

There are two ways you can cloak files. One is by folder. Keeping all your client documents in one folder for your use allows you to cloak the entire folder at one time. The other way to cloak files is by file type. You can cloak everything with a .png extension (Fireworks file) or a .doc extension (Microsoft Word file) and those files will be cloaked no matter where they reside on your site. You cannot cloak a specific file, however, just the folder or the entire file type. You will usually find that one or the other of these methods (or a combination of the two) will serve your cloaking needs quite nicely.

I have my site definitions all set up, and I am using localhost for my testing server, but have a remote hosting company for my remote files. During development, I am publishing my files only on the testing server. The problem is that Dreamweaver MX wants to publish my files to the remote location and not the testing server. Do I have to use localhost for my remote connection also and then change it? Why can't I set up my actual remote information now?

Click the Expand/Collapse button, which is located at the far right of the Site panel to expand the Site window to be as wide as your screen. The button icons located at the top left of the window govern which server is used. The remote site is selected by default. You can change that by clicking the Testing Server button, thus making the testing server active, both for viewing and for publishing. Click the Expand/Collapse button again to contract the window back into the Site panel again and now your files will upload to the testing server.

I'm trying to send my files to the remote server, but Dreamweaver MX keeps telling me that it can't determine the time on the remote server. What am I doing wrong?

This usually happens if there is a difference between the owner of the directory and the person logged into the site. We have also received this message when a remote server was down, even though we were able to connect. In the first case, you should be able to perform publishing functions and synchronization normally. If the latter is true, you will have to wait for the server to be available once again.

Summary

The new interface of Dreamweaver MX makes setting up site definitions easy. Novice users can take advantage of the *Basic* tab of the *Site Definition* window, with its question-and-answer format; Dreamweaver MX will create the site definition based on their answers. More experienced users can choose the *Advanced* interface, familiar to users of Dreamweaver 4 or UltraDev, and quickly fill in the choices themselves. The *Advanced* tab of the *Site Definition* window also has several options not available under the *Basic* tab, such as cloaking and Contribute options. In this chapter, we looked at how to use both tabs in the *Site Definition* window and finished off by answering some typical site definition questions.

In this Chapter

- Understanding databases

- Creating connections

- Working in ASP, ASP.NET, and ColdFusion

Author: Nancy Gill

Databases and Connections

Part of the power of Dreamweaver MX is the ability to connect to an online database and thereby create hundreds of web pages from just a handful. If you've looked at the *Application* panel in Dreamweaver MX, you probably noticed the *Databases* and *Bindings* tabs. These two tabs are used to connect to a database and use it in Dreamweaver MX.

This chapter will give you enough understanding to be able to set up Dreamweaver MX with the most commonly used databases. In this chapter we'll focus on ASP and ColdFusion. For more information on PHP and MySQL, see Chapter 6.

Understanding Databases

The type of database used most often in web site creation is a **relational database**. Relational databases hold information in **tables**, much like those in a spreadsheet. Each table has **columns**, which define what kind of information the database can hold, and **rows**, which contain the information itself. All the tables can be related to one another, and it is these **relationships** that allow for flexibility in putting the data to efficient use.

Let's start with a clear understanding of what a relationship is. We usually think of a relationship as a particular type of connection existing between people related to or having dealings with each other. For our purposes, the connection or relationship is not between people, but between tables in a database. By way of illustration, consider a simple product catalog, an example we'll be returning to later. Our first table is `Category` and it contains categories describing the kinds of products we will display. Sample records include `books`, `art`, and `toys`. Our second table is `Products` and it contains the actual products themselves. Included in the `Products` table is a Category ID from the `Category` table that represents what we call a "foreign key" and allows us to associate each product with a category.

Let's start with a clear understanding of what a relationship is.

We will probably wish to show all our toys on one product page. If the category ID of the toys category is 3, then to select all of the toys from the `Products` table, all we have to do is select all of the products with that category ID.

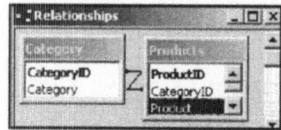

This relationship is shown visually in the preceding screen shot. Our `Category` table is on the left and contains a column of sequential `CategoryID`s and a text column for the names of the categories. The `Products` table on the right contains a sequential `ProductID` number and a text column for the name of the product, but it also includes the `CategoryID` column from the `Category` table. It is this column that enables us to join the information in the two tables together. The relationship is shown in the image by the line that connects the two tables on the common element, the `CategoryID`.

You will see this concept in practice shortly, but first we'll talk about available databases and how to choose the right one for your project.

Choosing a Database

Picking the correct database for your needs is important.

Microsoft Access

Probably the most familiar database to Dreamweaver users is Microsoft Access. It's easy to use and readily available since it comes as part of Microsoft Office. Chances are that you have it already. In addition, Access is easy to learn and makes database creation easy and fast.

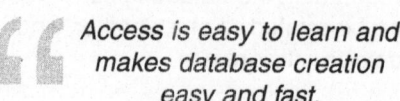

Access is easy to learn and makes database creation easy and fast.

There are a few problems, however, in using Access on a production web site. The biggest problem is that of simultaneous users. Though the documentation will tell you that Access can support 255 concurrent users, the truth of the matter is that when someone connects to the table, Access locks that portion, making more than just a few simultaneous users impossible. Access also has a history of data corruption when in use in a live situation, so you need to consider these factors carefully before choosing Access. Another consideration is the server platform you will use. Access limits you to Windows servers.

SQL Server

Access isn't the only solution available and, in fact, if you are anticipating a number of simultaneous users, you should move to a more robust database. Many choose Microsoft SQL Server because it is a powerful database and it is easy to upgrade for those who began with Access. Later versions of Access include an upsize wizard, which makes this transition easy and pretty much seamless. It is even possible through Access Projects in Access 2000 or 2002 to use SQL Server while keeping Access as the familiar front-end to work with the database. SQL Server can support many simultaneous connections, and it allows you to use stored procedures, which make it possible to execute simultaneous queries and batch updates.

SQL Server is an expensive option if you are planning to host your own server, but fortunately many hosting companies have assimilated the cost for you and you can gain use of SQL Server for an additional monthly fee. Like Access, however, SQL Server limits you to Windows servers, so we'll look at a few of the other options available and talk about how and where they will run.

Oracle

Another popular and extremely powerful database choice is Oracle. Oracle, like SQL Server, is powerful and allows for sophisticated queries and transactions. It runs well on Windows, Linux, or Sun Solaris servers. This makes Oracle a wonderful choice if your server is not Windows. In addition, Oracle works well with JSP servers while maintaining drivers that run either ColdFusion or ASP well. Oracle has download versions available at *http://www.oracle.com* for trial purposes.

DB2

The IBM equivalent of SQL Server and Oracle is DB2, another powerful, high-end database. DB2 is well integrated with IBM's WebSphere JSP server, making DB2 the number one choice if you are working with JSP and deploying on WebSphere. DB2 features a Control Center that makes creation of new databases fast and easy, and a high-level search engine that makes text searches practically painless.

DB2 runs well on most platforms, including Windows, Mac OS, Linux, Sun Solaris, and HP-UX. The commercial version is expensive, but you can obtain a developer's version and try out its features from the IBM web site at *http://www-3.ibm.com/software/data/db2/udb/downloads.html*. Be forewarned: the download is over 500MB.

2

Databases and Connections

MySQL

Gaining popularity among database developers is MySQL, the best-known open source database. Versions of MySQL are available for most any platform, making it flexible and available to everyone. MySQL in its native form, however, is difficult to learn and understand. The good news is that there are a multitude of front-end applications to make dealing with MySQL easier

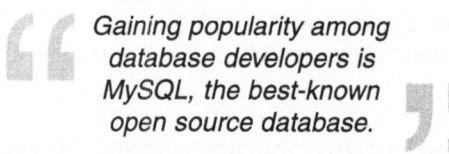

Gaining popularity among database developers is MySQL, the best-known open source database.

In many cases, MySQL is free to download and use. In some scenarios, purchase of a commercial license is necessary—check the details at *http://www.mysql.com*. Chapter 6 is dedicated to MySQL issues.

PostgreSQL

PostgreSQL has been, until recently, the little-known mysterious open source brother of MySQL. However, this rapidly evolving database is gaining in popularity, particularly for PHP sites. PostgreSQL is less limiting, has more available by way of database features, and is more powerful than MySQL. PostgreSQL runs well on a variety of platforms, including Linux and Mac OS X, and there is now a version of PostgreSQL available for Windows as well. There are a variety of mirror sites from which to download PostgreSQL. Get them at *http://www.postgresql.com/mirrors-ftp.html*.

Other Databases

Balancing these factors is important in choosing the best solution.

There are other players in the field of course—FoxPro, Paradox, dBASE, and others—but the previous listing contains the most common databases used with dynamic web sites. Consider your needs carefully when choosing the database for your application. Take into account the number of users, the size of the database, the speed with which you will need to deploy data to your users, and the cost involved. Balancing these factors is important in choosing the best solution before you start your project so that you won't waste time and money changing later.

Designing Your Database

Once you have chosen which database will work best, creating an efficient database is an art in itself. It is important that you put some planning time into what you need your database to do before constructing it so that it will be useful as you create the pages in Dreamweaver MX. When we begin a new database project, we usually sit down with a pad of paper and pen and outline what the application needs to do before we start. We make a list of what tables we think we will need, and we draw out a flowchart of how it might look to someone who was trying to make use of the application. There are programs available to help in this, such as Microsoft Visio, but a notepad works well for most purposes.

An Example Database

To aid your understanding of database design, you'll create a small database for a product catalog. You are going to use Microsoft Access for this project since, as discussed above, that database is easy to understand and use, and it's also readily available. Your product catalog will have three categories of products: books, art, and toys. Each category will have a product page listing the available products in that category, and each product listing will have a product detail page showing detail, pricing information, and a picture of the product, and giving an option to order.

Begin by opening Microsoft Access and selecting *File > New* from the menu bar. That opens up a dialog box for selecting the new item you wish to create. Select *Database* and click *OK*.

The next screen asks where you wish to store the database. The default is My Documents, but you can store your database anywhere on your computer because the database connection will tell Dreamweaver MX where to look for it. We find it easiest to store the database within the folder that we store the site in. Navigate to the folder where you will store yours, give it a name that makes sense in terms of your project, and click *Create*.

The next dialog box gives you three ways to create the first data table. You can create tables in Design View by using a wizard, or you can enter data in Datasheet View. Novice users will probably want to use the *Question and Answer Wizard* because most of the work is done for them by the application and the chance of making a mistake is less by this method. Creating your table in Datasheet View will automatically name the columns Field 1, Field 2, and so on. You have to go back and either change them in Design View or right-click on the field name and rename. We find this cumbersome and like to create our tables in Design View where we can quickly enter the name of our field and the data type and be finished.

Databases and Connections

Let's create a table using this method.

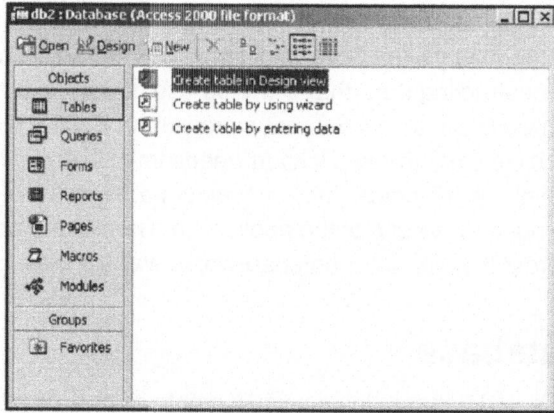

Double-click the option to *Create a Table in Design View* or click *New* at the top of the little database window and choose *Design View* from the *New Table* window that appears. Click *OK*.

The window that opens has three columns. The *Field Name* is the title for the data field or column. The *Data Type* is the type format for this column. Clicking in the right of the *Data Type* field reveals a drop-down list of the data types available.

It is an important practice in every data table to create a **primary key**. This is a field (or combination of fields) that uniquely identifies that data record from any other in the table. In Access, it is often an AutoNumber field so that two records in a given table can never have the same number. Access assigns these numbers sequentially. If you delete a record for any reason, it is gone, but its number won't be used again; there will just be a hole in the numbering system.

When naming the fields, it's important not to put spaces in them. Access, like many Microsoft programs, will actually allow you to use spaces, but this is an important habit to avoid. Servers other than Windows do not understand spaces in field names, so plan now to get in the habit of closing up the space between parts of the field name or use an underscore (for example, `Product_Description`) if you must.

The first table is called `Category` and has two fields. `CategoryID` is an AutoNumber field, and it's the primary key for this table. The second is a text field and called `Category`. It will hold the names of your categories, namely books, art, and toys.

The second table is `Products`. The first field will be the AutoNumber `ProductID`, and the second will be the text field `Product`, which will hold the name of the product. You might also have `ProductDescription`, `ProductPrice`, and `ProductPhoto` fields, to name a few.

With the exception of the AutoNumber ID field, all the others are going to be text fields. The `ProductPhoto` field is going to hold the path to where the uploaded photo is located. It is possible to load the actual photo into the database, but that would greatly inflate its size of the database, so we do not recommend taking this route.

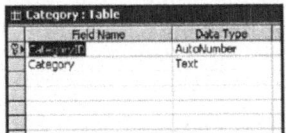

The following screen shot shows our `Category` and `Products` tables in Datasheet View:

You will usually need several more tables than this to create a complete database, but this is enough for this example. Let's move forward to creating a connection in Dreamweaver MX to the database for ASP, ASP.NET, or ColdFusion. Connections in PHP are discussed in Chapter 6.

Creating the Connection

Now that you have created a database for your site, you need to define a connection for Dreamweaver MX to use. This is done in different ways depending on the server model you have chosen for the site. For the most part, Dreamweaver MX saves the connection file in a special folder entitled `Connections`, which is uploaded to the server. So changing the connection method or file in Dreamweaver MX involves just changing the one file because all the other pages in the site refer to this connection. Other programs write the connection information in every page, making it very cumbersome to effect changes later.

ASP

ASP can be coded with either VBScript or JScript, but the connection methods are the same in both. The most common method to connect to the database for ASP sites is to use Open Database Connectivity (ODBC). You can also use an ADO connection string to create the database connection. Let's look at these methods one at a time.

ODBC

ODBC comes preinstalled with Windows and so is naturally widely used. The ODBC driver establishes compatibility between databases and creates needed communication between the commands you write and the database. To use ODBC, you create a Data Source Name (DSN) on the machine that points to the database. It can be located on your machine or on another machine in the network. As long as the DSN is pointing to the database, it will establish a connection.

Creating a Local DSN

To create a DSN, go to the Control Panel (*Start > Settings > Control Panel > Administrative Tools* on Windows 2000 or *Start > Settings > Control Panel > OBDC* on Windows 98) of the computer and double-click the icon called *Data Sources (OBDC)*. Choose the *System DSN* tab and click *Add*. A list of database drivers will appear. Select the *Microsoft Access Driver* (for this example) and click *Finish*. A new dialog box will open. Add your chosen DSN name in the field marked *Data Source Name*. Click *Select...* and browse to the database you wish to apply the DSN to. Click *OK*, and then *OK* again to close the dialog box. If you are using a database other than Access, the Microsoft Data Access Components (MDAC) driver listing provides a variety of drivers that will create a DSN connection to most common databases. If you are using a database not included in the MDAC driver listing, consult your database manufacturer about the appropriate driver.

Creating a Remote DSN

Creating a DSN on a remote machine is pretty much the same as on a local machine, but the host administrator will have to create the remote DSN for you unless you have a Control Panel on your site that allows you to do this yourself. The DSN must be identical in both spelling and case to the one you created on your machine. Once this DSN is created, return to the *Connection* panel in Dreamweaver MX and change the button that says *Use DSN on this machine* to *Use Remote DSN*.

Using the DSN in Dreamweaver

To use the DSN in Dreamweaver, you need to create a connection. In the *Databases* tab of the *Application* panel, click + > *Data Source Name (DSN)*. A dialog box will appear (as shown later) that asks for details regarding the connection.

First, you need to decide what you are going to call the connection. It is good practice to start your connection names with `conn` and then the name. This tells you that any name you see beginning with `conn` is automatically a connection file. Find the appropriate DSN from the drop-down list. Since you created the DSN in the Control Panel, it should be on the list. If it is not, click the *Define* button to access the Data Sources administration window in the Windows Control Panel directly.

If the database requires a username or password, insert these in the appropriate boxes. Finally, select the *using local DSN* option since the DSN is on your machine. Click *Test* to check that the connection can be made. The response should be *Connection Successful*. Click *OK* to close the connection box.

It is good practice to start your connection names with conn and then the name.

Custom Connection Strings

A second method of connecting in ASP is to use an ActiveX data object (ADO) custom connection string. The connection is also created from the *Databases* panel of DMX, but you need to specify *Custom Connection String* as the method of connection.

Before you create a custom connection string, you will need to find the path from the root of the server to the database. Fortunately, extension developer Tom Muck has made it easy for you by creating an extension to do the work for you. Download the extension from *http://www.basic-ultradev.com* under the title *Get Database Path*. This extension will write the ASP code to a new page to make it easy to find the path to the database. Apply this extension to a new document, name it something like `path.asp`, and upload it to the server. When you browse to the file, the path to the database will be displayed for you.

Next, you need to define a connection string using this path. There is a wonderful list of sample connection strings available at *http://www.dwteam.com/Articles/ado/index.asp* for ASP connections. Simply create the connection string and paste it into the *Connection String* dialog box as shown below, and then test the connection.

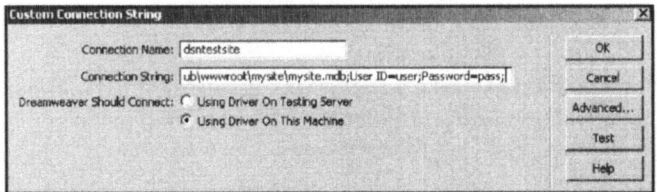

OLE DB Connections

ADO custom connections can be created in several ways, but the best way is to use OLE DB. This eliminates the ODBC wrapper and thus an extra step in establishing the connection, making OLE DB faster and more stable. It also means that you don't need to involve the web host in creating a DSN for you.

Here's a typical OLE DB connection string:

```
Provider=Microsoft.Jet.OLEDB.4.0;Data
Source=C:\Inetpub\wwwroot\mysite\mysite.mdb;User ID=user;Password=pass;
```

Note that the entire text is in one line in the *Custom Connection String* box, as shown in the previous screen shot.

ODBC DSN-less Connections

Another way of establishing an ASP custom connection is through the OBDC DSN-less connection. This also uses a connection string, like OLE DB, but it uses the OBDC wrapper. The advantage in this type of OBDC connection is that a system DSN doesn't have to be set up by the host administrator first. However, as mentioned previously, this string involves an extra step in the connection and is therefore not as quick or stable. Here's an example of an OBDC DSN-less connection string:

```
Driver={Microsoft Access Driver(*.mdb)};
Dbq=c:\Inetpub\wwwroot\mysite\mysite.mdb; Uid=user; Pwd=pass;
```

Using Server.Mappath in the Connection String

You can also use the `Server.Mappath` method for creating the connection string. This is useful when you don't know the exact path from the root of the server to your site. Sometimes, hosting companies will set up your access at a point that is not in the root of the server and you may not know this. With `Server.Mappath`, you don't have to guess whether you have found the root or not; you simply specify the relative path to the database on the server and `Server.Mappath` finds the rest of the path for you. You can do this with either OBDC or OLE DB connections. Here's an example of an OLE DB connection string using `Server.Mappath`:

```
"Provider=Microsoft.Jet.OLEDB.4.0;Data Source=" &
Server.Mappath("\database\mysite.mdb") & ";User ID=user;Password=pass;"
```

Once the connection is created, DMX will save the connection file in a `Connections` folder. Both the `.asp` file and the `Connections` folder must be uploaded to the server in order to work.

ASP.NET

Creating a connection for ASP.NET is very similar to creating an OLE DB connection. An OLE DB provider must be present on the server to create this connection, which is taken care of by the MDAC on Windows servers. It is very strongly suggested that version 2.7 of the MDAC is used when creating an ASP.NET application. This is freely downloadable from *http://www.microsoft.com/data/download.htm*.

> *Creating a connection for ASP.NET is very similar to creating an OLE DB connection.*

Alternatively, to connect to a Microsoft SQL Server database, you can use the Managed Data Provider for SQL Server that is supplied by the .NET Framework.

To create a database connection for ASP.NET, open an `.aspx` page and click *Databases* in the *Application* panel or select *Window > Databases* from the menu bar. Click the + button and choose *OLE DB*, or *SQL Server* if you are using a SQL Server database. Choose a name for your connection in the first text box.

To build an OLE DB connection string, Dreamweaver gives you the option of using the *Data Link Properties Wizard* or a predefined template. Clicking *Build* will open up the *Data Link Properties* and give you a Microsoft wizard to assist in building the connection. It is important to note that the *Data Link Properties Wizard* will only work if the OLE DB provider being used currently resides on the computer on which the connection is built. Supply the required information and the data goes into the *Connection String* text box. Test the connection and click *OK*.

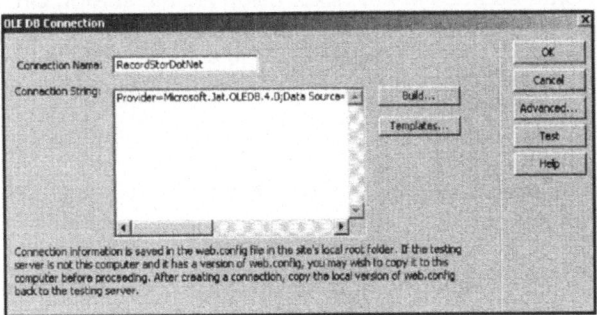

If you clicked the *Templates* option, you are given the option of selecting from several ready supplied connection strings for the most common databases. For others, consult the database provider or your server administrator. Select the one that is appropriate for your needs and the connection information will be put in place. You just need to fill in the blanks.

In ASP.NET, the connection is written directly to the pages so there is no connection folder or file to upload. Just upload the pages.

ColdFusion

In ColdFusion MX, connections use Java Database Connectivity (JD BC). JDBC is very similar to ODBC except that it is Java based. ColdFusion MX Server has the ability to use ODBC, JDBC, or a combination of the two. Which one is used is dictated by the database employed for the project.

Setting Up the Site

When your site definitions are created for a ColdFusion site, the URL prefix (specified in the *Site Definition* window) will vary depending on how you have set up the ColdFusion MX Server. If you are running ColdFusion on IIS, your URL prefix will still be *http://localhost/mysite*. If you are running the ColdFusion MX Server as a standalone web server, the URL prefix will be *http://localhost:8500/mysite*.

Once you have the testing server set up, the next step is to set up the Remote Development Service (RDS) connection in the ColdFusion Administrator. On a remote site, this may have to be routed through a server administrator, but for our purposes, we are assuming the ColdFusion server resides on your machine.

The RDS dialog box will prompt you for a password. The password needed is the one you used when installing ColdFusion MX. At that time, you had the option to select a unique RDS password or use the same one as you use for ColdFusion Administrator. Depending on the setup selection, enter the RDS password in this space and the RDS login information in the *Application > Databases* window should check off.

Adding a New Data Source

You can add a new data source via the ColdFusion Administrator. On a local machine this can be found at *http://localhost/cfide/administrator/* if installed on IIS or *http://localhost:8500/cfide/administrator/* if you're running ColdFusion as a standalone. You can access it quickly by clicking the *Modify Data Sources* button on the *Databases* tab of the *Application* panel in Dreamweaver MX.

To set up a data source, click the option *Data Sources*, which is under *Data & Services* in ColdFusion Administrator.

In the dialog box, enter a name for your data source, find the database driver for your database in the drop-down list, and click *Add*.

In the next window enter the location of your database in the *Database File* text box. You can find it by clicking the *Browse Server* button. Make sure *Use Default Username* is checked and click *Submit*. The new database will be visible in the *Connected Data Sources* table and you can click the *Verify Database* button to verify that the connection is working. An *OK* should appear to the far right of the window.

After this step, it is usually necessary to restart the ColdFusion server in order for the new data source to be recognized. This is similar to rebooting your computer after installing a new piece of software. After restarting the server, you should see that the remaining check boxes in the Dreamweaver Site dialog box have checked off, down to the Recordset creation.

it is usually necessary to restart the ColdFusion server in order for the new data source to be recognized.

In ASP, the connection was written to a separate file that needs to be uploaded to the server. In ColdFusion, the connection is written in the page as part of the code.

Getting Data from the Database

Now that you have created the connection, the next step is to start creating dynamic pages. In order to access database information from your tables, you will create a recordset in Dreamweaver that fits the needs of your page. This can be a recordset that contains an entire table or several columns of a table, or it can be a recordset created by joining two or more tables together.

To create a recordset, you need to click the + button in the *Data Bindings* window. The *Recordset* dialog box opens. Dreamweaver MX gives you two ways to create a recordset. The simple recordset box works well when you need to get data from one table or portions of one table with one filter and you want to sort records in either ascending or descending order.

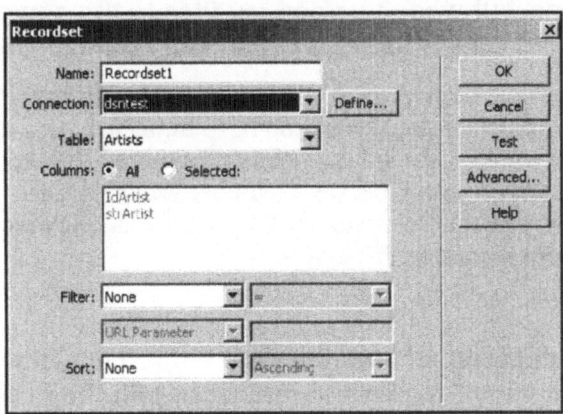

For more complicated recordsets, however, you will need to use the advanced *Recordset* window, accessed by clicking the *Advanced...* button.

This window allows you to type SQL queries directly into the window. It will also allow copying and pasting from a Query Builder such as the one in Access or SQL Server. Dreamweaver also has its own Query Builder of sorts; you can use the drop-down lists and buttons in the bottom window. You can highlight the fields in the tables to select, click *SELECT*, and they will appear as part of the SQL statement. You can continue in the same manner to add *WHERE* and *ORDER BY* statements in the SQL window. This window allows much more flexibility in your recordsets, giving you the ability to join tables, perform calculations, or use multiple filters on the data.

The middle window of the *Advanced Recordset* window is used for defining the variables used in the SQL statement. To add a new variable, you need to click the + button. Each variable is listed as it appears in the SQL statement and given both a default and a runtime value.

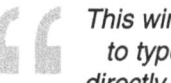
This window allows you to type SQL queries directly into the window.

Queries written into the *Advanced* dialog box are scripted in Structured Query Language (SQL). It is important that you have at least a basic knowledge of SQL in order to work with dynamic pages.

An excellent reference is the Apress book *Practical Web Database Design*, by Chris Auld et al. (ISBN 1-904151-20-5).

Frequently Asked Questions

I am using ASP and an Access database. I created a DSN connection that works on my machine, but when I upload my files to the server, I get a message that says "No Data Source or Driver Not Found". What do I do?

There are a couple of things that may have caused this. First, make sure that you uploaded the connection file to the server. Also, unless you have a way to create a DSN in a Control Panel provided by your host, you will have to ask the host administrator to create an identical DSN for you on the server. This DSN must be exactly the same, including case. Having to depend on the host administrator for this function is one reason a lot of people use DSN-less connections on a remote server.

I am working in ColdFusion. I created a data source in ColdFusion Administrator, and it says OK when verified, but still the Data Source option in Dreamweaver will not check off. I have gone through the same procedure over and over, but still it will not check off. What's wrong?

After you create the data source, make sure you stop and restart the ColdFusion Server in Admin Tools/Services of your Control Panel. Restarting the server will force the connection to be recognized and the item will then be checked off in Dreamweaver when you return to the program.

I can get an SQL query to work with a URL parameter, but DMX doesn't work when I have information coming from a form. What am I doing wrong?

If you are using the simple Recordset window, make sure that the drop-down box in the Filter section after the equal sign (=) is set to Form Variable rather than URL Parameter. If the Advanced Recordset window is used, make sure the Run Time Variable Value request method is Request.Form or just Request rather than Request.QueryString.

My database connection works on my local server, but when I upload the files to the remote server, I get a message that says "Data Source not found and no default driver specified". Why is this?

First, check to make sure that you uploaded all your files, including the connection folder and file. If you are sure everything is uploaded, make sure your path is correct and everything went to the right place. If nothing else works, make sure the driver for the database you are using is supported on the server.

I keep getting this message when I am trying to work with my database:

"Microsoft OLE DB Provider for ODBC Drivers (0x80004005) [Microsoft] [ODBC Microsoft Access Driver] The Microsoft Jet database engine cannot open the file '(unknown)'. It is already opened exclusively by another user, or you need permission to view its data."

What does it mean?

This means there is another source opening the database. Sometimes this is Dreamweaver itself because of the connection. Look for an .ldb file and try to delete it. If you can't, closing Dreamweaver and trying again will usually take care of this error.

Why can't I see my ColdFusion Administration panel?

This is probably because ColdFusion hasn't started up automatically when you booted up your machine. You'll need to start it manually.

Summary

Making the connection to the database is important to the success of a data-driven web site. In ASP, you can use a system DSN created on the server by the administrator, or through a client Control Panel or you can use an ADO (custom) connection that will allow you to create the connection yourself without administrator involvement. OLE DB connections are faster because they don't require the ODBC wrapper, which adds an extra layer of connectivity, thus slowing the process down.

In ASP.NET, you create the connection either in the *Microsoft Data Services Properties* dialog box or using one of several templates available in Dreamweaver MX.

In ColdFusion, you create a connection through the *Data Sources* selection of ColdFusion Administrator. ColdFusion Administrator is a part of ColdFusion MX. You will need to restart the ColdFusion server after creating the connection for it to be recognized.

Databases and Connections

3

In this Chapter

- Installing and setting up IIS

- Administering a web site

- Installing PHP for IIS

Author: Gareth Downes-Powell

Setting Up IIS for HTML, ASP, or PHP

This chapter is about setting up Internet Information Services (IIS) as a **development server** on a Windows machine so we can use it to develop HTML, ASP, and PHP pages.

In the first part of this chapter, we first look at installing IIS, a server that can handle HTML and ASP pages out of the box. This runs on and is included with various Windows platforms. We'll cover how to test whether the installation was successful and how to administer a basic web site, and we'll provide you with some handy troubleshooting tips to help solve any problems.

> *We'll cover how to test whether the installation was successful and how to administer a basic web site, and we'll provide you with some handy troubleshooting tips to help solve any problems.*

In the second half of this chapter, we look at how to install PHP on Windows. We'll cover how it can be integrated into IIS, so that PHP pages can be served by the web server. Finally, we present a troubleshooting guide to help solve any problems with the PHP installation.

Installing and Setting Up IIS

IIS was developed by Microsoft and runs only on the Windows Server operating systems (Windows NT, 2000, and XP Professional). Note that it's not available with Windows XP Home Edition. IIS has a built-in capability to run Active Server Pages (ASP) pages, since ASP was created by Microsoft. It can also run PHP pages, which we'll look at later in the chapter.

The current version of IIS, which comes with Windows XP Professional, is version 5.1, although version 6.0 is available with the .NET Server Packs.

To install IIS, you'll need to have your Windows operating system (OS) CD available. To start the install, insert the CD into your CD-ROM drive, and the disc should start automatically. You can then select *Install Optional Windows Components* or similar, and you will be able to select *Internet Information Services (IIS)*, as shown in the following screen shot:

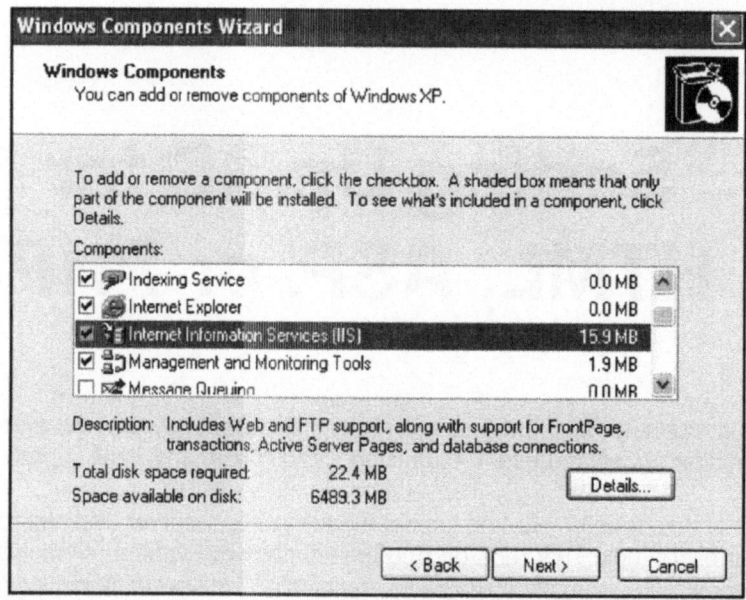

Alternatively, if the disc does not start automatically, you can go to the *Control Panel*, select *Add / Remove Programs* and *Add / Remove Windows Components*, and then select *IIS*. The wording may vary slightly depending on which Windows OS you are using, as will the location of your Windows directory. With Windows NT, the location of the Windows directory is `C:\winnt\`.

IIS is best installed leaving all options with their default values. Installation is fairly simple and needs very little user interaction.

Note that, once you have a server installed on your machine, it is very important that you make sure you have a firewall installed on your system to stop outsiders from connecting to your web server and potentially trying to hack into it. Many hackers scan for servers on home machines, as they are often fairly unprotected. It's also a good idea to keep your server up-to-date with all the latest patches from Microsoft (see *http://www.microsoft.com/security/*), so it behaves exactly like a production server would.

There are many firewalls available such as Norton Personal Firewall from Symantec (*http://www.symantec.com*) or Black Ice from ISS (*http://blackice.iss.net/index.php*). The firewall should be set up to disallow connections to your web server from outside your computer or network.

It is very important that you make sure you have a firewall installed on your system.

Checking the Installation

Once you have installed IIS, the next step is to check that the installation has worked successfully. Open up a new browser window, and in the address bar enter either

http://localhost/localstart.asp

or

http://computername/localstart.asp

Both *localhost* and *computername* refer to the computer that IIS is running on. Note that *computername* is the name assigned to your Windows system, which you can find by selecting the *System* option in the Windows *Control Panel*. When you enter one of these addresses, you should see the default IIS page, which is shown below:

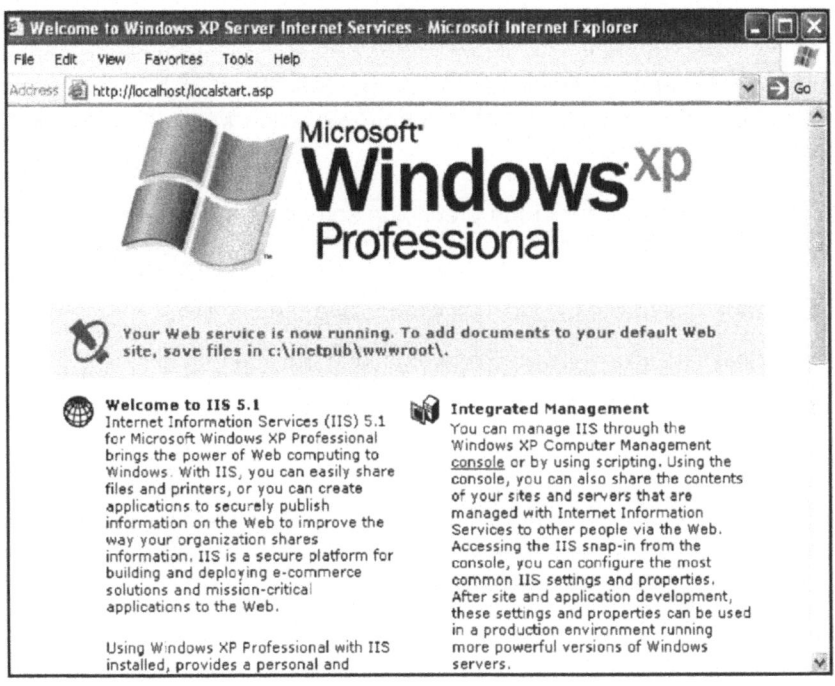

We'll look at testing your own HTML and ASP pages later in this chapter.

Administering a Basic Web Site

To administer your web site once IIS is installed, you need to use the *Internet Information Services* section of the **Microsoft Management Console** (MMC). To start the console, select *Internet Information Services* from *Administrative Tools* in your Windows *Start* menu. Otherwise, it can be opened from the Windows *Control Panel*. Once it opens, you can expand the tree on the left side to look something like the following screen shot (it will vary depending upon your setup).

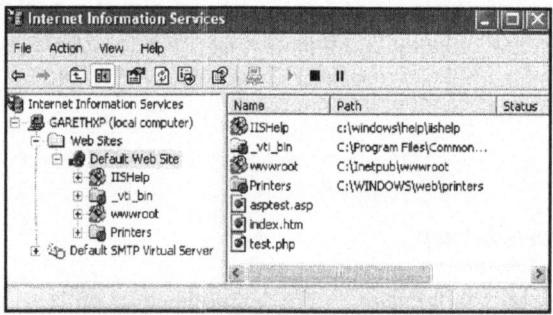

With most versions of IIS that come with Windows, you can only host one web site at a time. This is called the **default web site** and it can be browsed using the address *http://localhost/*.

However, as it's a development server you're setting up, you can easily get around the "one web site" rule by creating new directories under the default web site directory, storing a different web site in each directory. You can then browse each web site using the address *http://localhost/directoryname/*.

On the right side of the menu bar in the preceding screen shot, you can see three icons that allow you to control the web server:

- **A play icon** – This starts the web server, making the site live.

- **A stop icon** – This stops the web server, taking the site offline.

- **A pause icon** – This allows the web server to continue serving existing connections, while not accepting any new connections.

On the right side of the console itself, you'll see the directories and files that make up your web site. After a normal IIS install, there will be a number of files installed here, which are for the default IIS web site and help files.

The Home Directory

The home directory is a directory on your hard disk from which web pages are served. Usually, when you install IIS, the default home directory is set to `C:\Inetpub\wwwroot`.

All files that are placed in this directory are available through a browser, so creating your own web site is as simple as copying your web pages and images into this directory. The path to the home directory can be to a local directory on the PC or a shared folder on another computer in the network. You can change this directory if you wish, as detailed in the next section, so that you can leave the default IIS files in `C:\Inetpub\wwwroot` and start with a fresh directory for your new web site.

> *All files that are placed in this directory are available through a browser, so creating your own web site is as simple as copying your web pages and images into this directory.*

Changing the Web Site Settings

Right-click *Default Web Site* in the IIS console and select *Properties*. A new dialog box will appear, allowing you to change a number of settings related to the web site. There are many tabs on this dialog box, but most are for advanced uses on a production web server, so there are only a few we need to look at here.

Web Site

Under this tab, you can set the following options:

- **IP Address** – If you are unsure of your computer's IP address, you can leave this set to the default option of *All Unassigned*. Alternatively, if your computer has a local network IP address (for example, 192.168.0.1), you can enter it here.

- **TCP Port** – This is the port that the web server runs on. The standard value for this is 80. If you change the port number (for example, to port 81), you'll need to specify the new port number in the address bar when you call up a web page (for example, *http://localhost:81/*).

- You can also set a connection time-out value, which tells IIS how long to keep an idle connection open before it's closed, and the format in which IIS stores its web logs. These options are best left to the default settings.

Home Directory

As mentioned in the previous section, the home directory is where the files for your web site are located. Under this tab, you can change the default home directory from `C:\Inetpub\wwwroot` to another directory of your choice. This can be a directory on the server machine or another machine on your network. You can also specify whether *Directory Browsing* is allowed.

This means that if there is no default page found for a directory, the files in the directory are listed instead. This is a security risk on a production server and should be turned off, but on a development server it's often useful to leave the option on to allow you to easily select pages when you're testing the site.

The *Configuration* button is used to tell IIS the program that processes each different file extension—for example, the `.asp` or `.php` extensions. We'll look at this in more detail in the section about installing PHP into IIS.

Documents

The *Documents* tab allows you to set which web pages are loaded by default if no page is requested in the URL.

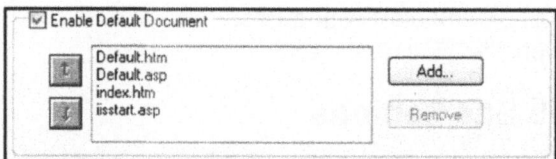

For example, if someone types the address *http://www.yoursite.com/,* your server would actually serve that user *http://www.yoursite.com/index.htm* or whichever file is specified as a default page. The list box allows you to specify which page names should be searched for in such situations, with the order of priority from top to bottom in the list.

In this section, you can also specify an HTML file that will be automatically added to the bottom of every page of your web site (for example, to display a copyright notice).

Checking That Web Pages Are Being Served Correctly

Now that you've looked at basic web site administration, you can check that the server can serve both HTML and ASP pages properly. Make sure that the web server is running by checking the IIS console first.

Checking HTML Pages

Create a new HTML page in Dreamweaver MX, and add a test message to be displayed if the server is serving documents properly. Save the file as `htmltest.htm` in the home directory for your web site (remember, the default is `C:\Inetpub\wwwroot\htmltest.htm`).

Now open a browser and go to *http://localhost/htmltest.htm.* If your message is displayed correctly, you can move on and check that the ASP pages are working.

If your page doesn't appear, check that the web server is actually running and that the directory in which you saved `htmltest.htm` is actually the home directory for your web site.

Checking ASP Pages

To check that ASP pages are running on your IIS installation, create a new page and add the following ASP code to the page body:

```
<html>
<head>
<title>ASP Test Page</title>
<meta http-equiv="Content-Type" content="text/html; charset=iso-8859-1">
</head>
<body>
<% ="ASP Pages are working<br>" %>
<% =("Your IP address is: " + Request.ServerVariables("REMOTE_ADDR") %>
</body>
</html>
```

Save this page as `asptest.asp` in your web site's home directory, and then open a browser and navigate to *http://localhost/asptest.asp*. When the page opens, it should display something similar to the following:

ASP Pages are working
Your IP Address is: 127.0.0.1

Again, if the page doesn't appear, check that it's saved in the web site's home directory and that the web server is running. The IP address *127.0.0.1* corresponds to your own computer and is the IP address equivalent of the hostname `localhost`. If you assigned an IP address in the IIS setup as a local network address (for example, *192.168.0.1*), it will be shown here instead of *127.0.0.1*.

Using an Access Database with ASP

If you want to use a Microsoft Access database with ASP, you'll need to have Microsoft Access installed on the server, or you can use the appropriate Microsoft MDAC and Jet files. These are available to download from *http://www.microsoft.com/data/*.

You can then set up a Data Source Name (DSN), which is a database connection that ASP uses to communicate with the Access database, unless you will be using DSN-less connections in your ASP code. A DSN is a connection between your ASP code and the database that allows your code to work with the data stored in the database.

Open the Windows *Control Panel* and select *Data Sources (ODBC)*. In the dialog box that opens, select the *System DSN* tab and click the *Add* button. From the list of data sources that appears, select *Microsoft Access Driver (*.mdb)* and then click *Finish*. A dialog box similar to the following will appear:

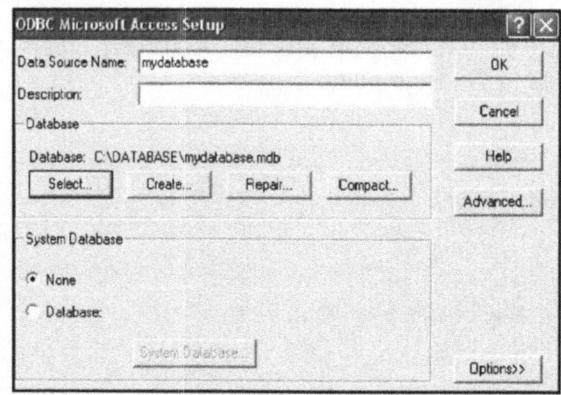

You can then enter the name of the DSN in the *Data Source Name* box. The DSN can be called anything you choose, but it cannot be the same as any others already set up on the server. A good idea is to name the DSN after your database, so that it's easy to see which database the DSN works with. You cannot have any spaces in the DSN name.

A good idea is to name the DSN after your database, so that it's easy to see which database the DSN works with.

Next, click the *Select...* button to select the database that the DSN is used to connect to. The database is normally located in a directory outside your web root directory so that it cannot be accessed over the Internet, only by your code on the server for security reasons. Click *OK* to create this DSN, which you can then use in Dreamweaver MX to connect to the database

When you come to transfer the web site from your development server to the production server, you just need to create a DSN with the same name on the new server so that no changes are required in your code.

Troubleshooting IIS Install Problems

A detailed manual for IIS administration is copied to your server when you install IIS. You can view this manual by browsing to *http://localhost/iishelp/iis/misc/default.asp*. It's a good idea to read through this if you have not previously worked with IIS.

If you have problems installing or setting up IIS, you can get more information about IIS from the *Help* menu of the IIS console.

It's also worth taking a look at the IIS section of the Microsoft TechNet site, at *http://www.microsoft.com/technet/treeview/default.asp?url=/technet/prodtechnol/iis/ support/IISTopKB.asp*. This site contains the IIS Knowledge Base and a large number of articles that will help you troubleshoot any difficulties.

Another good web site for IIS information is IISFAQ.com, located at *http://www.iisfaq.com/*, which also has a large amount of helpful information and links to other IIS-related sites.

It's extremely likely that you're not the first person to have a specific problem, so it's well worth doing a search on the Internet for more information. An excellent source for information is the Usenet newsgroups, which can be easily searched on the Web using Google Groups at *http://groups.google.com/*. It's very likely that you'll find that someone else has posted the same problem you're encountering, along with a solution. It's a good idea to search for the specific error message or number that occurs, as that will take you directly to information about the specific error.

 An excellent source for information is the Usenet newsgroups.

Installing PHP for IIS

In this section we'll describe how to add PHP functionality to IIS, so that you can use IIS to serve PHP pages. We assume that at this stage that your IIS server is set up and running correctly.

Downloading PHP

The first step to installing PHP is to download the package from the PHP web site. In your browser, go to *http://www.php.net/downloads.php*.

Next, scroll down to the section called *Windows Binaries*. At the time of this writing, there are two packages offered for Windows: the *PHP 4.3.0 Installer* and a larger package labeled *PHP 4.3.0 Zip Package*. The file that you should download is the larger of the two, the *Zip Package*. Whichever version of PHP is current when you visit the download page, it will always be the *Zip Package* that you need. This package offers support for MySQL and other PHP extensions, so is much better for developers.

Once you have the *Zip Package*, you'll be taken to another page that offers mirror sites in many different countries from which you can download the file. It's best to choose the country nearest to you, as it will offer a faster download by providing a shorter route between you and the download server.

Installing PHP

First unzip the PHP `.zip` file to your hard drive. It's a good idea to unzip the files to a directory called `php` on your `c` drive (that is, `C:\php`). If you don't use `C:\php`, it's important not to unzip the files into a directory with spaces in it, such as `C:\Program Files\php`, because spaces in the directory name can cause problems for PHP.

Next, open Windows Explorer and browse to the `C:\php` directory. You should see a subdirectory layout similar to the one shown in the next screen shot.

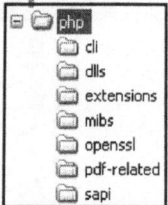

Don't worry if your directory structure isn't exactly the same as that shown in the image. Because PHP is a fast-moving language, with new versions released frequently, the structure may change.

You should see a file called `install.txt`. It's important to read this file, as it documents many aspects of installing and setting up PHP. Most important, it will contain any special instructions that are needed for the latest PHP version. There is also a Windows-specific installation page in the online PHP manual at *http://www.php.net/manual/en/install.windows.php*.

There are currently two ways of installing PHP: a CGI program and an ISAPI module. The ISAPI module integrates into IIS and offers improved performance, so it is the one we recommend. More details about both methods of installation are given at the previous address.

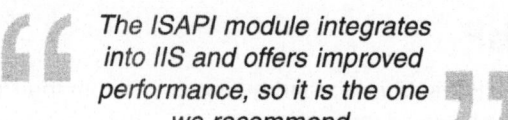

The ISAPI module integrates into IIS and offers improved performance, so it is the one we recommend.

For the ISAPI module install, you need then to open the `sapi` directory and copy the file named `php4isapi.dll` into the `php` root directory (for example, from `C:\php\sapi\php4isapi.dll` to `C:\php\php4isapi.dll`). If you chose the CGI install, you can skip the previous step, as `php4isapi.dll` isn't used with this method.

If you opt for the ISAPI install, as recommended, then your PHP scripts are processed by the `php4isapi.dll` module. For a CGI install, the PHP scripts are processed by the `php.exe` file. Another important file used for processing the PHP scripts is the `php4ts.dll` file, already located in the PHP installation directory.

Next, inside the `php` directory, create a new folder named `temp`. Inside `temp`, create another two folders, one called `sessions` and one called `uploads`. The former will be used to hold temporary files associated with session variables, and the latter will contain any files that are uploaded from a web page.

Creating a php.ini File

The next stage is to configure PHP, which is done in a settings file called `php.ini`. Because `php.ini` contains so many options, you don't create the file from scratch; instead you use a default `php.ini` file, which is included in the installation, and customize it for your needs.

There are two versions of `php.ini` in the `php` directory:

- `php.ini-dist` is used for running on a development server. It contains the best settings for development purposes, and so it is the one you'll be using.

- `php.ini-recommended` contains settings that lock down PHP for security purposes. It contains the optimal set of options for running on a production web server. However, because it's locked down, some older PHP scripts may not run as intended. It's worth reading the comments at the top of the `php.ini-recommended` file, as they discuss the techniques used to lock down the server.

Although you can stick with the default values in the `php.ini-dist` file for most options, there are a few options you **must** change, as they supply PHP with the paths it needs to run properly.

doc_root

`doc_root` needs to be set to the root path of the web server, meaning the site's home directory in IIS. If you used IIS's default settings when you installed it, then `doc_root` should be set like this:

```
doc_root = "C:\Inetpub\wwwroot"
```

Note that you need the quotation marks around the path.

extension_dir

This setting should contain the path to the PHP extension files. If you installed PHP in `C:\php`, then you should set `extension_dir` like this:

```
extension_dir = "C:\php\extensions\"
```

so that it points to the path of the DLL files needed for the PHP extensions to run, which are in the `extensions` folder of your PHP installation. Note that it's important that you include the backslash (\) on the end.

session.save_path

`session.save_path` is responsible for most of the problems PHP users have, as a session can't be used unless it's set to a valid directory, and the default setting is `/tmp`, which isn't a valid directory on a normal Windows installation. In this case, you need to set it to the directory you set up earlier to hold temporary session information. If you unpacked the files to `C:\php`, this will be

```
session_save_path = "C:\php\temp\sessions"
```

upload_tmp_dir

Again, this needs to be pointed to the temporary directory you created earlier, which stores files that have been uploaded temporarily before they are moved to their proper location. If you unpacked the files to `C:\php`, this will be

```
upload_temp_dir = "C:\php\temp\uploads"
```

If there is a semicolon (`;`) at the start of the setting, it will need to be removed so that the option is not treated as a comment.

cgi.force_redirect (CGI Install Only)

If you are installing PHP as a CGI module, you need to look for the following line. It is treated as a comment because of the semicolon at the front of the line.

```
;cgi.force_redirect = 1
```

This option needs to be uncommented (by removing the semicolon) and set to 0 rather than 1, as follows:

```
cgi.force_redirect = 0
```

That completes the main settings needed to get PHP running, so you can save the `php.ini` file and move on.

Adding PHP to IIS

Now that the PHP files are in the correct places and your `php.ini` file contains the correct paths, you can actually add PHP to IIS.

The first step is to open the IIS console as you did earlier. If the tree on the left side is minimized, expand it until you can see *Default Web Site*. Right-click *Default Web Site* and then select *Properties* from the drop-down menu that appears.

The *Properties* dialog box will open:

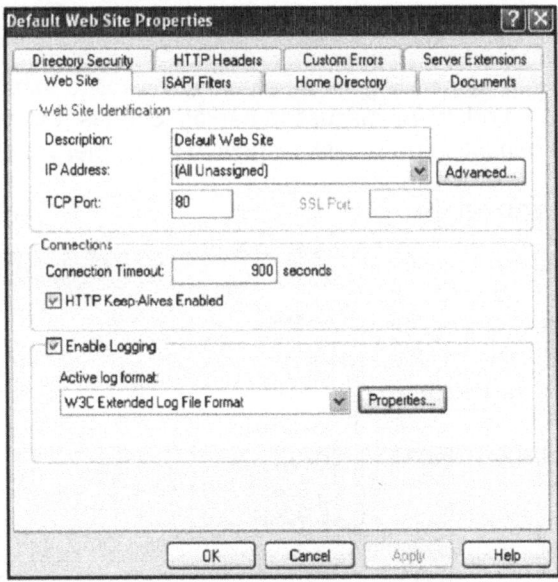

Select the *Home Directory* tab and click the *Configuration* button. A new dialog box similar to the following will open:

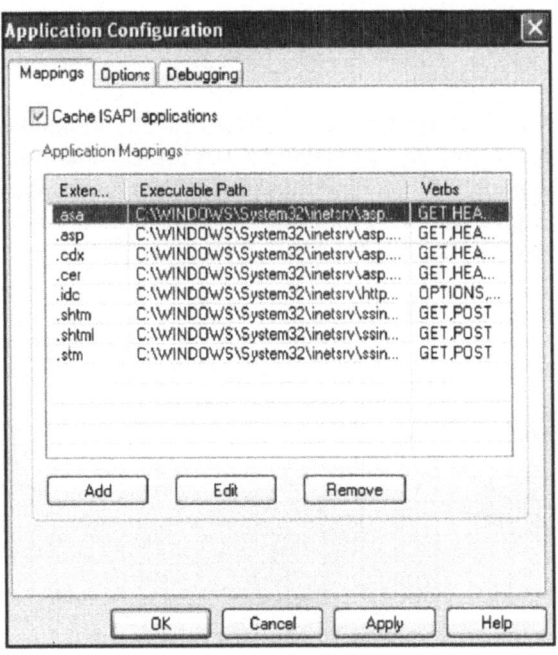

This section tells IIS which programs should handle pages with specific page extensions. You need to tell IIS to use the PHP interpreter to process `.php` page extensions, so click the *Add* button to add a new entry.

You now have two choices, depending on whether you want to install PHP as a CGI executable or as an ISAPI module. As discussed earlier, ISAPI is recommended because it can offer performance benefits, but we'll show how to add either type.

PHP As a CGI Executable

To install PHP as a CGI executable, click the *Browse...* button and navigate to the directory into which you unzipped the PHP files. If you have been following this guide, then this directory will be `c:\php\`. Once there, select `php.exe`, as shown in the adjacent screen shot.

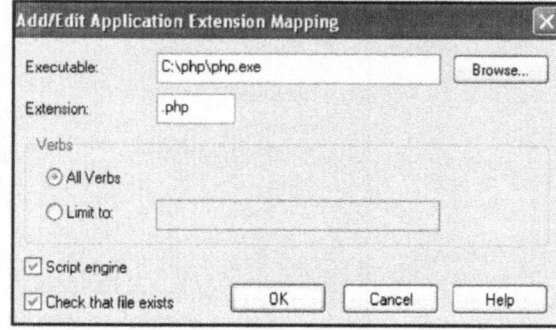

For the *Extension*, enter `.php`. Make sure that the options for *Script engine* and *Check that file exists* are both selected, and then click *OK*.

You now need to restart IIS, as discussed after the next section on installing PHP as an ISAPI module.

PHP As an ISAPI Module

Installing PHP as an ISAPI module is a very similar process to installing PHP as a CGI executable, except that a different file is selected. Click the *Browse...* button and go to the directory into which you extracted the PHP files. Select the file `php4isapi.dll` that you copied from the `C:\php\sapi` directory into the `C:\php\` directory earlier. You may need to change the drop-down menu for the file type so that it will display `.dll` files instead of `.exe` files.

For the *Extension*, enter `.php`. Make sure that the options for *Script engine* and *Check that file exists* are both selected, and click the *OK* button to add this new mapping.

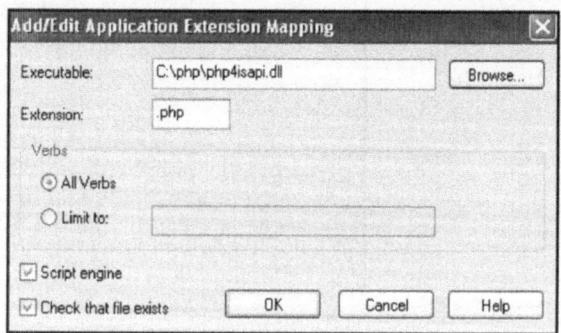

Checking the Mapping

Whichever method you used, you should now have the PHP mapping added, as shown in the following screen shot. Note that only IIS version 5.0 and above display the mappings as in the screen shot.

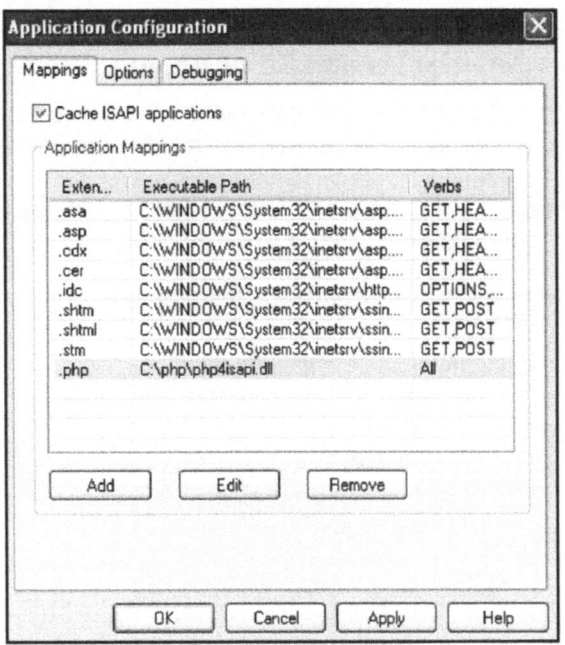

Click *OK* to keep your changes. You now need to completely restart IIS as described in the next section.

Restarting IIS

Whenever you make any changes to IIS settings, you need to restart IIS to make sure that it reads the new options and your changes take effect. How you restart IIS depends on which version of IIS you have.

> *Whenever you make any changes to IIS settings, you need to restart IIS.*

All IIS Versions

Open a new DOS box, usually by selecting *Command Prompt* from the Windows *Start* menu. First enter the command

```
NET STOP IISADMIN
```

This stops all the Internet services running on the server. You may be asked to confirm that you want to shut down the Internet services, in which case type y and press Enter.

Now that the Internet services have been stopped, you can restart the web server by using the command

```
NET START W3SVC
```

You should now see a message stating that *The World Wide Web Publishing service was started successfully.*

Internet Information Services Version 5.1 or Above

If you have IIS version 5.1 or above, you can restart the server straight from the IIS console without having to open a DOS box, which is much more convenient.

Select the *local computer* entry at the top of the tree. Right-click the entry, select *All Tasks,* and then *Restart IIS....* The following dialog box will display:

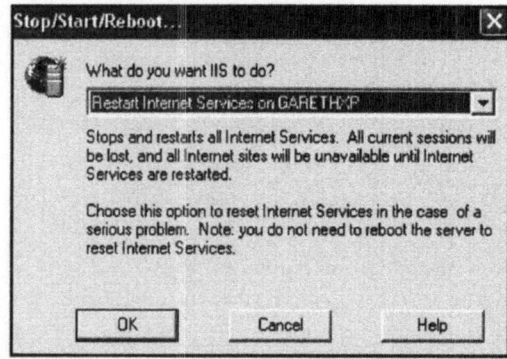

The default option is *Restart Internet Services on ...,* so you can just click *OK* to restart the server.

Testing PHP Pages

The next step is to check that PHP is actually working properly. Create a page in Dreamweaver containing the following HTML and PHP to use as a simple test:

```
<html>
<head>
<title>PHP Test Page</title>
<meta http-equiv="Content-Type" content="text/html; charset=iso-8859-1">
</head>
<body>
<?php phpinfo(); ?>
</body>
</html>
```

Save the page as `phptest.php` in the root directory for the default web site. If you installed IIS using the default settings, this will be

```
C:\Inetpub\wwwroot\
```

Next, open a browser and type in the following address:

```
http://localhost/phptest.php
```

If everything is working correctly, you should see a long page containing the entire PHP configuration, a small section of which is shown in the following screen shot.

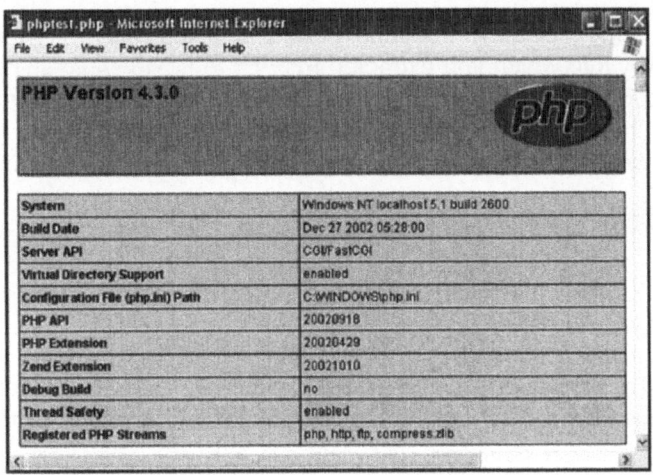

Note that if you installed PHP as a CGI module, the *Server API* setting will show as *CGI/FastCGI* or similar. If you opted for an ISAPI install, it will show *ISAPI*.

If you can see the preceding PHP configuration screen, PHP has been successfully installed. If PHP doesn't appear to work, check back over this section to make sure that everything is correct, and also have a look at the "Troubleshooting PHP" section later in the chapter.

Installing PHP Extensions

One of the great features of PHP is that it has a wide range of extensions that can be added to include extra commands and functionality in PHP. Note that the MySQL extension no longer needs to be installed separately; it is installed by default by PHP.

If you open `php.ini` (from `C:\windows\php.ini`) in a text editor and scroll down, you'll come to the extension section, a small block of which is shown below (and can be found around line 439):

```
;extension=php_bz2.dll
;extension=php_ctype.dll
;extension=php_cpdf.dll
;extension=php_curl.dll
```

You'll notice that each extension has a semicolon (`;`) at the start of the line, meaning that the line is treated as a comment and ignored. To make the extension active, you need to remove the semicolon and then save the file.

Next, you need to copy the relevant extension DLL file from its home in the `extension` folder in the directory into which you extracted PHP (`C:\php\extensions` if you installed to the recommended location), into your `Windows\System32` folder. For example, if you wanted to activate the PDF extension that allows you to create PDF files, which is called `php_pdf.dll`, you would copy

```
C:\php\extensions\php_pdf.dll
```

to

```
C:\Windows\System32\php_pdf.dll
```

If your `System32` directory is in a different folder such as `C:\winnt\`, then you need to copy the file there instead. You should then restart IIS as described in the previous section.

Note that it's very important that before you enable an extension, you read its entry in the online PHP manual at *http://www.php.net/docs.php*. Some extensions will need extra files or packages installed, and this will be mentioned in the manual.

Troubleshooting PHP

If you're having problems with getting PHP working successfully, first check back over all the topics covered so far and make sure that each stage is correct. You can then work through the checks and advice in this section.

CGI and ISAPI

- Check that `php.ini` exists in your main Windows directory.
- Check in your `php.ini` file that the paths for the `doc_root` and `extension_dir` settings are correct. Make sure that the case of the paths is correct and matches the actual directory name, and that the path is surrounded by quote marks. For example:

```
doc_root = "C:\Inetpub\wwwroot"
```

- In the IIS console, right-click *Default Web Site* and select *Properties*. Click the *Home Directory* tab and click the *Configuration* button. On the *Mappings* tab, select the entry for `.php` extensions and click *Edit*. Check that the path points to the correct file: `php.exe` for a CGI module install or `php4isapi.dll` for a ISAPI module.

- Try copying the following files from the folder you extracted PHP into to your Windows `System32` directory (assuming you extracted the files to `C:\php`):
  `C:\php\php4ts.dll`
  All files in `C:\php\dll`
  All files in `C:\php\extensions`

- Make sure that every time you change an option in `php.ini`, for example, you restart IIS so that the new changes will take effect.

- If you still can't get one version of PHP working, it's always worth trying the alternative version. For instance, if you can't get the CGI version to work, try using the ISAPI version.

CGI Specific

- Open your `php.ini` file and check that following setting exists:

  ```
  cgi.force_redirect = 0
  ```

ISAPI Specific

- Copy the file `C:\php\sapi\php4isapi.dll` to your `System32` directory, usually `C:\windows\system32` or `C:\winnt\system32`.

Sessions

- If you can't get sessions to work under PHP, open your `php.ini` file and check that the path is correct and the directory exists for the setting:

  ```
  session.save_path = "C:\php\temp\sessions";
  ```

  This directory is where the data for session variables is stored—for session variables to work, this directory must exist, and PHP needs to be able to write to it.

File Uploads

If you're having problems uploading a file through a browser, open your `php.ini` file and check the following settings:

- `file_uploads = On`

  This setting governs whether file uploads are allowed or not, and it should be set to `On` if you want to allow file uploading through a browser.

- `upload_tmp_dir = "C:\php\temp\uploads"`

  This setting tells PHP where it can temporarily store files that have been uploaded. Check the path is correct and that the directory it points to exists.

- `upload_max_filesize = 2M`

  This setting sets the maximum file size of files that can be uploaded through a browser, specified in megabytes.

Summary

In this chapter we've looked at how to install and set up IIS to use as a development server, so that pages can be tested locally on your computer without needing an active Internet connection. We've looked at the basic IIS settings to set up and control a web site, and we've presented some troubleshooting tips that can help to solve any problems with the installation.

We then looked at installing PHP into IIS, as either a CGI module or an ISAPI module, and we covered how to add a mapping to IIS so that it could process PHP pages. You learned how to create a `php.ini` file and which settings you must set before PHP will run. Finally, we looked at testing PHP, and we offered some tips that can help you to troubleshoot if the PHP installation isn't working as it should.

If you installed PHP into IIS, then it's a good idea to also look at the chapter in this book that explains how to set up a MySQL server, so you can develop and test PHP/MySQL pages without needing an Internet connection.

4

In this Chapter

- Installing Apache on Windows

- Configuring Apache

- Using PHP with Apache

Author: Gareth Downes-Powell

Apache and Windows

In this chapter, we first look at installing the Apache web server on a Microsoft Windows operating system. We'll discuss a few of the advantages Apache has to offer, cover how to configure Apache, and show how to test and troubleshoot the installation.

In the second part of the chapter, we'll show how to integrate PHP with Apache, giving Apache the capability to process PHP pages. PHP is an excellent choice for server-side scripting, being easy to learn and offering a powerful set of features. We look how to test and troubleshoot the installation and how to expand PHP's functionality using extra extensions.

Apache

Apache is a web server that was created by the Apache Software Foundation (*http://www.apache.org/*). It is based on the **HTTP Daemon**, which was developed by Rob McCool at the National Center for Supercomputing Applications at the University of Illinois in the early 1990s. It is an open source project, free to use, and it runs on Linux, Windows, Mac OS X, and a wide variety of other operating systems. Apache is one of the leading web servers in use throughout the world. In a survey carried out in January 2003 by Netcraft (*http://www.netcraft.com*) looking at 35,424,956 different web sites, 62% of them were found to be running Apache, compared to 27% running Microsoft IIS.

> *Apache is one of the leading web servers in use throughout the world.*

Apache can be run on all Windows systems and is not limited to the expensive Windows Server operating systems, such as Windows NT, 2000, or XP Professional. It's ideal if you have Windows XP Home Edition, which doesn't include a web server.

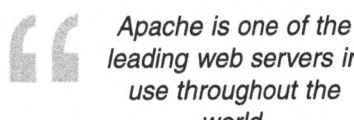

To learn how Apache can be run and installed on Linux, see Chapter 5.

Apache can support PHP pages, and it is the web server that is actually used for this task in real hosting environments. As such, Apache is great for working with Dreamweaver MX's PHP and MySQL server model (we'll look at setting up MySQL on Windows in Chapter 6).

Which Version of Apache?

Apache 2.0 offers better memory management and use of system resources than its predecessor, but since Apache has always been a very efficient program, the adoption rate remains quite low.

There are currently two versions of Apache available: the Apache 1.3 series and the newer Apache 2.0 series. In this chapter we're going to focus on Apache 1.3, because Apache 2.0's support for PHP is still only experimental. For the same reason, most production web servers still use the Apache 1.3.x series at the moment. If you do want to install Apache 2.0, this guide should still be useful to you because Apache 2.0 has a fairly similar installation process to its predecessor. Be aware, however, that Apache 2.0 is incompatible with versions of PHP prior to 4.2.1, so you will need to use at least PHP version 4.3.0 with it. In any case, the optimum PHP package to use will always be the most recent one available, regardless of *which* version of Apache you choose to work with.

Security

Before we look at installing Apache, it's important that you set up a firewall on the machine that will be hosting it. This will allow users on your local network to connect to the web server, while preventing people outside the network

Any web server can act as a potential point of entry to your network for malicious users. Security is never optional.

from doing so. You do this because, unless you were to run the web server as if it was in a live environment—installing every single patch that became available for it, as soon as it was released—the web server could act as a point of entry for malicious users outside your network wishing to compromise your system or the network as a whole. This is true of web servers in general, of course, and would be just as advisable for users of an IIS development server.

There are many firewalls available, both free and commercial. There is also a built-in firewall in Windows XP, but it must be enabled before it will work, and it is not as comprehensive as many of the commercial offerings.

Instructions on how to enable the Windows XP firewall can be found at *http://www.microsoft.com/windowsxp/pro/using/howto/networking/icf.asp*.

Some good examples of the commercial offerings available are Norton Personal Firewall from Symantec (*http://www.symantec.com/*) and Black Ice from ISS (*http://blackice.iss.net/ index.php*). Both of these allow packet filtering and enable you to choose which connections to your machine to allow and which ports can be used.

Downloading Apache

Apache can be downloaded free of charge from the *HTTPD Server* section of the Apache web site (*http://httpd.apache.org/*). Go to the downloads page at *http://httpd.apache.org/ download.cgi* and select a package to download. At the time of this writing, the latest version of Apache (series 1.3.x) was Apache 1.3.27. If there is a later version than this in the 1.3.x series by the time you get to read this book, then you should download that instead. The correct package to download is the one labeled *Win 32 Binary (MSI Installer)*.

In the case of Apache 1.3.27, this file is only 2.9MB in size, so it should be fairly quick to download, even on a dial-up Internet connection. Note that if you haven't got the MSI installer on your system, you can download that from the Microsoft downloads page (*http://www.microsoft.com/downloads*).

Installing Apache

Now that you have Apache 1.3.27 for Windows downloaded, you can start the installation by simply double-clicking the downloaded file. You'll see the installation dialog box appear, as shown in the following screen shot.

Click the *Next* button to continue the installation. The next dialog box shows you the Apache License Agreement. In order to carry on with the installation, you need to select the option saying that you agree to the license. Once you have done this, you can click the *Next* button to continue.

The next dialog box holds a small text file with information about the installation. It's worth reading the notes here before you click *Next* and move on.

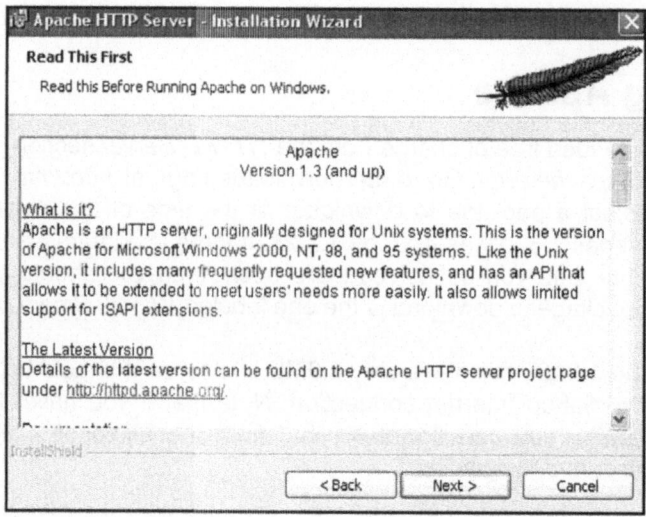

The next dialog box, shown below, allows you to enter the *Network Domain*, *Server Name*, and the *Administrator's Email Address*. As you're setting up a development server, it's not very likely that you'll have a domain name for it, so you can use the following:

- `127.0.0.1` for the *Network Domain* (this always points to your computer)

- `localhost` for the *Server Name* (again, this points to your computer)

- `admin@localhost` for the *Administrator's Email Address*

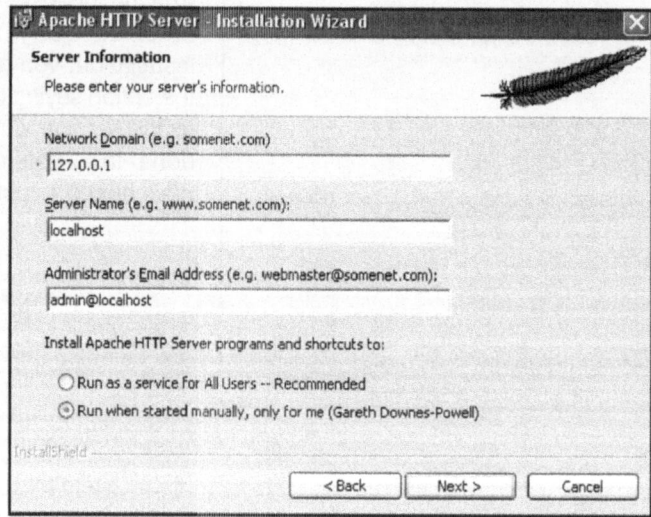

The second set of options in the dialog box allows you to choose whether to **run Apache as a service**, meaning that it will start up whenever Windows starts and is always available to serve web pages. The alternative is to **run only when you start it manually**. For a development server, we prefer to go for this second option, so that Apache is only running when it is actually in use, instead of all the time. There is no real point in letting Apache consume system resources while it is not being used. We will discuss how to manually start and stop the server in a moment.

Even after you've installed Apache, it is still possible to change the settings at a later date and make Apache run as a service. You can find a detailed description of the steps involved in the Apache online documentation (*http://httpd.apache.org/docs/win_service.html*).

Once you've selected the relevant options, click the *Next* button to continue. The next dialog box allows you to set a *Complete* or *Custom* install.

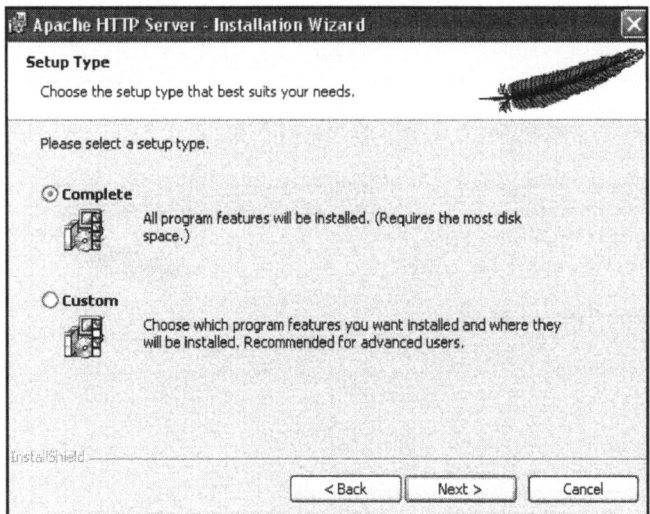

Since Apache takes up very little disk space, it is usually best to go for the *Complete* install option. Select that option and click *Next*.

The next dialog box allows you to set the directory in which to install Apache. For this guide, it's recommended that you leave this as the default option: `C:\Program Files\Apache Group\`. Click the *Next* button to continue.

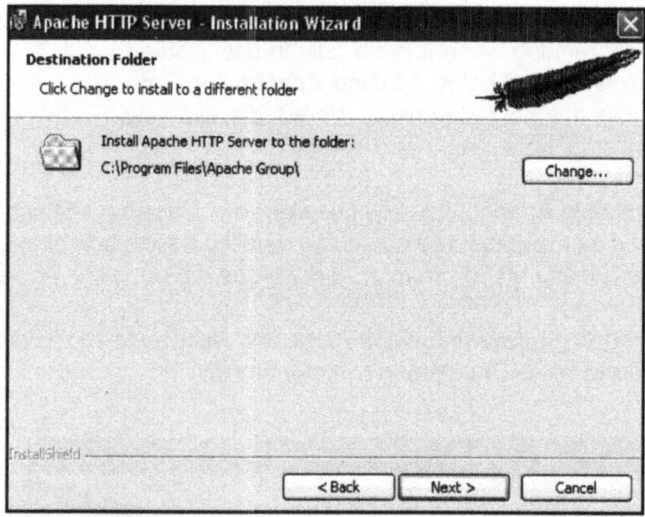

Finally, to complete the installation, click the *Install* button.

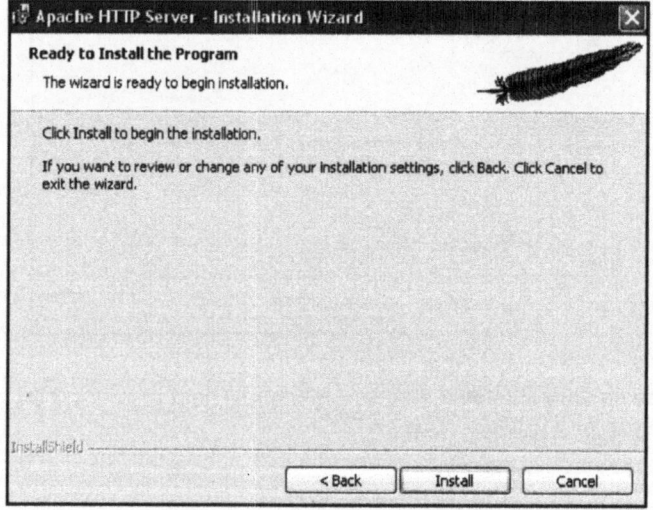

Apache will then install all its files and, after a short period, you should see the following dialog box, which lets you know that the installation has been successful. Click *Finish* to close the dialog box.

Apache should now be installed. You can move on to the next step: configuring Apache for your system.

Apache's Configuration Files

In this section we look at how to configure Apache and set it up as a development server. We assume that you installed Apache into the default location (`C:\Program Files\Apache Group`). All the Apache files should now be in a directory tree located at `C:\Program Files\Apache Group\Apache`.

All Apache's configuration files are stored in a single directory: `C:\Program Files\Apache Group\Apache\conf`.

The most important configuration file is called `httpd.conf` (short for **HTTP Daemon Configuration**). It contains the main settings for the web server, so this is the file that you are going to edit.

There are two other configuration files that you will see have also been created: `srm.conf` and `access.conf`. These files are, in fact, no longer used. They're included simply for legacy reasons and are usually left empty. These days, all configuration options should be set using the `httpd.conf` file. In fact, if you use Apache 2.0, these files won't be installed at all.

Make sure you open `httpd.conf` in a text editor, such as Notepad. If you open the file in a word processor, it may insert hidden formatting characters that will stop Apache from being able to read the file correctly.

You'll find that the `httpd.conf` file is quite lengthy and contains a huge number of options. It can look quite daunting at first, but you'll find that most of the options are actually not enabled anyway, and there are extensive comments that explain what each one does. In fact, most settings can be left as they are. There are only a few that need altering. Let's now go through setting up each option in turn.

ServerRoot

The `ServerRoot` is the directory into which you installed Apache. It tells Apache where to find files such as configuration files and logs. You will find that this setting is currently

```
ServerRoot "C:/Program Files/Apache Group/Apache"
```

This is where Apache has installed itself by default, so if you chose the default option during the installation process, there is no change required. If you installed Apache somewhere else, you'll need to change this path to point to your install directory. Don't forget to add the extra directory name, `/Apache` , to the end of your install path. Note that, unlike the normal Windows path format, which uses backslashes to delimit directory names, Apache uses the UNIX-style forward slash (/) instead.

Port

To get to the `Port` option, you'll have to scroll quite a way down the file.

The port setting allows you to set the port that the web server listens to requests on. Normally this is port `80`, but if you wish, you can use a different port number on your system. If you do set it to a different port, you'll have to specify the port number of the server in the URL whenever you request pages. For example:

You could jump straight to the `Port` option by doing a search for the word "Port". In Notepad, you activate the search facility by pressing CTRL+f.

http://localhost:81/

It's sometimes useful to be able to change the port number, so that you can run more than one web server on the same machine, each using a different port. For example, you could have IIS running on port `80` for testing ASP scripts and Apache running on port `81` for running PHP.

If you do wish to use another port, you will obviously need to select one that isn't currently being used by another service. There is a list available of which ports are normally used and which are free at *http://www.iss.net/security_center/advice/Exploits/Ports/*.

Typical alternative ports given for a web server are 81, 82, 83, 1080, 8080 or 8088. If you enter a port that's already in use, you'll get an error message when you start Apache, so simply try another of the ports listed previously and you'll soon find one that's free.

DocumentRoot

The path set for the DocumentRoot option is very important. It sets the physical directory on your drive system that will act as the root web directory of your web site. Everything placed in this directory and its subdirectories is made available by the web server. The default setting is

```
DocumentRoot "C:/Program Files/Apache Group/Apache/htdocs"
```

This is the equivalent to IIS's c:\inetpub\wwwroot directory.

However, this isn't very user-friendly. I would recommend changing this setting to point somewhere else, for example DocumentRoot "C:/web server".

If you do change the DocumentRoot path, you'll need to make sure that the path you entered points to a valid directory. If the directory does not exist, simply create it. In fact, the directory chosen doesn't even need to be on the same machine as the server that uses it: you could use a shared folder on another computer on your network. If you subsequently get a *404 Not Found* error when you try to access a web page after making this change, it's always worth checking that you haven't made any mistakes with the DocumentRoot setting.

A couple of paragraphs down from DocumentRoot is another option called Directory, which will be set to

```
<Directory "C:/Program Files/Apache Group/Apache/
htdocs">
```

If you are using Notepad, make sure it does not append the file extension .txt, resulting in a file called httpd.conf.txt *which Apache won't recognize. You can prevent it doing this by selecting All Files from the Save As Type option in Notepad's Save As dialog.*

You need to change this path so it's the same path that you used for the DocumentRoot setting. For example:

```
<Directory "C:/web server">
```

This completes the basic setup, so you can now save httpd.conf.

Apache only reads its httpd.conf file when it is starting up, so if your web server is already running, you will have to stop it and restart it in order for your changes to take effect. Let's now see how to do this.

Checking the Apache Installation

Now that Apache has been installed and configured, the next stage is to test the installation. To do this, create a new HTML document and add a message to the body. Save this file as `index.htm` into the directory specified for the `DocumentRoot` option in the `httpd.conf` file. If you used the path we recommended earlier, this will be

```
C:\web server\index.htm
```

Now that Apache has a file to serve, let's start the web server itself.

In the `Apache` directory, you will find the program called `Apache.exe`. If you opted for the manual Apache start-up, you can just double-click on its icon in Explorer whenever you want to start the server. When you do this, a new DOS window will open. It will remain open all the time Apache is running (although it can be minimized).

To stop Apache, all you need to do is to close this DOS box. When it is started in this way, the Apache web server runs as a child process of this DOS window, so shutting the DOS window kills the Apache process as well.

Alternatively, in a new DOS window, you can enter the command

```
C:\Program Files\Apache Group\Apache> apache -k shutdown
```

If you right-click the Apache.exe icon and select Create Shortcut, you can then drag this new shortcut straight onto your desktop. This makes it easier to find whenever you want to start the server.

This will kill the Apache process and close any of its log or system files that are open.

If you chose to run Apache as a service (only possible on NT-based systems), you can make sure the service has started by opening a new DOS prompt and entering the following command:

```
NET START APACHE
```

If the Apache service is already running, you'll get a message to that effect:

```
C:\>NET START APACHE
The requested service has already been started.
```

To stop the service, you use the following command:

```
NET STOP APACHE
```

You can also enter these commands straight into the *Run* option from the *Start* menu. Alternatively, you can check the status of the server and start and stop the service from the *Services* section of the Windows *Control Panel*.

Either way, if all went well with the installation, the DOS box will show a message similar to the following:

```
Apache/1.3.27 (Win 32) running…
```

If there is a problem, a message will be displayed in addition to the previous one, and the error will show details of which file is involved.

Apache also has an optional switch that allows it to check that all its configuration files have the correct syntax without actually starting the server up. It can alert you to any errors it finds. Do this with the following command from the DOS prompt:

```
C:\Program Files\Apache Group\Apache>apache -t
```

If the configuration files are OK, you'll see a message similar to this:

```
c:/program files/apache group/apache/conf/httpd.conf: Syntax OK
```

If any errors are found, you'll get a message showing the error, the setting it occurred with, and the line number in the `httpd.conf` file. This makes it easy to go straight to the relevant setting and correct it.

Now that Apache is installed and running, you can open a web browser and type in the following address:

```
http://localhost/index.htm
```

Alternatively, you can use your computer name instead of `localhost`. Your machine name will be listed under the *System* section of the Windows *Control Panel*. If you have assigned a domain name to the server, you could use that instead, of course.

If everything is working, then you should see the test page you created displayed in your browser.

Troubleshooting Guide

If you have any problems with Apache, your first job is to double-check that all the paths are correct in the Apache `httpd.conf` file.

If you have large-scale problems with the installation, you can remove Apache by opening the same file that you used to install it. It should recognize that Apache is installed and offer to repair or remove the installation. You can then remove Apache and reinstall it. Note, however, that the *remove Apache* option does not remove Apache's configuration files, so these should be manually erased before you reinstall, if you want to make a clean start.

The complete manual for Apache can be found online (*http://httpd.apache.org/docs/*).

> *Because Apache has been around so long and is so widely used, there is a wealth of supporting documentation for it available on the Web.*

Because Apache has been around so long and is so widely used, it has been the subject of a huge number of guides, tutorials, and Frequently Asked Questions (FAQ) documents, which you can find on the Internet. A quick trip to a good search engine with a description of the error can usually offer a solution.

Another excellent resource is the Usenet archive (*http://groups.google.com/*), which contains a vast number of Usenet messages that can be easily searched.

Apache Modules

Because Apache is so popular, many extra modules have been created that integrate with it to provide extra functionality. The PHP module (also called `mod.php` or `mod_php`) is one such module. It allows Apache to serve PHP pages.

A complete list of other modules can be found at *http://httpd.apache.org/docs/mod/ index-bytype.html*. For a development server, you probably won't need to install any extra modules apart from PHP, but it's worth knowing that these modules exist.

Once modules have been installed to their correct location, they can be enabled or disabled in the Apache configuration file, `httpd.conf`. You'll look at this in depth in the next section, when you add the PHP module to Apache.

Installing PHP with Apache on Windows

Let's now install PHP into Apache so it can process PHP pages and static HTML pages. We assume that you have installed and tested Apache according to the steps outlined thus far.

Downloading PHP

The first step is to download PHP, which is available from the PHP downloads page at *http://www.php.net/downloads.php*.

Scroll down the downloads page until you find the section labeled *Windows Binaries*. The current version at the time of this writing is PHP 4.3.0, and there are two different

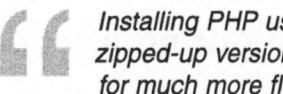

Installing PHP using the zipped-up version allows for much more flexibility.

packages available: a .zip file and an installer package. The .zip file is the larger of the two, and it is the one that should be downloaded, since it allows you much more choice when it comes to configuring PHP and adding extensions. If you have worked through Chapter 3, you will have already downloaded this file, and you just need to unzip it to a different location.

Once you've selected the .zip file, you'll be taken to a list of mirror sites from where you can download the file. It helps to pick a mirror site in a country close to you, as this will be the fastest way to download.

Installing PHP

Before you install PHP, make sure you have stopped Apache, as explained in the previous section. If you have a MySQL server running as well, it's a good idea to stop that, too.

The first step is to unzip the PHP .zip file you downloaded. It's recommended that you extract it to a somewhere fairly logical, such as C:\php. It is best not to use a directory path that includes directory names with spaces in them, such as C:\Program Files\php, since this can cause complications.

You'll find that there is a file called install.txt in the directory you extracted PHP into. Before you start, you should read this file. It may contain special instructions for newer versions of PHP.

There will also be a number of subdirectories relevant to running PHP. Two are especially so: the extensions directory and the sapi directory. The extensions directory, as its name suggests, contains the DLLs required to run extra PHP modules. The sapi directory contains important **Server API** DLLs, which form the heart of PHP. The PHP module has a different core DLL file, designed for each web server that supports PHP. The one you need for Apache is named php4apache.dll. You need to copy this from the sapi directory into the main php directory—in our case, from C:\php\sapi\php4apache.dll to C:\php\php4apache.dll.

PHP also needs a temporary directory, which it will use to store certain information when it is running. This can be anywhere on your file system, but we advise that you create a directory called temp in the php directory (for example, C:\php\temp).

Inside the newly created temp directory, create a directory called sessions and a directory called uploads. You'll refer to these directories later when you configure PHP.

There are only two more steps left: you need to configure Apache to recognize the PHP modules, and you need to create a php.ini file. We'll look at each step separately.

Configuring Apache for PHP

Configuring Apache to use the PHP module is fairly simple. It involves simply editing the main Apache configuration file, `httpd.conf`. If you installed Apache according to the guide in this chapter, then you will find the `httpd.conf` file at `C:\Program Files\Apache Group\Apache\conf\httpd.conf`.

The first section that needs editing is the one that tells Apache which modules to include when it starts up. Each module that you want to add requires an entry in the section under the heading

```
Dynamic Shared Object (DSO) Support
```

DSO support allows you to add extra modules to Apache without changing the main Apache program itself. You'll see a number of entries already in the list, such as the following:

```
#LoadModule vhost_alias_module modules/mod_vhost_alias.so
#LoadModule mime_magic_module modules/mod_mime_magic.so
#LoadModule status_module modules/mod_status.so
```

The `LoadModule` directive tells Apache to load in a module. However, the pound sign (#) at the start of the `LoadModule` line effectively comments it out and tells Apache to ignore it. To make the module active, you just need to remove the # sign from the front, save the `httpd.conf` file, and restart Apache.

In this case, you need to add a line to tell Apache to load in the PHP module. This needs entering on a new line underneath the existing ones.

```
LoadModule php4_module c:/php/php4apache.dll
```

If you didn't extract PHP to `c:\php`, then you'll need to change the path accordingly, of course.

Right below the `LoadModule` section is a corresponding section for `AddModule` lines, a few of which are as follows:

```
#AddModule mod_vhost_alias.c
AddModule mod_env.c
AddModule mod_log_config.c
```

Every entry in the `LoadModule` section needs a corresponding entry in the `AddModule` section. In the case of PHP, you need to add the following line just beneath the other `AddModule` directives:

```
AddModule mod_php4.c
```

Note that you don't need to add a path to the AddModule entry.

Finally, this command needs to be added just beneath the last `AddModule` line:

```
AddType application/x-httpd-php .php
```

This line tells Apache to process all pages with the extension `.php` using the PHP module. If you want to have other extensions processed by PHP, just add a duplicate copy of this command with the extra page extension for the types of page you want processed by PHP.

These are all the changes that are needed in the Apache `httpd.conf` file, so you can now simply save the file and close it.

Configuring PHP

Now that you've set up Apache, the next step is to configure PHP. PHP uses a configuration file called `php.ini`. This file can add to or modify the options built into the PHP module when it was compiled, and it allows you to reconfigure it as you wish without having to recompile it. This file has to be manually created, but this is not as hard as it may sound, because PHP comes with two template configuration files to use as a starting point. These two files are as follows:

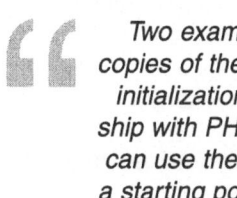
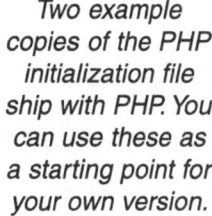

Two example copies of the PHP initialization file ship with PHP. You can use these as a starting point for your own version.

- **php.ini-dist** – This file contains a default PHP configuration, which is tailored for a development server. This is the file you are going to use as the basis for your own file, as this a development server that you're setting up.

- **php.ini-recommended** – This file is tailored for a real web server, and it is locked down, security-wise. All the notes regarding this file are placed as comments at the top of the file, and it's worth reading these to see the differences between the two versions of `php.ini`.

Creating the php.ini File

Open `php.ini-dist` in a text editor. If you extracted PHP to `C:\php`, then the location of this file will be `C:\php\php-ini.dist`. Before you edit the file, first save it as `php.ini` in your main Windows directory (such as `C:\Windows\php.ini`). That way, you will still have a backup copy of the original configuration file.

Although `php.ini` contains a large number of settings, you need to look at only a few to get the PHP installation up and running. They are for more advanced configurations. Let's look at the settings in the same order as they appear in the file.

Resource Limits

The first two settings we're going to look at are in the section labeled `Resource Limits`.

Error Reporting and Logging

- **error_reporting**

  This setting defines the level of error reporting that PHP uses. The default value is

  ```
  error_reporting  =  E_ALL & ~E_NOTICE
  ```

  This tells PHP to show all PHP errors and warnings, but not to display notices. If you want PHP to show notices as well, then you would change the setting to

  ```
  error_reporting  =  E_ALL
  ```

  Normally, notices cause more problems than they solve, so it's easier to leave them turned off. This setting can be overridden by the PHP `error_reporting()` command, so it's best to leave notices turned off here and then turn them on as desired in your PHP scripts.

Paths and Directives

Here you can set up the paths that PHP uses.

- **doc_root**

  This setting tells PHP which directory on the server's hard disk represents the root directory of your web site. It needs to match the `DocumentRoot` setting in the Apache `httpd.conf` file. If you configured Apache according to this guide, then this should be set to

  ```
  doc_root = "C:\web server"
  ```

- **extension_dir**

  This setting tells PHP where its extension DLLs are located. If you extracted PHP to `c:\php`, then this should be set to

  ```
  extension_dir = "C:\php\extensions\"
  ```

File Uploads

Scroll down to the section labeled `File Uploads`, which governs settings concerning file uploading from a web page.

- **file_uploads**

  This setting can be on or off. It tells PHP whether to allow file uploading through a browser or not. The default setting is

  ```
  file_uploads = On
  ```

- **upload_tmp_dir**

  This setting sets the location where uploaded files are stored temporarily until they are moved to their proper location. This should be changed to the `temp` directory that was created after the PHP files were extracted:

  ```
  upload_tmp_dir = "C:\php\temp\uploads"
  ```

- **upload_max_filesize**

  This setting specifies the maximum file size (in MB) that can be uploaded through a PHP web page. The default setting is

  ```
  upload_max_filesize = 2M
  ```

Sessions

The final setting in `php.ini` that we are going to look at is in the `Sessions` section.

- **session_save_path**

  This setting is the main cause of problems with session variables under Windows, as the default setting is

  ```
  Session_save_path = /tmp
  ```

  Because this `/tmp` directory doesn't exist, session data can't be saved, and sessions don't work. To fix this, you're going to change the path to the `temp` directory you created earlier, so this setting should be changed to

  ```
  session.save_path = C:\php\temp\sessions
  ```

This completes configuration of the main PHP settings, so you can save `php.ini` and then close the text editor.

Restarting Apache

As you've edited both the Apache configuration file, `httpd.conf`, and the PHP configuration file, `php.ini`, you need to restart Apache (if it's running) for the new settings to take effect. Refer back to the "Checking the Apache Installation" section for details of how to do this.

Now that the server has been restarted, you can move on to check that the installation was successful and that PHP pages are being processed.

Testing Apache and PHP

When you restarted Apache, you will have received a message similar to the following (if you used the manual install):

```
Apache/1.3.27 (Win 32) PHP/4.3.0 running...
```

You should see that, in addition to the main Apache message, there is a message saying that PHP is running. If you get an error message, it should tell you in which configuration file the error was found and the setting that caused it. You can then correct the error and restart Apache.

To test PHP, open Dreamweaver MX and create a new page with the following code:

```html
<html>
<head>
<title>PHP Test Page</title>
<meta http-equiv="Content-Type" content="text/html; charset=iso-8859-1">
</head>
<body>
<?php phpinfo(); ?>
</body>
</html>
```

Save this file as `phptest.php` in the directory set as Apache's document root. If you followed this guide, you would save the file as

```
C:\web server\phptest.php
```

Now that the file has been saved in the web server's document root directory, it's now available through Apache. Open a new browser window and enter the following address:

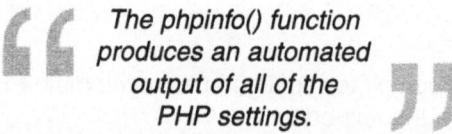

The phpinfo() function produces an automated output of all of the PHP settings.

```
http://localhost/phptest.
php
```

If the installation was successful, you should see a screen similar to the screen shot shown here. The call to the `phpinfo()` function simply produces an automated output of all of the PHP settings.

Note that the *Server API* section will show *Apache* for an ISAPI install or *CGI/FastCGI* for a CGI install.

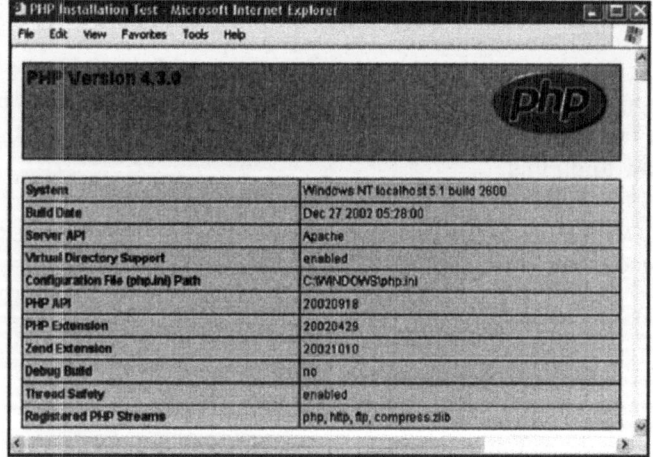

Troubleshooting a PHP Installation

If you have a problem with the installation, it likely has its roots in the `php.ini` file. First check that `php.ini` is located in your Windows directory (such as `C:\windows`), so it can be found and the settings can be read.

Open the `php.ini` file in a text editor and go back through the settings you've looked at in this chapter. Make sure that all the values and paths you entered are correct.

If you get a *404 – Page not found* error when you know that the page exists in Apache's document root directory, it may mean that the document root given in the `php.ini` file is incorrect. This must be changed so that it exactly matches the document root specified in the Apache `httpd.conf` file and the location of the folder holding your web site.

Open the Apache `httpd.conf` file and check in the `LoadModule` section that the correct path to PHP is given, and that you have entries for both `LoadModule` and `AddModule`.

If you later discover that you have problems with session variables not working or files not uploading through a browser, check that the path to the PHP `temp` directory is correct. If you have followed the steps in this guide, then the path for session variables is `c:\php\temp\sessions`, and the path for file uploads is `c:\php\temp\uploads`.

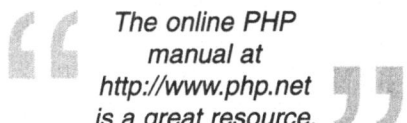

The online PHP manual at http://www.php.net is a great resource.

If all else fails, try copying all the DLL files from the PHP install directory into your `Windows\system32` directory. If you've had a previous version of PHP installed, you'll need to allow Windows to overwrite any existing PHP files.

The online PHP manual at *http://www.php.net* is a great resource. There are many user comments added to the manual pages that show how others have solved real-life problems. Have a read through the *configuration* and *installation* sections of the manual, and you're more than likely to find information that will help you track down the cause of any trouble.

It's also useful to do a search of the Web and Usenet. Because PHP has so many users, it's likely that someone else has experienced a similar problem to your own and has documented how he or she solved it.

PHP Extensions

Like Apache, PHP can also use modules to provide extra functionality. To use these modules, first look in the online manual at *http://www.php.net/* for the relevant page for the extension concerned. This is a must, as some PHP extensions require other software or DLL files to be installed that are external to PHP. For example, the XSLT extension requires an application called Sablotron.

If you want to use these extensions, you must first copy all files from the `dlls` directory, which was created when you extracted PHP. Assuming you followed this guide, the path to this directory is `C:\php\dlls`. All the DLL files in this directory need to be copied into your `Windows\system32` directory. Note that only the files themselves should be copied to `C:\Windows\system32`, not the directory.

The DLL files for the extensions themselves are located at `C:\php\extensions`. Again, the DLL files for the extensions you want to use should be copied to your `Windows\system32` directory.

Finally, open your `php.ini` file with a text editor and scroll down to the `Windows Extensions` section, where you'll see entries similar to the following:

```
;extension=php_bz2.dll
;extension=php_ctype.dll
;extension=php_cpdf.dll
;extension=php_curl.dll
;extension=php_cybercash.dll
```

All the current extensions are listed here, but they have a semicolon (`;`) at the start of their entries. This indicates that PHP should ignore the line, so the extension isn't actually loaded. To activate an extension, simply remove the semicolon from the front of the line and resave the `php.ini` file. If the extension needs any external files or software, you should install them now and restart Apache as described earlier so that the changes will take effect.

Summary

In this chapter, you learned how to

- Install the Apache web server on Windows.
- Configure and test the Apache installation.

In the second half of this chapter, you looked at how to integrate PHP into Apache. You learned how to

- Download PHP and extract it to a location on the server machine.
- Configure Apache to load the PHP module.
- Create a `php.ini` file, which gives the PHP process important start-up information.
- Test and troubleshoot the Apache and PHP installation.

Now that you have Apache and PHP installed, it's recommended that you also install MySQL, as detailed in Chapter 8, so that you can work locally with the Dreamweaver MX PHP/MySQL server model.

5

In this Chapter

- Linux

- Installing Apache on Linux

- Installing PHP for Apache

Author: Gareth Downes-Powell

Apache and PHP Setup on Linux

In this chapter, we look at installing Apache and PHP on a GNU/Linux operating system. This is a bit more involved than the Windows Apache install we covered in the last chapter, as it's done using a command line from a system shell.

In the first section we examine some additional utilities that can make working with the Linux server easier, enabling you to control it remotely from another computer.

We then cover how to install the Apache web server, first looking at where to download the Apache installation file and then how to extract it. We will show you how to create a directory structure that makes Apache easy to upgrade in the future, without your needing to make major changes to its configuration files. Next, we look at compiling Apache, turning the source code into a working program, and testing and troubleshooting the installation.

In the second half of this chapter, we look at how to plug PHP into Apache, so that Apache can serve and process PHP pages. We describe where to download PHP for Linux and provide step-by-step instructions for how to compile PHP as an Apache Dynamic Shared Object (DSO) module, since this integrates it better with Apache and can easily be upgraded in the future without your having to recompile the Apache program. Next, we look at how to configure Apache to recognize PHP and how to create a custom configuration file to control the way PHP works. Finally, we look at testing and troubleshooting the PHP installation, and how to extend PHP's functionality using extra PHP modules.

Linux

Linux is an excellent choice for use on a development server because it can run quite happily on a much lower specification machine than Windows needs. This makes it an excellent option for reusing older, "retired" systems. Many an old Pentium has been resurrected and given a new lease on life as a Linux server.

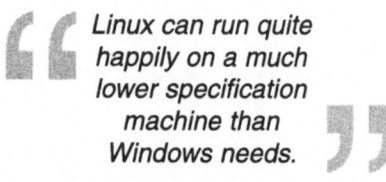

Linux can run quite happily on a much lower specification machine than Windows needs.

You can quite easily connect remotely to a Linux machine and control it through your usual desktop computer. This way, the Linux machine doesn't even require a monitor and can be hidden away in a corner of your office. You gain a double advantage of not having to run a resource-greedy desktop on what is, essentially, a web server, and you don't need to run a web server on your desktop machine.

Linux has the added bonus that it can be purchased on CD very cheaply. Alternatively, if you have a broadband connection, the ISO images can be downloaded free of charge so that you can burn your own CDs.

Many different Linux distributions available are available, including

- **Red Hat** – *http://www.redhat.com/*
- **Slackware** – *http://www.slackware.com/*
- **SuSE** – *http://www.suse.com/index_us.html*

It's a good idea to compare the support available from the different Linux vendors—in particular, check how good their after-sales service is. Different support packages are available from different vendors, and you should make sure the support offered meets your needs.

Recommended Software

Before we actually look at Apache and how to install it, it's recommended that you install some additional software that will allow you to tuck the Linux server away in a corner and control it remotely from a main Windows PC or Apple Mac that you use for Dreamweaver MX. The following recommended packages are free and likely already included in your Linux distribution.

Note that you don't have to install this software in order to install Apache. If you wish, you can skip this section and work directly on the Linux server itself rather than administering it remotely. The firewall section, though, should be essential reading.

Telnet

To administer the Linux server remotely, it's essential to have Telnet on your desktop machine. We find it much easier to use our desktop machine for everything so we don't have to keep moving back and forth between computers. Any computer that has a Telnet program available for it can be used to connect to your Linux server. Like Windows, Mac OS X comes with a UNIX version of Telnet preinstalled.

It's likely that a Telnet server is installed on your Linux server, but it is equally likely that it will be disabled by default. On Linux distributions that run *xinetd*, the program that controls the main Internet services, you need to log into the server as the user root and use the following command:

```
cd /etc/xinetd.d/
```

This takes you into the directory for the server that runs Telnet, *xinetd*.

Note that some installations may use *inetd* instead.

What is `xinetd`/`inetd`? Well, its name is short for the **Internet daemon**, a master server that listens for connection requests or messages for certain ports. Particular services on any machine are served by their respective servers (or **daemons**, as they are sometimes also called, with reference to the spirits in ancient Greek mythology who acted as intermediaries between gods and mortals). Some daemons, such as Apache (the **HTTP Daemon**) run constantly, waiting for requests for their services. Not all servers need to be run in this way. It is often more efficient for a daemon to be started up only for the duration of its work and then shut down again. This is `inetd`'s job. It starts server programs to perform the services associated with a given port, in response to a call from or to that port, shutting them down again once the task is completed. With respect to Telnet, `inetd` listens for requests on port 23, Telnet's port, and it will start Telnet up whenever it receives such a request.

In the `/etc/xinetd.d/` directory, there should be a file called `telnet` (the Telnet configuration file), which you can open using this command:

```
pico telnet
```

This invokes the Pico text editor and opens the Telnet configuration file for editing. At the bottom of the text in this file, there should be a setting similar to the following:

```
disable = yes
```

Change this to

```
disable = no
```

Press *Ctrl* and *x* to exit Pico, entering *y* when asked whether you want to save the file. Next, the `xinetd` server needs to be restarted using this command:

```
/etc/rc.d/init.d/xinetd restart
```

This is similar to the NET START command on Windows server systems.

Telnet should now be enabled.

These instructions may need altering for your particular Linux installation, depending on what extra software it ships with. To get more information, you should read the manuals for whichever version of Linux you have chosen.

To connect to your Linux server remotely from Windows or Mac OS X, you need to enter the following command from the command line:

```
telnet
```

On OS X, simply launch a Terminal program. On Windows, select *Run* from the Windows *Start* menu and type in the command `telnet`. Once Telnet has opened, you can connect to the Linux server using the following command:

```
open <IP_ADDRESS>
```

where `<IP_ADDRESS>` is the IP address that you have assigned to the Linux server. Once you have logged into the server, you can type in commands just as if you were sitting at the Linux machine itself.

You may find that you cannot see what you are typing in when the Telnet session is open. This is because the LOCAL_ECHO option is not enabled in the Telnet client running on your desktop machine. To change this, close the connection by typing in the `exit` command and turn LOCAL_ECHO on by entering the command Set LOCAL_ECHO. Retry your connection, and everything should be fine. Note that you can get a list of Telnet settings using the command `set ?` in Telnet.

Samba

Samba allows your Windows network to connect to your Linux server, as if it was running Windows. For example, you could connect to the Linux machine from your main Windows PC and access its hard disk in Windows Explorer, just as if it too was running Windows. The Samba web site is *http://www.samba.org/*.

With both Telnet and Samba running, you can control the Linux server completely on your Windows PC or Mac. This is extremely useful, as it means you don't have to keep moving from one computer to another.

Firewall

If your Linux server is directly connected to the Internet, it's essential that you install a firewall so that no one can get at your server from outside your network. If you have a paid-for distribution, it is likely that there is a firewall included with it.

If not, a good firewall for Linux is **ipchains**. There are a great many guides and tutorials on the Internet that detail how to set up and configure ipchains on your Linux server. Paul Russell maintains an in-depth resource for ipchains users here: *http://qslinux.org/docs/ howtos/ipchains/IPCHAINS-HOWTO.html*.

The Apache Web Server

There are currently two different versions of Apache: the original 1.3.x series and the newer Apache 2.x series. In this guide, we're going to look at the latest version of the 1.3.x series, which is Apache 1.3.27 at the time of this writing. We're using this version because PHP support for the Apache 2.0 series is still experimental. Also, most web servers you are likely to find offered by hosting companies will still be running Apache 1.3. So, unless you are willing to pay the cost of running your own dedicated server, Apache 1.3 is likely to be what you'll end up using for some time to come.

 Apache has a huge following, especially on the Linux platform.

Apache has a huge following, so there's a wealth of information on the Web about it, and a large number of modules have been written that add new functionality to it. Your first step is to download the package from the Apache web site, which you'll look at now.

Downloading Apache

Apache is free to download from the Apache web site: *http://httpd.apache.org/ download.cgi /*.

Once on the download page, you need to scroll down to the section labeled *Apache 1.3.27*. The file that you need to download is labeled *Unix Source: apache_1.3.27.tar.gz*. You don't need to download this file directly onto your Linux machine, however. You could download it onto your desktop computer and then transfer it across.

The file is around only 2.3MB, so it shouldn't take too long to download.

The reason the file is so small is that is has been compressed using an archiving utility called **GNU tar**, "tar" being short for "tape archive." The utility was originally written back in the mid-1980s for use with magnetic tape devices. Nowadays, it is normally used for combining multiple files and directories into a single file. When combined with the **GNU zip** utility, `gzip`, `tar` has an effect similar to the PKZIP format from PKWARE, Inc., common on Windows platforms, or the StuffIt archives used on Macs, in that it compacts, as well as archives, the files it contains.

Once you have downloaded the file, transfer it onto your Linux machine's `/usr/local/` directory for installation.

Installing Apache

This guide assumes that you're installing Apache through a shell prompt, either on the Linux server itself or through a Telnet session from another computer. You'll need to be logged in as the **root** user. If you're not already the root user, you can change using the Linux `su` command:

```
su root
```

You'll then need to enter the root user password.

The `su` command is short for "switch user" and allows you to change to another user without having to log out and log in again. You can become another user only if you have the correct permissions and know the user's password.

Creating the Required Directory Structure

Before you can install Apache, you need to extract the Apache file downloaded from the Apache web site and create the correct directory structure ready for the installation.

In this guide, you're going to install Apache to the following path:

```
/usr/local/apache
```

This directory doesn't exist by default, so you need to create it using the following commands:

```
cd /usr/local
mkdir apache
cd apache
```

The next step is to copy the Apache archive file that you just downloaded (`apache_1.3.27.gz`, in our case) to this location. You can do this with the following command (inserting your own filename, as necessary):

```
cp /usr/local/apache_1.3.27.tar.gz /usr/local/apache/
```

Now that the file is in the correct place, you need to extract the files it contains. Move to the `/usr/local/apache` directory:

```
cd /usr/local/apache
```

Enter the following command:

```
tar -xzvf ./apache_1.3.27.tar.gz
```

When the command is run, a new directory is created within `usr/local/apache/` called `apache_1.3.27`, which contains all the necessary files for Apache to run.

The options used with the `tar` command have the following meaning: `x` = extract file (rather than archive it), `z` = unzip the compressed `gzip` archive, `v` = use the "verbose" option, which means "show all the file names as each one is extracted", and `f` = work on the archive file named in the command.

The archive will unpack the files and directories, and output a scrolling list showing each one as it is extracted.

To make life easier, you next create a **symbolic link** between the `apache_1.3.27` directory and a directory called `httpd` using the following command:

```
ln -s /usr/local/apache/apache_1.3.27 /usr/local/apache/httpd
```

A symbolic link has now been set up so that you can refer to the `apache_1.3.27` directory as if it were called `httpd`. In effect, you've given the directory `apache_1.3.27` another name. Either name can now be used to access the directory. Understand, however, that `httpd` is not a *copy* of `apache_1.3.27`; both are names for the same directory. The concept is similar to that of a shortcut in Windows or an alias in OS X.

Creating the symbolic link has several advantages:

- It's much easier to type `httpd` in a path than it is to type `apache_1.3.27`.

- If in the future you install a later version of Apache, you can just change the symbolic link that `httpd` uses to the new Apache directory. This keeps each version of Apache separate from any others, and you don't have to change any configuration files (which are set to point to the `httpd` directory).

5

Apache and PHP Setup on Linux

Should you have problems installing the new version, you can just change `httpd` to point back to the old version, and you'll have a working version of Apache again without losing any development time.

Symbolic links do add slightly to the system overhead, but on a development server this shouldn't be a problem.

The Apache Layout

To keep the installation neat and easy to upgrade, you're going to split the installation into two separate locations. One location will hold dependent files specific to the running of Apache, and the other will hold the configuration and log files, as these are not specific to the Apache version. This means that you can upgrade to later Apache versions without having to change your configuration files.

You need to create these directories in the following location:

`/home`

If you don't already have a `home` directory, use the following commands to create one in the server's root directory, `/`.

```
cd /
mkdir home
cd home
```

Now that you're in the `/home` directory, you're going to create a new subdirectory called `www` and then three subdirectories under that for different types of files. Type the following commands to make the directories:

```
mkdir www
cd www
mkdir conf
mkdir logs
mkdir webroot
```

`www` is your base directory and will contain all of the non-version-specific files. `conf` will contain the Apache configuration files, `logs` will hold the Apache log files, and `webroot` will be the directory that web pages are served from.

To recap, you now have two separate directory structures:

- `/usr/local/apache/httpd` – For version-dependent files
- `/home/www` – For version-independent files

Now that you have the two directory structures set up, you can start the Apache installation.

Starting the Apache DSO Installation

Use the following command to change to the location to which Apache was extracted:

```
cd /usr/local/apache/httpd
```

Installation on Linux systems is very different from Windows systems. You have to actually create the program files themselves. The file that you downloaded from the Apache web site contains the source code for Apache, written in C, rather than a ready-to-run installation package. To turn this source code into a working program, you need to compile it using a C compiler. This isn't as difficult as it sounds, though, since it's largely an automated process.

There are two ways you can build Apache, and which one you use will be determined by how you want it to run:

- If you choose a **static build**, then every time you want to install a new module into it, you need to recompile the whole Apache program again from the source code, including the new module into the build.
- The alternative method, which is the one you are going to use, is to build what is called a **DSO installation**. This installation allows you to add and remove modules without having to recompile the Apache program. In addtion to the performance advantages this offers, it makes it much easier to install the PHP module, which you will be looking at in the second section of this chapter. Building a DSO installation also makes it easier to update Apache. You can find a more detailed explanation of the DSO system at *http://httpd.apache.org/docs/dso.html*.

To build the DSO installation, you first have to use the `configure` command. You can supply further options as parameters that dictate how Apache will behave. We're only going to cover a basic setup, so the only parameters you'll use are the ones that tell Apache where to place the compiled program files. Type the following command to start the compile process:

```
./configure -prefix=/usr/local/apache/httpd -sysconfdir=/home/www/conf -
enable-module=so
```

The `-prefix` parameter indicates where to install the Apache program files, and the `-sysconfdir` option defines the directory where Apache will store its configuration files.

Once you've entered the command, the compile process will start. It may take a minute or two, during which time you'll see various information about the process displayed. When the `configure` command has completed, you'll be returned to the command prompt. All the relevant pieces of source code needed to build Apache have been pulled together according to the options that were specified.

Next, you need to compile the parts of Apache that the `configure` command has prepared to make it into an executable file, which you can do by entering the following command:

```
make
```

While the `make` command is compiling all the code, you'll see the lists of the current files being compiled. The process may take a couple of minutes, especially on an older machine. Don't worry if you're not sure what the output means; you just need to wait for the `make` command to finish. If the program compiled successfully, then you'll just be returned to the command prompt. Otherwise, an error message indicating what the problem is will be output before returning you to the command prompt.

At some stages of `make` (and `make install`, which is the next command we look at), it may appear as if nothing is happening. It's very unlikely that the server has hung, though, so just be patient and wait for the command to finish.

If there is an error, it's usually because the libraries on the server Apache needs to compile are older versions than the ones Apache requires. If this is the case, the error message will show which package is too old and which version Apache needs to compile. You can then download the newer library versions and install them if necessary. If you do update any libraries, you need to execute the following command, so that the newer library versions can be found:

```
/sbin/ldconfig
```

You should then run the Apache `configure` and `make` commands again. As long as the correct versions of the libraries it needs are present, Apache will be compiled successfully.

You need to enter one final command:

```
make install
```

This copies all of Apache's files to the correct location and sets the correct file permissions for the files and directories used. Again, everything `make install` is doing is shown on the screen.

Once everything is complete, you should see a message similar to the following:

```
+--------------------------------------------------------------+
| You now have successfully built and installed the            |
| Apache 1.3 HTTP server. To verify that Apache actually       |
| works correctly you now should first check the               |
| (initially created or preserved) configuration files         |
|                                                              |
|   /home/www/conf/httpd.conf                                  |
|                                                              |
| and then you should be able to immediately fire up           |
| Apache the first time by running:                            |
|                                                              |
|   /usr/local/apache/httpd/bin/apachectl start                |
|                                                              |
| Thanks for using Apache.         The Apache Group            |
|                                  http://www.apache.org/      |
+--------------------------------------------------------------+
```

Apache has installed successfully, but before you can start it, you need to change a few options in the Apache configuration file.

Configuring Apache

Now that Apache is installed, you need to set some options specific to your server in its main configuration file, which is called `httpd.conf`. The location of this file will be

`/home/www/conf/httpd.conf`

If you're opening the file on a Windows system, you'll need to use a text editor such as Notepad, as a word processor may insert hidden formatting codes that will cause problems when Apache tries to read the file.

If you're editing the file on the Linux server itself, you can use the `pico` or `vi` editors.

During the install process documented in the previous section, most of the correct paths are placed in the `httpd.conf` file, but it's a good idea to go through and check certain key settings.

ServerRoot

The first setting that is of importance to you is the `ServerRoot` setting, as this tells Apache where its program and system files are located. The setting should currently read

```
ServerRoot "/usr/local/apache/httpd"
```

This is correct because you specified it in your earlier `./configure` call, so it can be left as it is.

Port

The `Port` setting is in the second section of the `httpd.conf` file, which is quite a ways down the page. To jump to it quickly, you can use the *Find* function of your text editor. The default setting is

```
Port 80
```

This governs the port that Apache listens to requests on. Port 80 is the standard port for running a web server, but if you wish, you can change the port to another value, as long as the port number you choose isn't already in use. If you do decide to change the port, then whenever you make a request to the web server you will need to specify the port number in the URL. For example, *http://localhost:81/page.php.*

DocumentRoot

The `DocumentRoot` setting defines the directory on the server that web pages are served from the root directory of your web site. By default, this setting should be

```
DocumentRoot "/home/www/webroot"
```

Again, this is correct, so you can leave it as is.

Slightly further down, you'll also see the following line:

```
<Directory "/home/www/webroot/">
```

The paths in these two settings must always match each other, so if you change the `DocumentRoot` setting in the future, you must also change the path for the `Directory` setting.

AllowOverride

The `AllowOverride` option sets whether or not you can override the settings in `httpd.conf` by using `.htaccess` files. The default setting for this option is

```
AllowOverride None
```

This means that no settings in `httpd.conf` can be overridden by an `.htaccess` file. This isn't very convenient for a development server, and it can be changed to `All` to allow any setting to be overridden. This is what you would want on a development server. Other options include the following: `Options`, `FileInfo`, `AuthConfig`, `Limit`, or `None`. These govern which sections of the `httpd.conf` file can be overridden, where `All` means that all options can be overridden, and `None` means no options can be overridden. The other options allow you to specify that certain parts of the `httpd.conf` file can be overridden, and you can find a list of the directives they apply to at *http://httpd.apache.org/docs/mod/core.html#allowoverride.*

ErrorLog

This setting dictates where the file that logs errors is stored. Following installation, it will be set to its default location:

```
ErrorLog /usr/local/apache/httpd/logs/error_log
```

You want the log files to be in your www directory, however, so you need to change this setting to the following:

```
ErrorLog /home/www/logs/error_log
```

CustomLog

This setting governs where the normal Apache log files are stored. By default this will be

```
CustomLog /usr/local/apache/httpd/logs/access_log common
```

Again, this needs changing to

```
CustomLog /home/www/logs/access_log common
```

These options are the main ones that need to be checked, so you can now save the file and close it.

Controlling the Apache Server

To start Apache, you need to use the apachectl (short for "Apache control") control:

```
/usr/local/apache/httpd/bin/apachectl start
```

Similarly, to stop the server, you would use this command:

```
/usr/local/apache/httpd/bin/apachectl stop
```

There is also a restart command, but it can sometimes be unreliable, and it is more useful on a live server. If you want to restart a test server, we recommend that you just stop the server and then start it up again.

It's a good idea for a Linux development server to have Apache start itself during bootup. How you do this will depend on your version and distribution of Linux, but there are many guides on the Web on how to set Apache to run on start-up. Instructions can also usually be found in the manual for your particular Linux distribution.

Note that you can shut down your whole Linux server so that it can be powered off, using the command

```
/sbin/shutdown -h now
```

and you can do this remotely through a Telnet session.

Testing Apache

Once you have Apache started, you can create a test page that you can view in your browser to check that Apache is correctly serving web pages.

If you have followed this guide so far, the root of your web site will be at the location `/home/www/webroot`.

You can now copy the default Apache `index.htm` file from the `httpd/htdocs` directory, using the following command:

```
cp /usr/local/apache/httpd/htdocs/index.html.en
/home/www/webroot/index.html
```

Open a web browser and, if you're working on the server, enter this URL:

```
http://localhost/index.html
```

If you're working remotely, you can use this URL:

```
http://serveripaddress/index.html
```

And if everything is working correctly, you'll see the Apache test page.

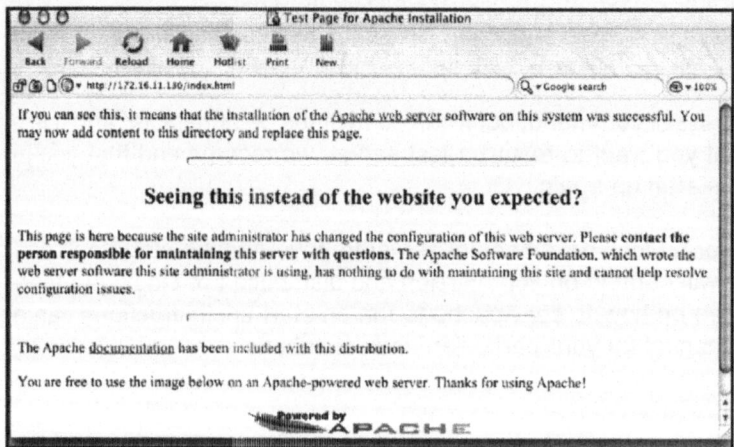

Actually, you probably won't see the graphic, `apache_pb.gif`, at the bottom of the page in your copy of the page, because it's still located in Apache's default `webroot` folder. If you want to see it, you'll have to copy it across to your new `webroot` folder by entering the command

```
cp /usr/local/apache/httpd/htdocs/apache_pb.gif /home/www/webroot/
```

Reload the page and the image should appear.

Troubleshooting the Apache Installation

If you get a *404 - Page Not Found* error, open up the main Apache configuration file, `httpd.conf` from

```
/home/www/conf/httpd.conf
```

You then need to check that all the paths you entered are correct. Fix any errors and save the file. You'll then need to restart Apache so it will read the new settings. You can also check that the Apache configuration files do not have any syntax errors using the `apachectl` command you use to start and stop the web server. You do this by passing it the argument `configtest`, as follows:

```
/usr/local/apache/httpd/bin/apachectl configtest
```

This will point out any syntax errors it finds in the configuration files.

You can also check the Apache log files, especially `error_log`, which, in our case, is found at the following location:

```
/home/www/logs/error_log
```

This should provide some helpful information.

Note the `error_log` file has no file extension. This is perfectly valid on Linux; it's just a normal text file. You can read it and edit it using a text editor such as Notepad or Pico.

Don't forget that Apache needs to be started by the root user.

There are a large number of frequently asked questions and troubleshooting tips that will help you sort out any problems at the **Red Hat Apache Knowledgebase** (*http://www.redhat.com/support/resources/faqs/RH-apache-FAQ/book1.html*).

Apache and PHP Setup on Linux

Apache Modules

Apache can be extended by a number of modules that you add when you compile Apache or later. A current list that's divided into groups depending on the module type can be found at *http://httpd.apache.org/docs/mod/index-bytype.html.* Although you probably won't use any of these modules yet, it's useful to know they exist and can be installed later on if you wish.

In the next section, you will install the PHP module that allows Apache to serve PHP pages.

Installing PHP into Apache

In this section, we look at how to install PHP into Apache. The first step is to download it from the PHP web site. There are other sources for PHP around the Web, but it is much easier to get it from the source.

Downloading PHP

PHP is available as a free download from the PHP web site, *http://www.php.net/downloads.php.* The file that you need to download is at the top of the page, in the section labeled *Complete Source Code.*

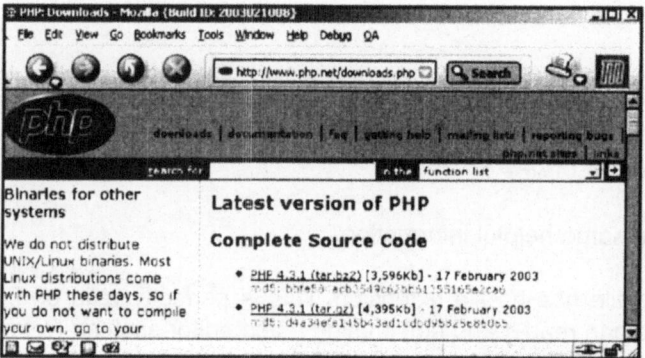

The current file at the time of this writing was for PHP 4.3.1. Its entry looks like this:

PHP 4.3.1(tar.gz) [4,395Kb] – 17 February 2003

Development of PHP

New versions of PHP are released frequently. At the time of this writing, PHP 5 is currently being tested and is likely to be released soon. It is unlikely that Dreamweaver MX will offer extensive support for PHP 5, however, so you should download the most recent version of PHP 4 if you wish to use Dreamweaver's design features with PHP. PHP 5 is something of a new digression in PHP development. Because of this, advances and improvements to PHP 4 will continue, even after the release of PHP 5.

Once you've clicked on the file, you'll be taken to a mirror page where you can select a country nearest to you to download from so you can get a faster download. Download the file to your /usr/local directory, as that is where you'll be installing the file.

Now that you have the required file, you can move on to extract it and start the installation. Note that you need to install PHP as the Linux root user.

Extracting the PHP File

You are going to install PHP into the location

```
/usr/local/
```

First, you need to create a php directory in this location, and then you need to move the PHP file to that location. This can be done with the following commands:

```
cd /usr/local/
mkdir php
cd php
cp /usr/local/php-4.3.1.tar.gz ./
```

Note that the PHP file contains the version number within it. If you have downloaded a later version, you'll need to change the preceding filename to reference the name of the file you downloaded. You should now be in the directory

```
/usr/local/php/
```

And there should be a copy of php-4.3.1.tar.gz at that location. To extract this file, enter the following command:

```
tar -xzvf php-4.3.1.tar.gz
```

This will extract the archive, and you should now see another directory at the following location:

```
/usr/local/php/php-4.3.1
```

As with the Apache installation previously, you're going to create a symbolic link between the php-4.3.0 directory with the name php. In your configuration files, you can then refer to this symbolic link, and in future the link can easily be changed to point to later PHP versions as and when you install them. This allows new versions to be installed without having to change any configuration options.

To create the symbolic link, enter the following command:

```
ln -s php-4.3.0 php
```

From now on, you can refer to the directory php as if you were referring to the directory php-4.3.0. You also need to create a new directory, which will be used later by PHP to store temporary files. This directory needs to be called tmp and you'll need to create it at the following location:

```
/usr/local/php/
```

Do this with the command

```
mkdir /usr/local/php/tmp
```

You are going to be installing PHP as a DSO module. To do this, Apache must have been originally built to allow DSO support, as described in the first section of this chapter. If you're upgrading a previous version of Apache, you can check that Apache has been built with DSO support with the following command:

```
/usr/local/apache/bin/httpd -l
```

Note that the argument passed is a lowercase 1, not a numeric 1, and that you won't need to do this at all if you installed Apache as outlined in the first part of this chapter. If Apache has been built with DSO support, the preceding command will return something similar to the following:

```
Compiled-in modules:
  http_core.c
  mod_so.c
```

If you see the two previously listed files, http_core.c and mod_so.c, it means that Apache has been built with DSO support. If not, you'll need to recompile Apache to allow DSO support.

To add PHP as a DSO module for Apache, you must tell PHP the path to the Apache apxs program, which integrates the module with Apache. If you built Apache as per the first part of this guide, then the path to the Apache apxs command will be as follows:

```
/usr/local/apache/httpd/bin/apxs
```

You also need to tell PHP where its php.ini file will be located. Because the two are so closely related, it's convenient to store the php.ini file (a file that PHP will use to set configuration options at start-up) in the same directory as the Apache configuration files. Again, if you followed the first section of the chapter, this location will be

```
/home/www/conf/
```

Now that you have the correct paths, you can start the process of compiling PHP, which you can do by using the following command (from the location /usr/local/php/php on your Linux machine's drive system):

```
./configure --with-apxs=/usr/local/apache/httpd/bin/apxs --with-config-file-path=/home/www/conf --with-mysql
```

There are many options available for configuring PHP. The options shown here are for a basic installation. If you wish, you can add more extensions later on by recompiling PHP. A complete list of options can be found in the online PHP manual at *http://www.php.net/*.

Once you have entered the configure command, you'll see various checks being executed, such as making sure that the path to the apxs command is correct. Once everything has completed, you will be returned to the command prompt.

Compiling PHP and Configuring Apache

You now need to start the actual compile process, which turns the PHP source code into a working program. To start this process, enter the following command:

```
make
```

This process may take a while longer than the time needed to compile Apache in any case, because PHP is a much larger program. As a guideline, we found that on a machine fitted with an AMD K6/2-266 MHz CPU, the process took around 10 minutes, whereas on another Pentium III 500 MHz machine with 256MB of RAM, a time of around 7 minutes was experienced. You'll need to be patient. If everything goes successfully, you'll be returned to the command prompt with no error messages.

Now you can complete the installation. First, stop your Apache server:

```
/usr/local/apache/httpd/bin/apachectl stop
```

Now execute the following command:

```
make install
```

Again, this will take a couple of minutes, so be patient while the compile takes place. Once the process is complete, you should see a message indicating that the operation was successful and that PHP is now installed.

If There Are Any Errors in the PHP make Process

If there are any errors in the process, it will be because PHP cannot find some software that it needs or, alternatively, the version number of installed software is lower than PHP requires. If this is the case, you'll receive an error message that will tell you the problem, which software is needed, and also the version number required. You can then search on the Internet for the required software and install it. Once the correct software is installed, you will need to restart the installation from the configure command. However, before you enter the configure command, you will need to delete a file at the following location:

```
/usr/local/php/php/config.cache
```

You can do this with the command

```
rm /usr/local/php/php/config.cache
```

It's important to do this, as it means that PHP will recheck all the software installed and register the new version number.

When you extract PHP into the usr/local/php/ directory, it creates a further directory called php-4.3.0. As with Apache, we've created a symbolic link to it called php. Under the main usr/local/php/ directory go all the different versions of PHP. You just set the symbolic link, php, to point to the relevant version. This means the path is always /usr/local/php/php/.

Before you can restart Apache with PHP, you need to configure both Apache and PHP to talk to each other, which you will do next.

Configuring Apache

The Apache configuration file is changed automatically during the PHP installation, but it's important to check that the correct settings have been made. You also have to add some extra information.

Open the Apache configuration file, `httpd.conf`, in a text editor. You will find it at the following location:

```
/home/www/conf/httpd.conf
```

The section that you need to look at is just before the second section of the configuration file and is labeled `#Dynamic Shared Object (DSO) Support`. You need to check that the following line is present:

```
LoadModule php4_module          libexec/libphp4.so
```

This tells Apache to load the PHP module, named `libphp4.so` and located in the Apache `libexec` directory. `libphp4.so` should have been copied to the Apache `libexec` directory, but it's worth checking that the file has been correctly copied to this location. The full path to check is

```
/usr/local/apache/httpd/libexec/libphp4.so
```

If the file isn't there, you should copy it to this location from the PHP installation directories.

You also need to add a new setting to the end of this section:

```
AddType application/x-httpd-php .php
```

This tells Apache to process any files with the file extension `.php` using the PHP module. If you wish to process other page extensions, you just need to copy the preceding line and change the page extension to the one you wish to use.

Another optional setting you may wish to add is as follows:

```
AddType application/x-httpd-php-source .phps
```

This adds a new feature that allows pages with extension `.phps` to be displayed as PHP source code with syntax highlighting. This is useful if you wish to display PHP code on a web site. You can control the colors used for the formatting in the `php.ini` file. The lines may already exist, but they may be commented out with a semicolon. If this is the case, just remove the semicolon from the front of the line and the line becomes active.

This completes the configuration of Apache, so save `httpd.conf`. You now need to configure PHP to complete the configuration process.

Apache and PHP Setup on Linux

Configuring PHP

To configure PHP, you edit a file called php.ini, which contains all the PHP settings. You need to create this file, but because of the large number of settings involved, you don't create it from scratch. The PHP directory to which you extracted PHP will contain two templates for the php.ini file, each for different uses.

php.ini-dist

This file is a template for the php.ini file for a development server, and it contains settings that are ideal for code development.

php.ini-recommended

This file is a template for the php.ini file of a production web server. It contains settings that lock down PHP and offer optimum security settings for scripts running on the server.

As you are setting up a development server, you are going to use the file php.ini-dist as your base. You need to copy this file from the PHP installation directory to the directory you specified in the configure command, in this case

```
/home/www/conf
```

To do this, use the following command:

```
cp /usr/local/php/php/php.ini-dist /home/www/conf/php.ini
```

This has created your base php.ini file at the following location:

```
/home/www/conf/php.ini
```

You can now open the php.ini file in a text editor and configure it for the server.

There are a number of important settings, and we'll look at these one by one, working from the top of the file to the bottom. The first setting is found roughly one quarter of the way into the file.

max_execution_time

This setting defines the maximum time that a PHP script can run before being shut down, specified in seconds. The default setting is

```
max_execution_time = 30
```

If you're running a PHP script that does a lot of processing, you may need to increase this value to allow the script to complete its work.

memory_limit

This setting governs the amount of memory a PHP script can use, and it is specified in megabytes. The default setting is

```
memory_limit = 8M
```

It's important that this setting isn't too high. A number of scripts using a large amount of memory and running at once could overload a server, so this value is best left at its default setting unless you happen to know that you have a particularly large script you need to run.

error_reporting

This setting controls the level of error reporting that PHP uses. The default option is

```
error_reporting  =  E_ALL & ~E_NOTICE
```

This displays all errors and warnings, but not notices. This is usually the best setting, as notices can sometimes cause problems. Notices show noncritical information about a script. For instance, if a PHP script is making reference to a variable for the first time, the variable name will not be recognized by the interpreter. A notice would interrupt the execution of the page to insert a message to this effect.

doc_root

This setting is quite a way down the page from the previous one, so you'll need to scroll down a bit to get to it. It serves the same function as Apache's `DocumentRoot` setting, and it should be set to the same directory:

```
doc_root = /home/www/webroot
```

extension_dir

This should be set to the path where the PHP extensions folder is located, which is the extension folder at the location where you installed PHP. For this installation, it should be set to

```
extension_dir = /usr/local/php/php/extensions
```

file_uploads

This option specifies whether to allow file uploads through a web browser. The default setting is

```
file_uploads = On
```

which allows file uploads. Set this to `off` if you don't want to allow uploads, although on a development server this setting is often set to `On`.

upload_tmp_dir

This setting tells PHP where it can temporarily store files that have been uploaded through a web browser. The path needs to be changed to the tmp directory that you created earlier:

```
upload_tmp_dir = /usr/local/php/tmp
```

upload_max_filesize

This sets the maximum size for files that can be uploaded through a web browser, and the default setting is as follows (in megabytes):

```
upload_max_filesize = 2M
```

You should use a setting just larger than the maximum file size you expect to be uploading.

session_save_path

This setting is again some distance down the page, so you'll need to scroll down to get to it. It should be set to the path of the tmp directory created earlier. This will allow PHP to store temporary session data. This should be set as shown here:

```
session_save_path = /usr/local/php/tmp
```

This completes the PHP configuration, so save and close the php.ini file. You now need to restart Apache so that it uses your new settings.

Restarting Apache

To restart Apache, you need to use the apachectl command to stop the server and then start it up again. You do this with the following commands:

```
/usr/local/apache/httpd/bin/apachectl stop
```

which should return the message

```
/usr/local/apache/httpd/bin/apachectl stop: httpd stopped
```

Then to start the server, use

```
/usr/local/apache/httpd/bin/apachectl start
```

which should return the message

```
/usr/local/apache/httpd/bin/apachectl start: httpd started
```

If you get any error messages when you restart Apache, it's usually because of an incorrect setting in either `httpd.conf` or `php.ini`. If this is the case, the error message should let you know which file the error is located in and which setting is at fault. You can then correct the error and restart Apache.

Once Apache has started successfully, you can test it to make sure it's serving PHP pages.

Testing Apache and PHP

To test Apache and PHP, you need to create a new PHP page and add the following PHP function call to the page body:

```
<?php phpinfo(); ?>
```

Save this page as `phptest.php` in the directory you specified as the `documentroot` in the `httpd.conf` file. For the installation we have outlined in this chapter, the file should be saved at the following location:

```
/home/www/webroot/phptest.php
```

You can now open a new web browser window and use the URL

http://ipaddress/phptest.php

where *ipaddress* is the IP address of your Linux server.

If everything is running successfully, you should see the PHP Information screen as shown in the screen shot to the right, which shows information about both the Apache and PHP installation. It is, in itself, extremely useful for troubleshooting.

If you get a *404 - Page Not Found* error, check the troubleshooting guide in the next section. If you get what looks like a blank page, use the *View Source* option in your browser. It's likely you'll see the PHP command displayed, which means that although Apache is serving your file, it's not being processed by PHP, and again you can refer to the troubleshooting guide in the next section.

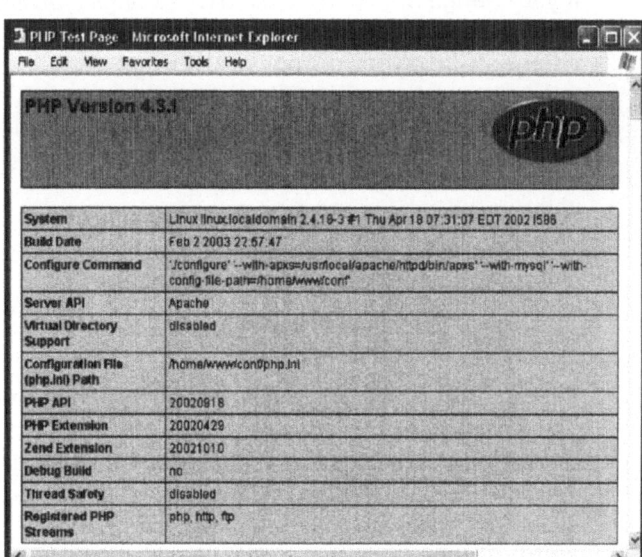

Troubleshooting the PHP Installation

The first step is to check the Apache `httpd.conf` file, which you have placed at the following location:

```
/home/www/conf/httpd.conf
```

Make sure that both of the following lines are present in the file:

```
LoadModule php4_module libexec/libphp4.so
```

```
AddType application/x-httpd-php .php
```

If PHP pages are being served by Apache but are not being processed by PHP, it's likely that the second line is missing.

If the preceding lines are correct, then you need to check the `php.ini` file, which you placed at the following location:

```
/home/www/conf/php.ini
```

Check that the paths for the following settings are correct:

```
doc_root = /home/www/webroot
extension_dir = /usr/local/php/php/extensions
```

If you change any of the preceding settings, you'll need to stop and then start Apache, so that the new settings take effect. You can then request the `phptest.php` page again to see if the installation is working.

If PHP is running, but you have problems with file uploading or sessions in your PHP scripts, open `php.ini` and check that the following paths are correct:

```
upload_tmp_dir = /usr/local/php/tmp
session.save_path = /usr/local/php/tmp
```

Check that you created the `tmp` folder in the preceding location and that Apache has permission to write to that folder.

If you still have problems, your first stop should be the online PHP manual (*http://www.php.net/docs.php*). Here, you'll find many troubleshooting suggestions and checks, as well as comments from real-life users detailing any problems they had and how they solved them. Since PHP and Apache are so popular, it's likely that someone has had a similar problem to your own and documented how he or she fixed it. A search at *http://www.google.com/* and *http://groups.google.com/* will help you come up with some information that can help solve any problems you may have.

Summary

In this chapter we first described how to install Apache on a GNU/Linux operating system. We covered where to download Apache and how to extract the downloaded installation file. We then looked at creating a directory structure that separates the version-dependent and version-independent files, so that Apache can be easily upgraded in the future. We covered how to compile Apache for DSO support and turn the Apache source code into a working program. Finally, we looked at testing and troubleshooting the installation.

In the second half of the chapter, we explored how to add PHP to Apache. We described where to download the PHP installation file from, how to extract it, and how to compile the code. We then looked at configuring Apache to recognize PHP and covered how to create a custom `php.ini` file. Finally, we looked at testing and troubleshooting the PHP installation.

5

Apache and PHP Setup on Linux

6

In this Chapter

- Installing MySQL on Windows and Linux

- Configuring MySQL

- Working with Databases

Author: Gareth Downes-Powell

MySQL Setup

In this chapter, you'll learn how to install the popular open source database, MySQL. MySQL was created by MySQL AB and is free to download from the MySQL web site at *http://www.mysql.com/*. We'll explain how to install and set up a local MySQL server, so that you can use and work with MySQL databases while you're developing your site, without needing to be connected to the Internet.

We will cover the following areas:

- How to download and install MySQL on a Windows system

- How to install MySQL on Linux, using RPM packages to make the installation easy

- How to administer the MySQL server

- Some typical questions about MySQL

If you've only worked with Microsoft Access, then MySQL may take some getting used to—the two database systems are totally different. Microsoft Access stores a database in a single file, and you create the database and tables graphically through the Microsoft Access program. MySQL is actually a server rather than a program, and it is administered mainly through a command prompt by default (although programs are available to give MySQL a Windows-based interface). MySQL is much more powerful than Access and can cater to many more concurrent users. It is used by companies such as NASA, Google, and Hewlett-Packard for heavy-duty, mission-critical applications, and it is viewed as a powerful alternative to proprietary systems from Oracle, IBM, and Informix.

We'll focus on Linux and PC versions of MySQL in this chapter. We recommend that Mac users use the MySQL installation package made available by Marc Liyanage at: http://www.entropy.ch/software/ macosx/mysql/.

Installing MySQL on Windows

We'll look at three stages: downloading, installing, and starting the server.

Downloading MySQL

The first step to installing MySQL on Windows is to download the installation file. Open your browser and browse to *http://www.mysql.com/downloads/index.html*, which is the MySQL downloads page. You need to select the option *MySQL 3.23 Production release (recommended)*. This will take you to a new page where you can select the package to download. For Windows, there's only one file, which at the time of writing is listed as

Windows 95/98/NT/2000/XP   Version 3.23.55 Size 13.3M

Download this file ready for the install by selecting the "Pick a mirror" link, so you can choose the download location closest to you. New versions are released frequently, but the actual setup procedure should remain the same.

It is worth noting that a new version of MySQL (version 4) is under development and at the time of this writing is still undergoing testing. You can find out more about the MySQL version 4 release at the following URL: *http://www.mysql.com/doc/en/ MySQL_4.0_In_A_Nutshell.html*.

Installing MySQL

The downloaded install file is a `.zip` file, so you'll need to extract the contents of this file to a temporary location on your hard drive. Run the setup program by double-clicking `setup.exe`. This will start the install process, and you'll see the following dialog box:

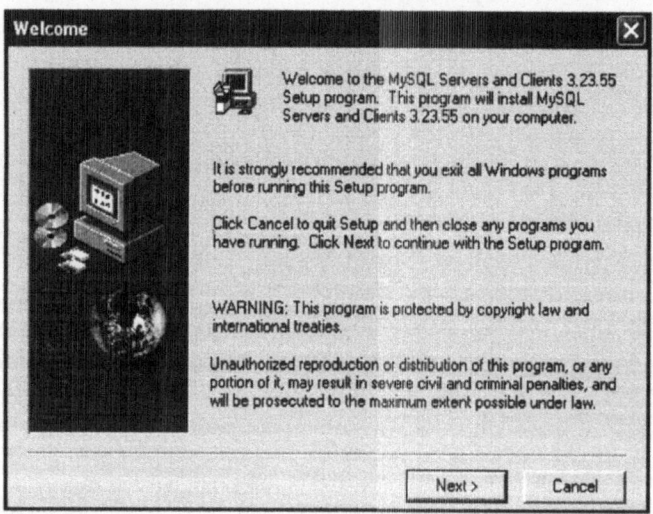

Click *Next* to start the installation and you'll then see the following dialog box:

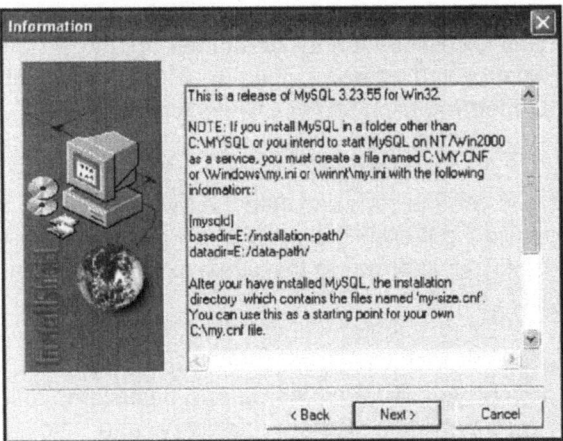

This dialog box gives extra information about the installation. It's important to read this information in case it applies to your installation. You can then click *Next* to continue.

In the next dialog box, you can select the directory into which MySQL is installed. It's recommended that you leave this directory as the default, which is `C:\mysql`. If you change it, you will need to configure MySQL later to use your chosen path.

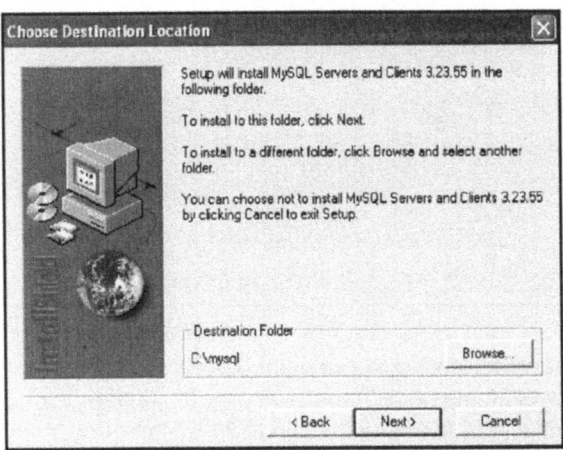

Click *Next* to continue to the next dialog box, which allows you to select an installation type. It's recommended that you stick to the default option. Click *Next* to continue and then *Finish* to complete the installation.

Starting the MySQL Server

Now that the MySQL server package has been installed, you need to start the server before you can perform any administration tasks and set up a new database. To start the server, open Windows Explorer and browse to the directory in which you installed MySQL. If you followed this guide, then the location is `C:\mysql`.

Next, change to the `bin` subdirectory. Here you should see a tool called `winmysqladmin.exe`. This is used to start and stop the MySQL server, so to make it easier to get to, it's a good idea to right-click the `winmysqladmin.exe` file and select *Create Shortcut*. You can then drag this shortcut to the desktop to make it more accessible and easier to control the MySQL server.

To start the server, double-click the `winmysqladmin.exe` file. The first time you run `WinMySQLAdmin`, it will prompt you for a username and password, which it will store in a file called `my.ini` in your Windows system directory and use to access MySQL information.

The dialog box shown next will appear briefly and will then disappear.

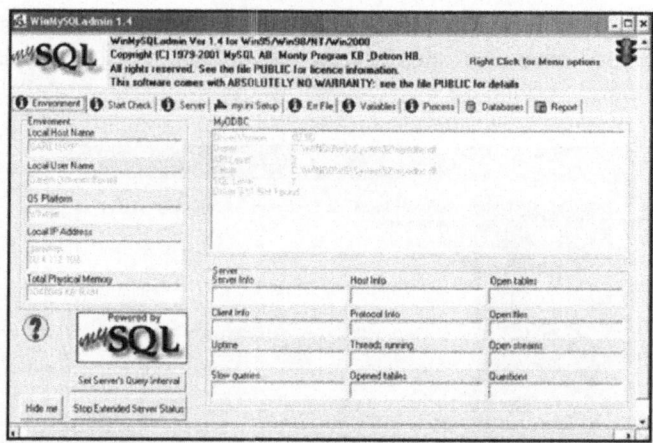

Note that the *Environment* tab, shown in the preceding screen shot, is useful for displaying information about the MySQL server. When the preceding dialog box has minimized, you'll be left with a green "traffic light" icon in your Windows System tray, similar to the following. This indicates that the MySQL server is running.

If the icon is red, the MySQL server is stopped.

If you right-click the MySQL "traffic light" icon and select *Show me*, the main `winmysqladmin.exe` screen is redisplayed. This tool allows you to see various categories of information about the server, such as the databases set up and how many users are connected to MySQL.

To start and stop the MySQL server, you can either right-click the MySQL icon in the system tray and use the menu to stop or start the server, or you can use the *Services* section of *Administrative tools* in the Windows *Control Panel*.

Now the server is installed and running, you can move on to the third part of the chapter, which explains how to administer MySQL and set up a new database and users.

Installing MySQL on Linux

In this section we look at how to install MySQL on a Linux Server, using the Linux shell prompt. You can use this shell either on the Linux server itself or remotely through a Telnet session. You will need to be logged in as the Linux root user.

Downloading MySQL

Most recent Linux distributions come with a copy of MySQL included, although not installed. You can either use the distribution package to install or download the latest version of MySQL from the MySQL web site at *http://www.mysql.com/downloads/index.html*.

Next, select the following option:

MySQL 3.23 – Production release (recommended)

MySQL 3.23 is the current stable production version; the other versions are still experimental and are not recommended for a production server.

You are going to install the RPM version of MySQL, as it's comparatively easy and MySQL needs little initial configuration. RPM stands for Redhat Package Manager, and it automates most of the installation process.

Scroll down the page to the section labeled

Linux x86 RPM downloads

There are currently five files available here:

- Server
- Benchmark/test suites
- Client programs
- Libraries and header files
- Dynamic client libraries

At the very least, you need to download the "Server" package. It's also recommended that you download the "Libraries and header files" and "Client programs" packages to allow other programs to link to MySQL. If you wish, you can also download the other packages, such as "Benchmark/test suites." You will notice that the filenames usually contain version numbers. You should make sure the packages you download are all for the same version, as mixing packages for different versions may cause problems.

Installing MySQL

You now need to use the Linux `rpm` program to install the RPM packages that you downloaded. Execute the following command to start the installation (remember this must be done as the root user):

```
rpm -ivh MySQL-3.23.55-1.i386.rpm
```

Make sure you type the command exactly at it is above, with the same case, as Linux filenames are case sensitive.

Once you've started the command, MySQL will install and you should see output similar to the following:

```
Preparing...             #########################################
[100%]
   1:MySQL                #########################################
[100%]
Preparing db table
Preparing host table
Preparing user table
Preparing func table
Preparing tables_priv table
Preparing columns_priv table
Installing all prepared tables
030206 21:22:35   /usr/sbin/mysqld: Shutdown Complete
```

```
PLEASE REMEMBER TO SET A PASSWORD FOR THE MySQL root USER !
This is done with:
/usr/bin/mysqladmin -u root  password 'new-password'
/usr/bin/mysqladmin -u root -h linux.localdomain  password 'new-
password'
See the manual for more instructions.

Please report any problems with the /usr/bin/mysqlbug script!

The latest information about MySQL is available on the web at
http://www.mysql.com
Support MySQL by buying support/licenses at https://order.mysql.com

Starting mysqld daemon with databases from /var/lib/mysql
```

This completes the MySQL installation. If you get any error messages, it's likely that your system lacks other packages that MySQL needs to install (the error messages should tell you which ones). Download and install these packages, then execute the rpm command again, and MySQL should then install successfully.

One of the nice things about the rpm command is that in future you can easily upgrade to a later version using the command

```
rpm -Uvh MySQL-latest-version.rpm
```

The u command tells RPM to update the existing installation, which it does automatically.

Installing the MySQL Libraries and Header Files

It's a good idea to also install the MySQL "Libraries and header files," as other packages that you install in the future may need these so they can use and connect to MySQL.

Before you can install the "Libraries and header files" package (MySQL-devel-3.23.55-1.i386.rpm), you need to install the MySQL client files, which are in the package MySQL-client-3.23.55-1.i386.rpm. Once you have downloaded the files, you can install the package using the following command:

```
rpm -ivh MySQL-client-3.23.55-1.i386.rpm
```

You should then see an output similar to the following:

```
Preparing...                     #############################################
[100%]
   1:MySQL-client                #############################################
[100%]
```

The MySQL client files are now installed, and you can go on to install the development files. Execute the following command to install the package:

```
rpm -ivh MySQL-devel-3.23.55-1.i386.rpm
```

You should then see output similar to the following:

```
Preparing...              #############################################
[100%]
   1:MySQL-devel           #############################################
[100%]
```

The MySQL development files are now installed.

Starting and Stopping the MySQL Server

When the MySQL RPM package is installed, it adds a start-up file to initiation files in the etc system directory. The full path is as follows:

```
/etc/rc.d/init.d/mysql
```

This means that MySQL will start when the server boots up. You can also use this file to start and stop the server.

To start the MySQL server, you need to execute the following command:

```
/etc/rc.d/init.d/mysql start
```

You should then see the following output:

```
Starting mysqld daemon with databases from /var/lib/mysql
```

To stop the MySQL server, you need to execute the following command:

```
/etc/rc.d/init.d/mysql stop
```

You should then see output similar to the following:

```
Killing mysqld with pid 10024
030206 22:17:04  mysqld ended
```

MySQL File Locations

It's useful to be able to see where the RPM packages installed the files contained within them. To do this, you can use the command

```
rpm -ql PackageName
```

where *PackageName* is the name of the installed package without file extensions. For example, look at the RPM file containing the MySQL files, which is called `MySQL-devel-3.23.55-1.i386.rpm`. Note, however, that some Linux distributions may use slightly different filenames. You can find the locations of its files with the command

```
rpm -ql MySQL-3.23.55-1
```

You can see that the `.i386.rpm` extension is removed in the preceding command. This will output the location of the files that the package installed, a small snippet of which is as follows:

```
/etc/logrotate.d/mysql
/etc/rc.d/init.d/mysql
/usr/bin/isamchk
/usr/bin/isamlog
/usr/bin/my_print_defaults
/usr/bin/myisamchk
/usr/bin/myisamlog
/usr/bin/myisampack
/usr/bin/mysql_convert_table_format
/usr/bin/mysql_fix_privilege_tables
/usr/bin/mysql_install_db
/usr/bin/mysql_setpermission
/usr/bin/mysql_zap
/usr/bin/mysqlbug
/usr/bin/mysqld_multi
/usr/bin/mysqldumpslow
/usr/bin/mysqlhotcopy
/usr/bin/mysqltest
/usr/bin/pack_isam
/usr/bin/perror
/usr/bin/replace
/usr/bin/resolve_stack_dump
/usr/bin/resolveip
/usr/bin/safe_mysqld
/usr/lib/mysql/mysqld.sym
/usr/sbin/mysqld
```

The snippet on the previous page shows the locations of the main program files. The development files install to the following locations:

```
/usr/include/mysql
/usr/lib/mysql
```

These are the locations you specify to another program when you're compiling in MySQL support. If you are ever unsure of where a certain file has been installed, you can use the preceding process to find the file.

If you decide at any point that you want to uninstall MySQL, it's important that you do it using the `rpm` command if you used RPM to install the program rather than deleting the files manually, as you may miss some files. Uninstalling with the `rpm` command ensures that everything is correctly removed. You can use the following command to uninstall a package:

```
rpm -e packagename
```

Although installing MySQL using an RPM is much easier, if you wish you can download and compile MySQL from source code yourself by downloading the source files from the MySQL web site. This allows you to optimize MySQL for your particular Linux configuration, although there is no real need for this on a testing server.

MySQL Server Setup and Configuration

Now that the MySQL server has been installed, you can configure the server and set up a new database to work with. Before you carry on, make sure the MySQL server is running.

Before the rest of the configuration, there is one OS-specific step:

- **Configuring MySQL under Windows**

  To administer MySQL under Microsoft Windows, you need to open a new command prompt and change to the following directory (assuming you installed MySQL to its default location): `C:\mysql\bin`.

- **Configuring MySQL under Linux**

  To configure MySQL under Linux, you need to open a new shell, either at the server itself or through a Telnet session. Log in as user root. You can then change to the following directory, where the MySQL program files are located: `/usr/bin`.

You can now follow the rest of this guide.

Setting the MySQL Root Password

The first job is to set the **root password** for the MySQL server. This is very important, as a password is not set by default, so anyone can connect to the MySQL server.

To set a new password, you need to enter the following command:

```
mysqladmin -u root password newpassword
```

where `newpassword` is the password you want to use for the MySQL root user. It's a good idea to set up another MySQL user under which you can still administer the server, but only give yourself the permissions you actually need, rather than everything the root user has.

Working with MySQL

To administer MySQL, you use the **MySQL monitor**. This sets up a connection to the MySQL database server and gives you a command-line interface through which you can type commands.

To start the MySQL monitor, you need to run the program `mysql.exe`, which is in the `bin` directory located in the directory to which you installed MySQL. When you start `mysql.exe` you need to pass the username you want to connect as. To start with, you are going to connect as the MySQL root user, which you can do with the following command:

```
mysql -u root -p
```

Because you used the parameter `-p`, you are asked for the password for the root user, so enter the password you set up in the previous section. The `-u` parameter indicates that a username is the next parameter. If you don't supply the `-p` command, you won't be asked for a password and you won't be able to log in. When the MySQL monitor has started, you'll see a message similar to the following:

```
Welcome to the MySQL monitor.  Commands end with ; or \g.
Your MySQL connection id is 4 to server version: 3.23.55

Type 'help;' or '\h' for help. Type '\c' to clear the buffer.

mysql>
```

Now that you have the MySQL prompt (`mysql>`), you are within the MySQL monitor and can enter commands to the MySQL server. If you get stuck at any time, you can type `\h`, which will show the help details. Note that when you type commands for the MySQL server, you need to end the command with a semicolon (`;`). If you forget the semicolon, the query gives you another line, and you can simply add it to this new line and it will complete the command.

If you make a mistake in your SQL, you can tell MySQL to ignore the current command by adding \c onto the end of the line, and the mistake will be ignored.

If you want to leave the MySQL monitor at any time, enter the following command:

```
exit;
```

You will be returned to a normal system command prompt.

Working with Databases

To view which databases are currently set up on the MySQL, you need to use the following command :

```
SHOW DATABASES;
```

This will return an output similar to the following on a newly installed system:

```
+----------+
| Database |
+----------+
| mysql    |
| test     |
+----------+
2 rows in set (0.00 sec)
```

This shows two databases that are set up automatically when MySQL is installed. The mysql database holds all the MySQL server information, such as users that can connect to the server. The test database allows users to test options without having to worry about causing problems to an important database.

To create a new database called *bookexamples*, you would use the command

```
CREATE DATABASE bookexamples;
```

This will output the following:

```
Query OK, 1 row affected (0.00 sec)
```

Now execute the following command to see a list of databases on the MySQL server:

```
SHOW DATABASES;
```

You'll get the following output, showing the database bookexamples has been created.

```
+----------------+
| Database       |
+----------------+
| bookexamples   |
```

```
| mysql         |
| test          |
+---------------+
3 rows in set (0.00 sec)
```

Now that you have a database to work with, you can tell MySQL to switch to that database by using this command:

```
USE bookexamples;
```

which will return the following:

```
Database changed
```

To delete the database (but don't delete it yet as you haven't finished with it!), you can use the following command:

```
DROP DATABASE bookexamples;
```

This command will delete the database along with all its data.

When you open the MySQL monitor, no database is set, so to work with a database you must first issue a use command to switch to the database you want to work with, as shown previously.

Working with Tables

Now that you have a database set up and you've switched to the correct database with the use command, you can start creating and working with the database tables.

Creating a New Table

To create a new table, use the SQL CREATE TABLE command, passing the name of the table, the columns, and the column data types that the table contains. For example, to set up a simple table, you could use the following command:

```
CREATE TABLE books (
bookname varchar(60),
description text
);
```

When you're typing the CREATE TABLE SQL, you can press the *Enter* key, and although you move to a new line, everything up to the semicolon is taken as a single command. Spreading the SQL over more than one line makes it easier to read.

This will create a new table called `books`, with two columns, `bookname` and `description`, and will show the following output, indicating the table has been created successfully:

```
Query OK, 0 rows affected (0.01 sec)
```

You can find all the column data types available to you and more options for table creation in the online MySQL manual at *http://www.mysql.com/doc/en/Reference.html*.

Finding Information About a Table

If you want to see the structure of an existing table in a database, you can retrieve what is known as the **table description** by using the SQL DESC command, which provides information about the table's columns. To view the description of the `books` table you just created, you can use the command

DESC books;

This will return the following output, which shows the table structure:

```
+-------------+-------------+------+-----+---------+-------+
| Field       | Type        | Null | Key | Default | Extra |
+-------------+-------------+------+-----+---------+-------+
| bookname    | varchar(60) | YES  |     | NULL    |       |
| description | text        | YES  |     | NULL    |       |
+-------------+-------------+------+-----+---------+-------+
2 rows in set (0.00 sec)
```

Deleting an Existing Table

To delete an existing table, you need to use the SQL DROP TABLE command. For example, to delete the example `books` table that you just created, you can use the following command:

```
DROP TABLE books;
```

This will delete the `books` table from the database. Be careful when you delete a table, as the deletion cannot be undone unless you restore from a backup of the database.

Working with Users

As we mentioned briefly earlier, the `mysql` database holds information relevant to the MySQL server itself. The main use is to hold details of users with permission to connect to the database.

We are going to work in the MySQL monitor, so start the monitor if it's not already started. Switch to the `mysql` database using the command

```
USE mysql
```

You can now use the `show tables` command, which will show a list of the tables in the `mysql` database:

```
SHOW TABLES;
```

This will return the following output:

```
+-----------------+
| Tables_in_mysql |
+-----------------+
| columns_priv    |
| db              |
| func            |
| host            |
| tables_priv     |
| user            |
+-----------------+
```

These tables contain the MySQL user and privileges information. We'll now look at the information that's contained in these tables in turn.

- `user` – The `user` table contains the global privileges for MySQL. It contains all the users that are allowed to connect to your MySQL server and what privileges they have once they are connected.

- `host` and `db` – The `host` and `db` tables contain information about specific hosts and databases. For example, a user could be allowed to log in from the server itself, using localhost, and connect to every single database with full privileges. However, if the same user connected from another network, you could limit his or her access to a certain database and give him or her lower privileges.

- `tables_priv` – The `tables_priv` table contains information about which users can use a certain table in a database. For example, a large business would have a database containing product information as well as staff information. You would want all users in the business to be able to use and query the products table, but you would only want certain people in the business being able to access the staff information table, as it contains sensitive information such as wage figures.

- `columns_priv` – The `columns_priv` table contains information relating to which columns in a database certain users can access. Using the previous example of a business, it may in fact be necessary for all staff to see and query the `staff` table, for example, to get contact information. However, you can allow only certain staff to see the `wages` column.

You can see that MySQL offers a huge amount of control over who can see what, although like any other computer system, to be secure it needs to be configured correctly.

These tables are listed in their order of priority, with the user table having the highest priority and the column table having the lowest priority. Privileges given in the higher priority tables will overrule those set in tables with a lower priority.

For example, if in the user table you give a user SELECT privileges, the user will be able to use SELECT queries on any database, table, or column in the system, even if the user is subsequently locked out of access to certain columns in the column table, since the user table has the highest priority.

As mentioned in the previous section, the user table holds details about the users who can connect to the MySQL server, and is the first table MySQL uses when you log into the MySQL server. The other tables are then read to see which databases, tables, and columns the user can view, edit, or delete.

Creating New Users

To create a new user, you have to add an entry to the MySQL user table. A description of the fields in the user table follows:

Field Name	Description	Typical Values
Host	The hostname that the user can connect from	localhost for pages running on the server. % is used to connect from any host.
User	Username	
Password	Password	Encrypted password. If you add an entry manually, you need to use the SQL PASSWORD() command to encrypt the password for you.
Select_priv	Allow user to execute SQL SELECT queries	Y or N. Note that a Y here means that the user can use SELECT on any database, table, or field. It's best to set this in a lower priority table. This also applies for the following five settings.
Insert_priv	Allow user to execute SQL INSERT commands	Y or N
Update_priv	Allow user to execute SQL UPDATE commands	Y or N
Delete_priv	Allow user to execute SQL DELETE commands	Y or N
Create_priv	Allow user to create new tables	Y or N

Field Name	Description	Typical Values
Drop_priv	Allow user to delete tables	Y or N
Reload_priv	Allow user to reload the MySQL server process	N. Only the MySQL root user should have this set to Y.
Shutdown_priv	Allow user to shutdown the MySQL server	N. Only the MySQL root user should have this set to Y.
Process_priv	Allow the user to control MySQL server processes	N. Only the MySQL root user should have this set to Y.
File_priv	Allows usage of SELECT ... INTO OUTFILE and LOAD DATA INFILE	N. Only the MySQL root user should have this set to Y.
Grant_priv	Specifies whether the user can grant MySQL privileges to other users	N. Only the MySQL administrator should have this set to Y.
Reference_priv	Not yet implemented	Y or N
Index_priv	Allows the user to create an Index	Y or N
Alter_priv	Allows the user to alter table structure	Y or N

The other privileges tables have similar field names to the user table, with the same options, but running at a lower priority.

To add a user to the table, you need to use a normal SQL insert query. You can type the query straight into the MySQL monitor. To add a new user to the table, you could use the following SQL:

```
INSERT INTO user (Host, User, Password) VALUES
("%","fred",PASSWORD("test"));
```

which would return the following if successful:

```
Query OK, 1 row affected (0.00 sec)
```

This has added a user with username fred, who can connect from any host (%) using the password test. The password for the user is stored encrypted, so you use the SQL PASSWORD command to encrypt the password test before it's stored in the user table.

Now you have a user set up but the user can't actually do anything. You didn't insert data into any of the privileges fields, so the value defaulted to N, turning off all privileges.

Granting Privileges to Users

The next step is to grant the user privileges, allowing the user to use the databases. You do this using the SQL GRANT command. The format of this command is

```
GRANT priv_type [(column_list)] [, priv_type [(column_list)] ...]
    ON {tbl_name | * | *.* | db_name.*}
    TO user_name [IDENTIFIED BY [PASSWORD] 'password']
        [, user_name [IDENTIFIED BY 'password'] ...]
    [WITH [GRANT OPTION | MAX_QUERIES_PER_HOUR # |
                          MAX_UPDATES_PER_HOUR # |
                          MAX_CONNECTIONS_PER_HOUR #]]
```

This shows the maximum set of options for the GRANT command. In practice, you work with only a few of these options. We'll look at each section of the GRANT command separately.

```
GRANT priv_type [(column_list)] [, priv_type [(column_list)] ...]
```

On this line, you can specify the privileges that you want to give the user. The following privileges are available:

```
ALL PRIVILEGES          FILE            RELOAD
ALTER                   INDEX           SELECT
CREATE                  INSERT          SHUTDOWN
DELETE                  PROCESS         UPDATE
DROP                    REFERENCES      USAGE
```

The description for these is the same as for the columns in the user table you looked at earlier. The field names in the relevant tables consist of the privilege with a suffix of _priv.

The (column_list) is a list of column names separated by commas.

```
    ON {tbl_name | * | *.* | db_name.*}
```

This line tells MySQL what to apply the privileges to. Here you have the following options:

- tbl_name – The name of a specific table
- * – All tables in the current database
- *.* – All tables in every database
- dbname.* – All tables in a specific database

In the preceding options, the asterisk (*) is used to match all tables or databases.

```
TO user_name [IDENTIFIED BY [PASSWORD] 'password']
    [, user_name [IDENTIFIED BY 'password'] ...]
```

The preceding line allows you to set the user that the privileges will be given to, IDENTIFIED BY the user's password, which you send unencrypted because MySQL will automatically encrypt it for you. Note that the username needs to be in the form of username@"host", for example fred@"%" or fred@"localhost".

```
[WITH [GRANT OPTION | MAX_QUERIES_PER_HOUR # |
                      MAX_UPDATES_PER_HOUR # |
                      MAX_CONNECTIONS_PER_HOUR #]]
```

The final section is optional and allows you to set extra options for the user that limit the use of the MySQL server.

It's well worth reading the online MySQL manual pages for the GRANT command, as it contains extra information that may be useful. You can go straight to this page using the following URL: *http://www.mysql.com/doc/en/GRANT.html*.

Although the GRANT command looks quite complicated, you often use only parts of the command at a time, which makes it easier to understand. Note that GRANT doesn't work on one specific table; it automatically selects the correct table to work on, depending on the privileges being set. Let's look at some examples of using the GRANT command to restrict users' access to the MySQL databases.

Administrator – Full Access

First we see how to set up an administrative user, who has full control and can connect to any database, from anywhere.

```
GRANT ALL PRIVILEGES ON *.* TO fred@"%" IDENTIFIED BY "test";
```

The preceding line will allow the user "fred" maximum privileges on all databases and database tables. "test" is fred's unencrypted password. The command will set all the privileges in the user table for fred at host % to Y.

Note that the following message returned from the GRANT command is slightly misleading:

```
Query OK, 0 rows affected (0.01 sec)
```

Although it says that 0 rows are affected, the GRANT operation has taken place successfully as long as it says "Query OK".

User – Full Access to a Specific Database

Next, we'll look at a user that has full control, but over a single database only:

```
GRANT ALL PRIVILEGES ON bookexamples.* TO fred@"%" IDENTIFIED BY "test";
```

This gives user `fred` full access to all tables in the `bookexamples` database.

User – Dreamweaver MX Connection

Dreamweaver connects to the MySQL server through the host `localhost`, so first you'll add a user to the database with the following command:

```
INSERT INTO user (Host,User,Password) VALUES
("localhost","dmx","dreampass");
```

This creates a new user with username "`dmx`" and password "`dreampass`". The user can connect to the server only as `localhost` (meaning the user can't connect from outside the server).

To make MySQL recognize the new user, you must tell it to reload its privileges data using the command

```
FLUSH PRIVILEGES;
```

Next, give the user permission to connect to the `bookexamples` database only, but with full control:

```
GRANT ALL PRIVILEGES ON bookexamples.* TO dmx@"localhost" IDENTIFIED BY
"dreampass";
```

You can now use the following parameters when you create your Dreamweaver MX MySQL connection:

- Host: localhost
- User: dmx
- Password: dreampass

User – Access to One Table Only in One Database

The last example that we are going to look at is to limit the user to a single table in a single database—for example, the `employees` table in the `bookexamples` database. This can be done with the following command:

```
GRANT ALL PRIVILEGES ON bookexamples.books TO fred@"%" IDENTIFIED BY
"test";
```

The user will now only be able to use the `books` table in the `bookexamples` database. If you wanted to restrict the user further, you could limit him or her to reading from the table and not being able to change or delete the data, which is done with the following command:

```
GRANT SELECT ON bookexamples.books TO fred@"%" IDENTIFIED BY "test";
```

This allows `fred` to open, and read from, the table `employees`, but not update, add new records, or delete records from the table.

Removing User Privileges

It's likely that at some point you may need to remove a user's privileges, and you can do this with the SQL REVOKE command, which is very like the SQL GRANT command you looked at earlier. The format for the REVOKE command is as follows:

```
REVOKE priv_type [(column_list)] [, priv_type [(column_list)] ...]
    ON {tbl_name | * | *.* | db_name.*}
    FROM user_name [, user_name ...]
```

Again, REVOKE works with the same privileges as the GRANT command. For example, to stop `fred` from being allowed to connect to the `bookexamples` database, you would use the command

```
REVOKE ALL PRIVILEGES ON bookexamples.books FROM fred@"%" IDENTIFIED BY
"test";
```

Note that once you've executed the preceding command, you'll need to run the FLUSH PRIVILEGES command for the new privileges to take effect.

Deleting Users

To delete a user, you use a standard SQL DELETE command, as follows:

```
DELETE FROM user WHERE User="fred" AND Host="%";
```

This would remove the user with username `fred`, password `test`, and host `%`. To check that the user has been deleted, you can view the `user` table content using

```
SELECT * FROM user
```

Frequently Asked Questions

How do I set up a MySQL connection in Dreamweaver MX?

This is an area that many people have problems with. Before you look at creating the connection itself, it's important to understand how Dreamweaver MX connects to a MySQL database. The system that Dreamweaver MX uses to connect to a MySQL database involves storing some hidden files on the web server. These hidden files are in a directory called `_mmServerScripts`, which is stored in the `root` directory of your web site. When Dreamweaver MX needs information about the MySQL database, it requests the files over the Internet, and the files relay back information about your database, such as table and field names.

The reason Dreamweaver MX uses this method is that many web hosts lock down their MySQL servers so that only connections coming from the server itself can connect to MySQL. Dreamweaver MX uses its hidden files to get round this situation, so that it can communicate with the database across the Internet, even if the MySQL server does not accept outside MySQL connections. It should be noted, however, that leaving these files on a server after development is a security risk.

The main cause of errors when Dreamweaver MX tries to work with the database is that it can't find or read the hidden files. The location of the hidden files is dependent on a correct site definition being set up. Site definition is covered in Chapter 1.

If you use your web host's server to test with, you enter the same details as for the remote information page.

Users often get confused about the difference between the remote server setup and the testing server setup, and this can cause problems with the MySQL connection. The remote server is always your web host's server. The testing server can be a computer on your local network that has a web server installed, or you can use your web host's server as the testing server if you don't have a local server available—in this case, you enter the same details in the testing server section as you do for the remote server. If you're setting up a dynamic site, then a testing server must be defined, as this is used to test your pages and connect to the MySQL server.

How do I use my web host's server as the testing server?

If you are using your web host's server as your testing server, you need to use the same options as you did for the remote server. Although Dreamweaver MX automatically copies the remote server details over to the testing server settings, double-check the URL Prefix setting, which should be set to the root address of your web site, such as *http://www.mysite.com/*, as Dreamweaver MX often fills this incorrectly so you may have to change it manually.

How do I use a local Windows server or a Linux server running Samba as the testing server?

If you are using a computer that runs Windows or a Linux server running Samba as a testing server, then you need to select *Local/Network* for the Access Type. You can then select the folder on the testing server's hard disk into which your web site files are to be placed. The other option you need to set is the address of the web site on your testing server. If you're working on the machine you use as the testing server, you need to enter the address *http://localhost/.* If you're using another computer, then enter the address in the form of *http://ipaddress/*; alternatively, you can use *http://computername/,* where *computername* is the name defined for the particular computer.

How do I use a Linux server as the testing server?

If you're using a Linux server, then you need to have an FTP server running on the Linux machine. You then select *FTP* for the Access Type and enter the server's IP address as the address to connect to. The URL Prefix should be in the form *http://ipaddress/* (for example, *http://192.168.0.2/*).

How do I create the MySQL connection?

In the *Application Panel,* select the tab labeled *Databases* and select *MySQL Connection.* The connection dialog box will then be displayed, similar to the following screen shot:

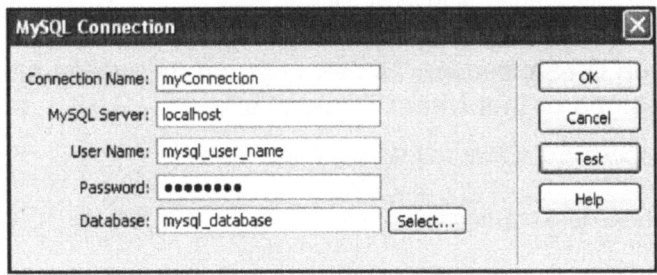

The *Connection Name* can be set to anything you choose.

The MySQL server needs to be set to *localhost,* as the connection to the actual MySQL server is made on the server, and it is a local rather than a remote connection. If your MySQL server is on a different computer, then you'll need to enter the IP address of the MySQL server.

The *User Name* and *Password* fields need to be set to your username and password for the MySQL server.

Finally, *Database* is set to the name of your MySQL database, and if everything is working correctly, clicking the *Select...* button will show a list of the databases on the MySQL server.

Once you've entered the previous settings, click the *Test* button to check the connection. Dreamweaver MX then uploads its hidden files to connect to the MySQL database. If the connection works, you'll see a box appear similar to the following one.

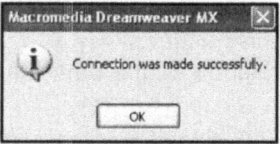

This shows a successful connection has been made, and you can now click *OK* to make the connection. Don't forget to upload the newly created `Connections` folder to your testing server.

How do I troubleshoot a MySQL connection?

In the following FAQs, we look at some of the problems that can occur when connecting to a MySQL database, and how to troubleshoot and solve them. As we mentioned earlier, the main problems occur with the Dreamweaver MX hidden files, which it uses to communicate between itself and the MySQL server.

What do I do when Dreamweaver MX can't upload its hidden files due to incorrect permissions or incorrect FTP details?

This gives an error message similar to the following:

HTTP Error Code 404 File Not Found

This can be diagnosed by looking at the Dreamweaver MX FTP log. The FTP log can be accessed from the *Results* panel, which is usually at the bottom of the screen. You may need to open it by clicking the white arrow. Alternatively, you can use the key combination *Ctrl+Shift+F12*. A screen shot of the FTP log window is shown here:

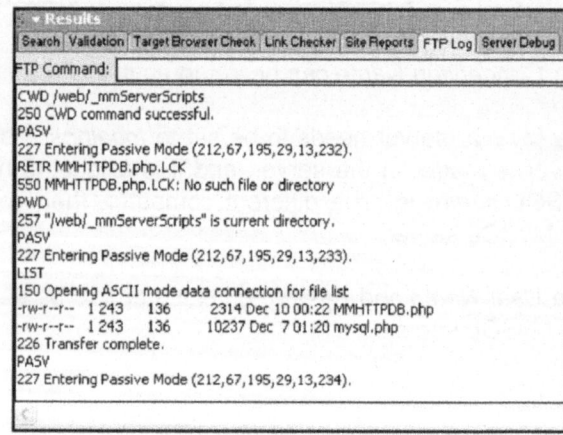

The FTP log shows all the commands sent from Dreamweaver MX to the FTP server. If the hidden files folder `_mmServerScripts` cannot be uploaded, it will be shown here. Usually it's because the permission set on the directory won't allow the FTP user to upload files. Either change the details for the FTP user in the site definition to a user who is allowed to upload files or change the permissions of the directory on the testing server. If you are running your own Windows server, the permissions can be changed from Windows Explorer; if it's a Linux server, you can use the `chmod` command. If you are using your web host's server, you will need to ask them how to change the permissions for your files. (This is usually explained in your host's support pages.)

What do I do when Dreamweaver MX can upload its hidden files, but it looks in the wrong place when it tries to read them back?

Another problem that frequently occurs is Dreamweaver MX uploading its hidden files successfully, but looking in the wrong place when it tries to read them back. This will give the same error message as for the previous section:

HTTP Error Code 404 File Not Found

This can occur if the URL Prefix option under the *Testing Server* tab in the site definition window is set incorrectly. This means that when Dreamweaver MX thinks it's looking at the root of the web site, where it would normally find its hidden folder, it's actually looking elsewhere. The URL should be the root address of your web site, such as *http://www.mydomain.com/*.

Double-check the URL Prefix option in your *Testing Server* section and make sure the address corresponds to the root address of your web site on the testing server.

What do I do when I get the "Access Denied for User: username@localhost" error?

An example of the next error we will look at is as follows:

This is caused by the MySQL login details that you entered in the *MySQL Database Connection* dialog box not having permission to connect to the MySQL server. There are two main connection types in MySQL: one for connections coming from pages on the MySQL server and another for connections to the MySQL server from outside the server. If the MySQL server is running on the same machine as your web server, you must allow the user to connect using host *localhost* or ask your web host to set this up for you. Even if you're connecting to a remote MySQL server, Dreamweaver MX still connects as a local user.

What do I do when I get the "HTTP Error Code 401 Unauthorized" error?

This error occurs if you have an `.htaccess` file in the root folder of your web site, so that web users can only access your pages if a password is entered. This stops Dreamweaver MX from being able to read its hidden files from the server. To solve this problem, you need to do the following.

Create a directory called `_mmServerScripts` in the root directory of your web site, if it doesn't already exist. In that directory, create a file called `.htaccess` that contains the following:

```
satisfy any
allow from all
```

This will turn off protection for the `_mmServerScripts` directory, allowing Dreamweaver MX to read back its hidden files, and a connection will be made successfully.

What do I do when I get the "An Unidentified Error Has Occurred" error?

This error message is also fairly common, but there is no definite single solution, as there can be a range of possible causes of this error. This error has its own tech note on the Macromedia web site, and this document contains a range of possible causes and solutions. This tech note is located here: *http://www.macromedia.com/support/ dreamweaver/ts/documents/ unidentified_error_mysql.htm.*

What do I do when I get the "2222 Error – Can't Connect to Local MySQL Server Through Socket "/tmp/MySQL.sock"" (Linux only) error?

This error is normally only seen if you have set up the MySQL server yourself, and the MySQL server is running on Linux. It means that MySQL can't create a socket for the connection. To fix this error, you will first need to log into your server through Telnet or through a local shell prompt. You will need to change to the root user before you run the following commands:

```
touch /tmp/mysql.sock
```

This creates the `mysql.sock` file that MySQL needs. Next, you need to create a new file in your `/etc` directory called `my.cnf`. You then need to add the following to the file, using a text editor:

```
[mysqld]
socket=/tmp/mysql.sock
```

```
[client]
socket=/tmp/mysql.sock
```

You can then save the file, restart your MySQL server, and you should be able to create a connection in Dreamweaver MX to it.

Why isn't my new user working?

One feature of MySQL that often catches people out is that once you have created a new user, or granted privileges to the new user, the changes don't take effect immediately. Instead, you have to reload the privileges so that MySQL knows the new settings. You can do this with the command

```
FLUSH PRIVILEGES;
```

Once you have issued this command, MySQL will start to use the new privileges that were specified.

How do I back up a database?

Backing up a MySQL database isn't the same as backing up some other database systems, such as Microsoft Access, as you can't just copy the files somewhere else. Instead, MySQL comes with a command that dumps the database to a file. This command is in the `bin` directory of your MySQL installation directory, and it is called `mysqldump`. This command is very easy to use, and it's essential to keep regular backups of your database if you value your data.

It is run through a command prompt on Windows or a shell on Linux, and both OSs use exactly the same commands. To get a list of all the options for `mysqldump`, you would use the command

```
mysqldump --help
```

How do I dump the database to a file?

To dump the database to a file, you need to run the following command:

```
mysqldump -u username -ppassword databasename > backup.txt
```

This will dump a copy of "`databasename`" into a file called `backup.txt` in the directory the command is run from. Note that on a development server, you'd use the user root in the command.

It's important that you don't have a space between the -p parameter and the password. Otherwise, you will be prompted for the password, but you won't be able to see the prompt or respond because all output is directed to the `backup.txt` file instead of the screen.

The text file produced doesn't just contain the data. It also includes SQL to build a complete replica of the original database with all the tables and field information.

How do I restore the database from a file?

To restore the database from the text file, first you need to have created a new database on the server using the SQL command

```
CREATE DATABASE databasename;
```

Next, from a system command prompt, enter the following command to populate the new database with the data stored in the MySQL backup text file:

```
mysql -u root -p databasename < backup.txt
```

where `backup.txt` is a text file produced by the `mysqldump` command, and `databasename` is the name of the empty database you created. If you want to back up to a database with the same name as the old database, you just need to delete the old database first using the `DROP` command, and then re-create the database with the same name:

```
DROP DATABASE databasename
```

When the command is run, it first creates the database structure, including the required tables, and then populates the tables with the original data.

Is there an easier way to administer MySQL?

Though it's essential to be able to know how to administer MySQL through the MySQL monitor, there are a number of third-party tools available that offer a graphical interface, which makes administering the server much easier. Another advantage is that if you're creating a new table, for example, the column types are usually listed, and you just have to select the option you want, which saves having to memorize all the settings.

A list of many third-party tools (some free, some commercial) is available at *http://www.mysql.com/portal/software/index.html*. Some programs allow you to convert other databases, such as Microsoft Access, into MySQL, and it's well worth having a browse through the utilities on offer. A couple of recommended tools are as follows.

MySQL Control Center

MySQL Control Center is available at *http://www.mysql.com/downloads/mysqlcc.html* and is created by the MySQL developers. Versions are available for both Windows and Linux, and it makes it much easier to administrate the MySQL server and databases, because it provides you with a graphical interface for administering the server, instead of your havign to use the command line in the MySQL monitor. An example of the interface is shown next:

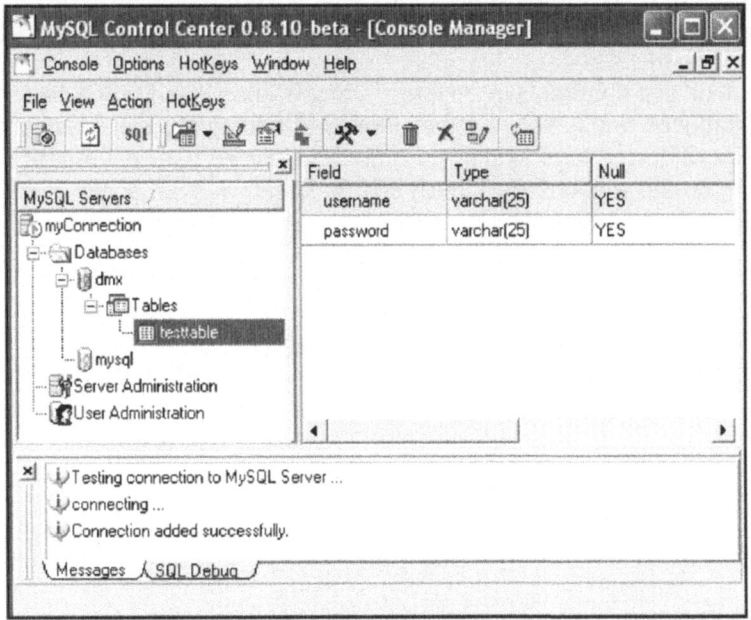

Winmysqlprofessional

Another excellent tool, and one we can really recommend, is Winmysqlprofessional from *http://www.winmysql.com/*. The tool is Windows based and makes it easy to administer the MySQL server, add users, and create databases and tables. It's great for working with data as well, because it allows you to dump data into a comma-separated variable (CSV) file to import into other programs. It can also read from a CSV file and import the data into your MySQL table.

PHPMyAdmin

PHPMyAdmin is extremely popular and allows easy administration of the MySQL database. PHPMyAdmin isn't actually a program—it's a set of web pages that run on a web server. As the name suggests, PHPMyAdmin is written in PHP, so your web server must be able to process PHP pages. It's available as a free download from *http://www.phpmyadmin.net* and requires some configuring. Full details can be found in the `Documentation.html` file that comes with the download.

Summary

In this chapter, we first looked at how to install MySQL on Microsoft Windows and showed you the installation process step by step. We then looked at the `winmysqladmin` program, which starts and stops the MySQL server and allows you to view many of the server settings.

In the second section, we covered installing MySQL on Linux, using an RPM package. We looked at all the packages available and showed how to install them onto the system.

In the third part of the chapter, we covered administering the MySQL database and creating new databases and tables. We then looked at adding MySQL users and showed how to use the MySQL privilege system to grant and revoke user privileges. Finally, we examined how to create a connection to MySQL in Dreamweaver, some of the common error messages, and other common questions.

7

In this Chapter

- Why use Cascading Style Sheets?
- CSS in Dreamweaver MX

Author: Rachel Andrew

CSS

Cascading Style Sheets (CSS) is a language developed by the World Wide Web Consortium (W3C, see *http://www.w3.org/Style/CSS/*) that can be used to dictate how HTML elements are displayed in the browser. For example, with CSS you can style text (changing the font style, size, color, line spacing, and also position) and position other elements on the page.

Why Use CSS for Text Styling Instead of <font> Tags?

If you are currently using `<font>` tags in order to style HTML elements, you probably feel that you need some concrete reasons why you should change your way of working. An obvious reason is that font tags are deprecated (which means they will be removed from future specifications of XHTML and may not be supported in future browsers). However, there are many other current and concrete reasons why you should move to CSS.

Separating Document Structure from Presentation

You will find this concept mentioned a lot as a benefit of moving to CSS. What this phrase actually means is that your document and content (the basic HTML document with structural tags such as `<p>`, `<h1>`, and `<li>`) are separated from the style (the way that it looks in the browser).

The following example demonstrates this separation and what it means in real terms. Here is a page using `<font>` tags:

```
<?xml version="1.0" encoding="iso-8859-1"?>
<!DOCTYPE html PUBLIC "-//W3C//DTD XHTML 1.0 Transitional//EN"
"http://www.w3.org/TR/xhtml1/DTD/xhtml1-transitional.dtd">
<html xmlns="http://www.w3.org/1999/xhtml">
<head>
<title>CSS Example</title>
<meta http-equiv="Content-Type" content="text/html; charset=iso-8859-1"
/>
</head>

<body bgcolor="#FFFFFF" text="#000000" link="#660099" vlink="#660099"
alink="#660099">
<h1><font color="#336699" size="5" face="Arial, Helvetica, sans-
serif">Look at my mock Latin</font></h1>
<p><font size="2" face="Arial, Helvetica, sans-serif">Lorem ipsum dolor
sit amet,
   consectetuer adipiscing elit. Curabitur vel nibh sed mauris hendrerit
gravida.
   Sed mollis neque id massa. Etiam eu wisi eget erat malesuada varius.
Sed faucibus
   nunc nec sapien. Quisque ullamcorper, purus in vestibulum scelerisque,
dui pede
   vulputate urna, nec condimentum magna odio non lacus. Praesent purus
sem, vehicula
   nec, viverra sit amet, posuere eu, felis. Vestibulum id massa nec leo
bibendum
   adipiscing. Cras ligula nulla, pellentesque non, facilisis nec, varius
id, dui.
</font></p>
<ul>
   <li><font color="#333366" size="2" face="Arial, Helvetica, sans-
serif">
      Quid rides vervex?</font></li>
   <li><font color="#333366" size="2" face="Arial, Helvetica, sans-
serif">
      Longos imitaris</font></li>
   <li><font color="#333366" size="2" face="Arial, Helvetica, sans-
serif">
      omnium mensarum assecula</font></li>
</ul>
<p><font size="2" face="Arial, Helvetica, sans-serif">Donec justo. In
diam nunc, congue
   ac, suscipit id, tincidunt in, diam. Praesent at quam. Proin et lorem
eu urna
```

```
   viverra malesuada. Cum sociis natoque penatibus et magnis dis
parturient montes,
   nascetur ridiculus mus. Fusce facilisis rhoncus mi. Proin luctus est
non arcu.
   Morbi a nulla et metus porta tempus. Pellentesque dapibus ornare
risus. Nam
   interdum volutpat nibh. Sed eget massa.</font></p>
<p><font size="2" face="Arial, Helvetica, sans-serif">You can get your
own mock
   Latin at <a
href="http://www.lipsum.com">http://www.lipsum.com</a></font></p>
</body>
</html>
```

If you look at the markup of the preceding document, you can see that every element has been wrapped in `<font>` tags. The browser is reading these `<font>` tags and rendering the text inside them in the style they dictate. This gets quite messy, particularly for items such as lists or tabular data, as you have to repeat the `<font>` tags for each list item or table cell. You also have to remember which `<font>` tags you have applied to which elements, so that you don't end up with your site looking inconsistent because you used Arial at size 2 on some pages for your main paragraph font and Verdana at size 3 on others. Most of the time, you want all HTML elements within a site to have a consistent feel—and here CSS can really make your life easier.

By attaching a CSS stylesheet to the preceding document, you can remove all of the `<font>` tags and still maintain the style of the page. In the following sections of this chapter, we will cover the mechanics of creating and attaching this stylesheet but, for now, let's just see the effect.

First, there is the stylesheet, which has sections within it that correspond to the different HTML elements that you were styling with `<font>` tags. Each section relates to a different HTML element, and the rules between the curly brackets show how you want that element to be styled:

```
body {
  background-color: #ffffff;
  color: #000000;
}

h1 {
  font-family: Arial, Helvetica, sans-serif;
  font-size: large;
  color: #336699;
}
```

```
p {
  font-family: Arial, Helvetica, sans-serif;
  font-size: x-small;
}

li {
  font-family: Arial, Helvetica, sans-serif;
  font-size: x-small;
  color: #333366;
}
```

You can then delete all of the `<font>` tags from within the document and, as long as the document has the stylesheet attached, the browser will look at the stylesheet before rendering the document and style the HTML elements in the manner set out there. The markup now looks like this:

```
<?xml version="1.0" encoding="iso-8859-1"?>
<!DOCTYPE html PUBLIC "-//W3C//DTD XHTML 1.0 Transitional//EN"
"http://www.w3.org/TR/xhtml1/DTD/xhtml1-transitional.dtd">
<html xmlns="http://www.w3.org/1999/xhtml">
<head>
<title>CSS Example</title>
<meta http-equiv="Content-Type" content="text/html; charset=iso-8859-1"
/>
<link href="ex1.css" rel="stylesheet" type="text/css" />
</head>

<body>
<h1>Look at my mock Latin</h1>
<p>Lorem ipsum dolor sit amet,
  consectetuer adipiscing elit. Curabitur vel nibh sed mauris hendrerit
gravida.
  Sed mollis neque id massa. Etiam eu wisi eget erat malesuada varius.
Sed faucibus
  nunc nec sapien. Quisque ullamcorper, purus in vestibulum scelerisque,
dui pede
  vulputate urna, nec condimentum magna odio non lacus. Praesent purus
sem, vehicula
  nec, viverra sit amet, posuere eu, felis. Vestibulum id massa nec leo
bibendum
  adipiscing. Cras ligula nulla, pellentesque non, facilisis nec, varius
id, dui.
  </p>
<ul>
  <li>Quid rides vervex?</li>
  <li>Longos imitaris</li>
  <li>omnium mensarum assecula</li>
</ul>
```

```
<p>Donec justo. In diam nunc, congue
   ac, suscipit id, tincidunt in, diam. Praesent at quam. Proin et lorem
eu urna
   viverra malesuada. Cum sociis natoque penatibus et magnis dis
parturient montes,
   nascetur ridiculus mus. Fusce facilisis rhoncus mi. Proin luctus est
non arcu.
   Morbi a nulla et metus porta tempus. Pellentesque dapibus ornare
risus. Nam
   interdum volutpat nibh. Sed eget massa.</p>
<p>You can get your own mock
   Latin at <a href="http://www.lipsum.com">http://www.lipsum.com</a></p>
</body>
</html>
```

In doing this, you have effectively separated the presentation of the document from the actual content and structure of the document. This has a range of benefits, which we describe in the following sections.

Consistency of Look and Feel

Once you have your stylesheet, you are not limited to applying the changes to only one page of your site. You can attach the stylesheet to all of your pages, ensuring that a level 1 heading or a list is always styled in a consistent way.

Sitewide Design Changes Made Simple

With your stylesheet attached to all pages of your site, when your client requests that all headings should be red instead of blue, you simply need to change one line in the stylesheet. No more going through all the pages of your site, changing each one and then having to reupload everything to your server.

Smaller File Sizes

As you have seen, changing to CSS means that you can remove a great deal of markup from your documents. This might not seem like a huge saving on your simple page, but on a complex page (particularly one that includes tabular data) you can trim your file size impressively, the saving being multiplied if the stylesheet is applied to multiple pages as the stylesheet will be cached.

Accessible to Alternative Devices and Search Engines

Many devices used to read web pages do not render color and style at all. An obvious example is a screen reader, which may be used by someone who is visually impaired to read out the content of pages, but also in this category are limited browsers such as those used by web-enabled phones, some PDAs, and also search engine robots looking for content to index.

Clean, structured markup is far easier for these limited devices to understand and, as they don't support any style information, they can simply ignore the stylesheet and deal with the content. Not only does this make your site more accessible to those who need to use an alternative device, but also it may get you a better ranking in search engines as they find a higher percentage of indexable content on your site. CSS is one way to assist in making your site accessible without compromising the way it looks.

 Not only does this make your site more accessible to those who need to use an alternative device, but also it may get you a better ranking in search engines as they find a higher percentage of indexable content on your site.

CSS Tools in Dreamweaver MX

Dreamweaver MX ships with a variety of tools that will help you learn CSS and use it on your web sites.

Preferences

To open the *Preferences* dialog box, select *Edit > Preferences*. In the dialog box that opens, select the category *CSS Styles*.

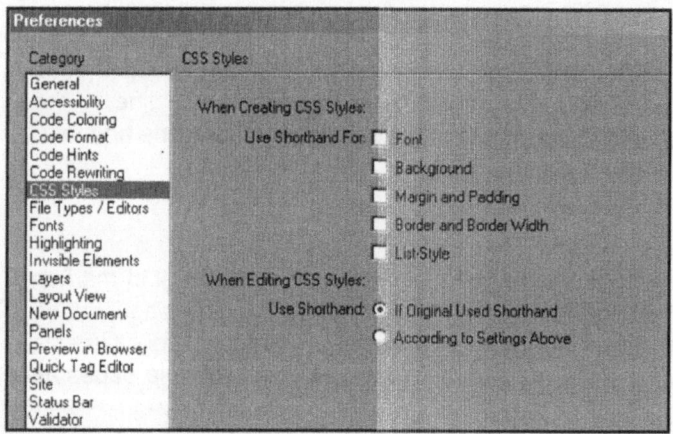

This dialog box lets you tell Dreamweaver whether it should write CSS using **shorthand.** But what is this?

Here is a typical set of CSS rules using longhand:

```
.longhand {
    font-family: Arial, Helvetica, sans-serif;
    font-size: small;
    color: #660066;
    text-decoration: underline;
}
```

Checking the *Use Shorthand For Font* box will force Dreamweaver to use the following shorthand syntax instead:

```
.shorthand {
  font: small Arial, Helvetica, sans-serif;
  color: #660066;
  text-decoration: underline;
}
```

Whether or not you use shorthand is mainly a personal preference. However, you may find that some browsers will accept a style when written in shorthand but not in longhand (there are many such examples in Netscape 4.x). So, if you know there are places in your stylesheet where you have used shorthand to get around a browser problem, ensure that the radio buttons at the bottom of the dialog box are set to *Use Shorthand: If Original Used Shorthand* so that Dreamweaver does not change your rules.

The CSS Styles Panel

The *CSS Styles* panel is part of the *Design* panel group. From this panel you can create, edit, and attach stylesheets to your pages. You will use the *CSS Styles* panel extensively in the remainder of this chapter, so here is a quick rundown on what you can do with this panel.

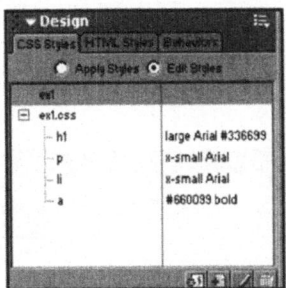

With the radio button *Apply Styles* checked, you can apply custom classes to elements on your page. This can also be achieved from the *Properties* inspector and by right-clicking the element in the tag selector. We will cover applying styles in the section "What About Special Cases?"

Your main use of the *CSS Styles* panel is to edit or create new styles. With the *Edit Styles* radio button checked, all of the styles that you have created will be displayed. Double-clicking them will launch the *New Styles* dialog box so that you can edit them.

The small buttons on the bottom right of the *CSS Styles* panel are as follows (from left to right):

- **Attach Style Sheet** – Attach a stylesheet to a document.
- **New CSS Style** – Create a new style.
- **Edit Style Sheet** – Edit the linked stylesheet.
- **Delete Style** – Select a style and click this button to delete it.

The Properties Inspector

By default, the *Properties* inspector still contains all of the tools for adding style with `<font>` tags to your documents. However, when working with CSS you can switch the *Properties* inspector to give you ways of applying custom CSS style classes that you have created for your documents instead of using `<font>` tags for styling. The default text *Properties* inspector looks like this:

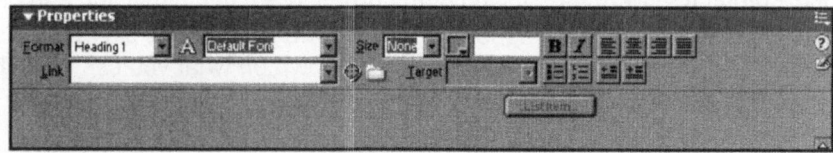

To toggle to the CSS mode, click on the yellow *A* after the *Format* drop-down list. The *Properties* inspector will now change to look like this:

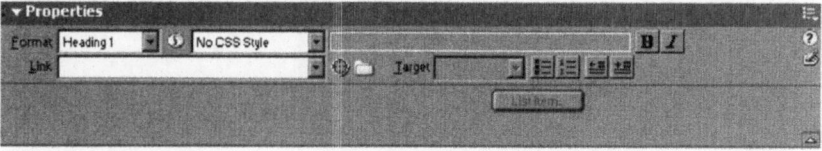

Now you can add defined CSS styles to selected page elements.

Frequently Asked Questions

How do I create a stylesheet in Dreamweaver?

To create a new external stylesheet in Dreamweaver, open a new blank document and then open the *CSS Styles* panel and click the *New CSS Style* button, which is the second button from the left at the bottom of the panel (circled in the following screen shot).

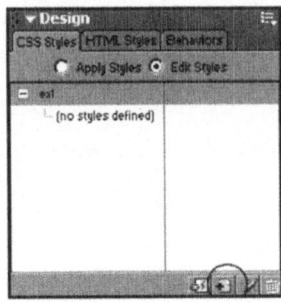

This will launch the *New CSS Style* dialog box:

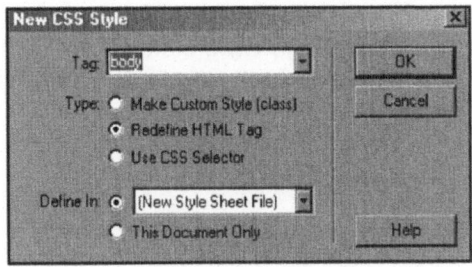

You will need to create a style definition in order to create a new stylesheet, so a good place to start is with the basic body font style. Click the radio button labeled *Redefine HTML tag* and then select *body* from the *Tag* drop-down list. Select the radio button to define in *New Style Sheet file* and click *OK*.

Since this is a new stylesheet, a *Save As* dialog box will appear so that you can save your stylesheet. Make sure that you add the .css extension on the end of your stylesheet name. Save this stylesheet and the following dialog box will appear:

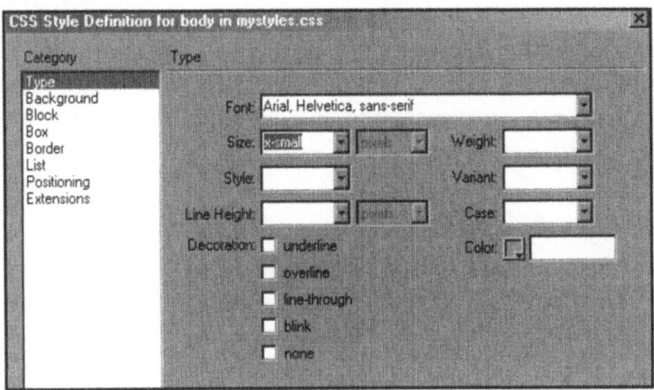

In this *CSS Style Definition* dialog box, you can set the rules for the tag or class that you are working with. For your `<body>` tag, you will want to select *Type* in the left list and choose a font face and size as in the previous screen shot. Then click *OK*.

If you create a style in a new stylesheet file while working in a document, Dreamweaver automatically attaches it to the document, so you should see your changes take effect immediately.

We have only specified this style for the body text. Because of differences in the way that browsers (particularly Netscape 4.x) interpret the CSS inheritance rules, they will display this differently. Some will apply this rule to all text (including that in tables, paragraphs, and lists) and some will not. To be on the safe side, you need to add this same set of rules to other page elements that you want to use the same font settings.

In the *CSS Styles* panel, click the *New CSS Style* button again. This time, select the `<p>` tag to redefine. As you now have a stylesheet attached to the document, Dreamweaver will have the name of the stylesheet displayed in the drop-down box next to *Define in*. You can attach multiple stylesheets to a page, but for the most part you will want to define your styles in the same sheet.

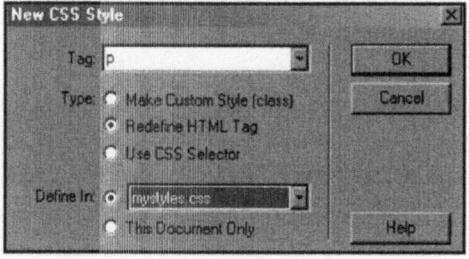

Clicking *OK* will take you straight into the *CSS Style Definition* dialog box. You will need to set the same styles for `<p>` as you did for `<body>`. Click *OK* and repeat the process for `<li>` and `<td>`.

You can redefine any of the standard HTML tags that you would like to be styled in the same way across all pages of your site that use this stylesheet. When starting on a new site, we usually begin by creating a stylesheet that contains basic styles for `<body>`, `<p>`, `<td>`, `<li>`, `<h1>`, `<h2>`, `<h3>`, and `<h4>`.

What about special cases?

You will often have a case where you don't want a heading, a list, or other page element to be styled in the same way as your basic font styles. Here you can create a "custom class" that you can apply to the element on the page.

To create the class, click the *New CSS Style* button of the *CSS Styles* panel as before, but this time select the *Make Custom Style (class)* radio button. In the text box at the top of the dialog box, enter a name for your class. This needs to begin with a period. Classes always begin with a period, whereas definitions for HTML tags do not.

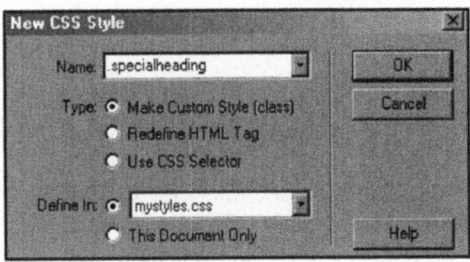

Click *OK* and the *CSS Style Definition* dialog box will open to let you create the style rules for this class. Click *OK* to save the definition.

You can now apply this style to a page element. In the example document at the beginning of the chapter, level 1 headings have the following style rules:

```
h1 {
  font-family: Arial, Helvetica, sans-serif;
  font-size: large;
  color: #336699;
}
```

These rules apply to all the level 1 headings of this site. However, on some pages we are using a different color scheme and we would like the level 1 headings on these pages to be red (#CC0000) and use a different font face. When we created the .specialheading class, we created a set of rules that looked like this:

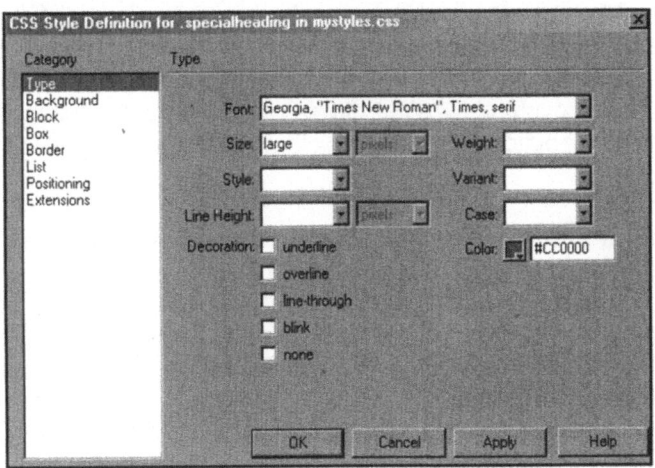

In the stylesheet, this class looks like this:

```
.specialheading {
  font-family: Georgia, "Times New Roman", Times, serif;
  font-size: large;
  color: #CC0000;
}
```

To apply these rules instead of the default ones, select the heading in the Design View of Dreamweaver MX and go to the *Properties* inspector. You should have the *Properties* inspector in CSS mode. Changing your *Properties* inspector to CSS mode is explained near the beginning of this chapter in the section "The CSS Properties Inspector." In the drop-down list (which will currently have *No CSS Style* selected), you should find the class name that you created.

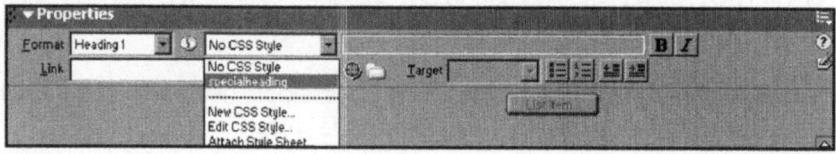

Select it, and the heading should now display in the style of this class instead of the default style.

You can follow this procedure to create custom classes for any other special cases within your site. If you have many classes it is a good idea to give them logical names, so that they are easy to locate and apply.

When naming CSS classes, do not use spaces or special characters. Many people like to name using the underscore character to separate words; do not do this with your CSS class names as they will not work!

How do I use the styles I created with new pages?

When we created our stylesheet, we linked it to the page we were working on at the time. When you are working on a site, you will need to link the stylesheet to multiple pages. After you have designed the stylesheet, the next step is to attach it to your documents. With your new document open, click the *Attach Style Sheet* button on the bottom of the *CSS Styles* panel. This is the button to the left of the *New CSS Style* button. The dialog box that appears allows you to browse for your stylesheet.

The two radio buttons underneath allow you to select how you would like to attach the stylesheet. The options are *Link* and *Import*.

Linking to the stylesheet is the more common way of attaching a stylesheet to your page. Selecting this option will attach your stylesheet to your page by way of the following markup:

```
<link href="mystyles.css" rel="stylesheet" type="text/css" />
```

This is the way that Dreamweaver attaches stylesheets by default and is supported by all CSS-enabled browsers. You should do this for all styles you need to be recognized by older browsers such as Netscape 4.x.

If you choose *Import*, the stylesheet will be attached with this markup:

```
<style type="text/css">
<!--
@import url("mystyles.css");
-->
</style>
```

which is recognized by newer CSS-enabled browsers.

How can I edit my stylesheet?

You can edit individual styles by simply double-clicking them in the *CSS Styles* panel. The *CSS Style Definitions* dialog box will appear for that item so that you can edit the definitions. You can also open the stylesheet within Dreamweaver by selecting the file after choosing *File > Open* or double-clicking the stylesheet file in the *Site* panel of the *Files* panel group.

Can I check that my stylesheet rules are valid?

Once you have created a stylesheet, it is a good idea to validate it, to check that the syntax is correct and to pick up any potential problems. If you are having problems with your CSS, very often validating and fixing any errors or warnings flagged up by the validator will solve the problem.

However, there is no way to validate your stylesheet directly within Dreamweaver. If you use TopStyle you can validate from that application. Otherwise, just visit the CSS Validator on the W3C web site at *http://jigsaw.w3.org/css-validator/*.

If your stylesheet has been uploaded to a web site, you can validate by the URI. Simply type the address of your stylesheet into the box. Otherwise, you can either paste the stylesheet into a text area or upload it to the W3C site. Whichever way you get your file to the validator, you will get a report telling you whether your stylesheet is valid and pointing you to errors or warnings in the stylesheet.

CSS

7

How do I remove underlines from my links?

Making changes to the styles used for links to other documents isn't as easy as adding styles for the <a> (anchor) tag. You also need to change the different states of that tag.

Going back to the old way of styling these tags with <font> tags, you would set a value for link (link), visited link (vlink), and active link (alink) in the <body> tag of your document. With CSS, you need to create declarations for these states too. You can also create declarations for the hover state: this gives the effect of the link changing when the user holds the mouse pointer over it.

To declare these states, click the *New CSS Style* button and in the dialog box select the *Use CSS Selector* radio button. You should get a drop-down list with the four states listed.

Select *a:link* and click *OK* to launch the *CSS Style Definition* dialog box.

You can now remove the underline from the link by checking the *none* check box under *Decoration* in the *CSS Style Definition* dialog box:

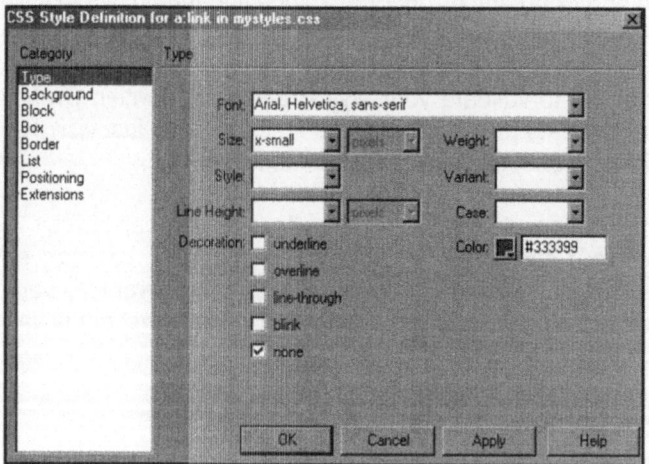

After setting the properties for `a:link`, click *OK*. You need to repeat the process for each of the other states. You could keep each state the same, but a common way to style the states is to have a different color for visited links in a document, so that the user knows he or she has been to that page already, and to add a method of highlighting the link on the hover state.

It is important to add these definitions in the correct order of link, visited, hover, active.

How do I have more than one style for links in one document?

Launch the *New CSS Style* dialog box again and proceed in the same way as you did to create your first set of links. This time, before clicking *OK*, edit the *Selector* field as in the following figure:

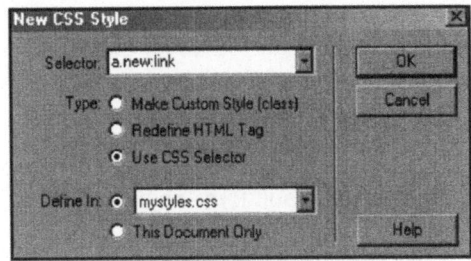

Click *OK* and define some different style rules from those for your first set of links. You need to do this for each selector in turn, remembering to add `.new` after the `a` each time.

You will now have two sets of links in your stylesheet: a basic set that will be applied to any links and a set that will be applied to any links with a `class` attribute name of `new`. To apply the `new` class to a link, you can use the *Properties* inspector. Select the link you would like to be in the secondary style, and then in the list in the *Properties* inspector select the class `new`.

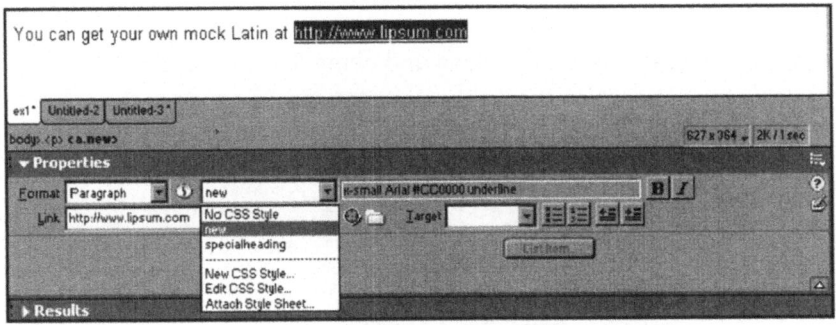

CSS

7

You can have as many different styles defined in your stylesheet for links as you want—just follow the preceding steps.

Tips for Styling Links

If you are removing the underline from your links, ensure that they still look like links! It is often better to create different styles for the links, using links with no decoration for navigation and retaining underlined links within the flow of the content, in order to demonstrate to the user what they are.

Take care not to change the size of the font for the different states; otherwise, your page will appear to jiggle when the links are in the `hover` state.

Adding an underline or overline, subtly changing the color, or adding a background color are all ways of creating an attractive effect for the hover state.

How can I make forms look nicer?

Another place where a simple use of CSS can really make a difference to the look of your site is in styling the rather ugly-looking default form objects.

Create a basic form in Dreamweaver with a text field, text area, and submit button. Attach your stylesheet to this page.

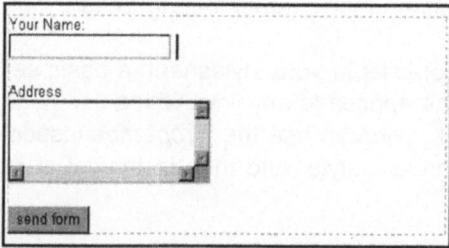

Within your stylesheet, create a custom class and name it `.textfield`.

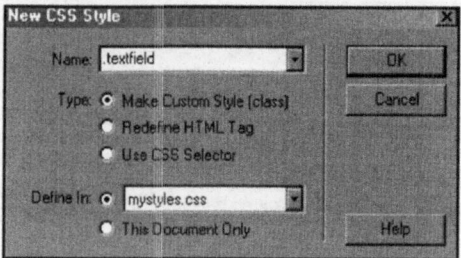

Click *OK* and add styles for the text field.

In the *Category* list, click *Border*. You can change the *Style*, *Width*, and *Color* of the border around the text field here. You can change the border all the way around an item (in Dreamweaver, checking the *Same for All* check box achieves this), or you can change the *Top*, *Left*, *Bottom*, and *Right* borders separately. By playing around with these, you can create nice effects. For this chapter's purposes, you are going to create a 1-pixel, solid blue border around the text field.

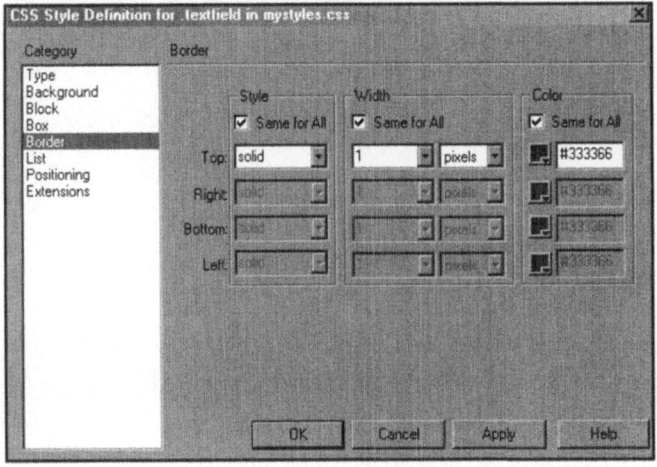

To change the background color of the field, select the *Background* category and choose a color. If you choose a dark background color, don't forget to select a text color (in the *Type* category) that will show up in the box.

You can also change the size of the field with CSS: select the *Box* category and in the field for *Width* type a width in pixels.

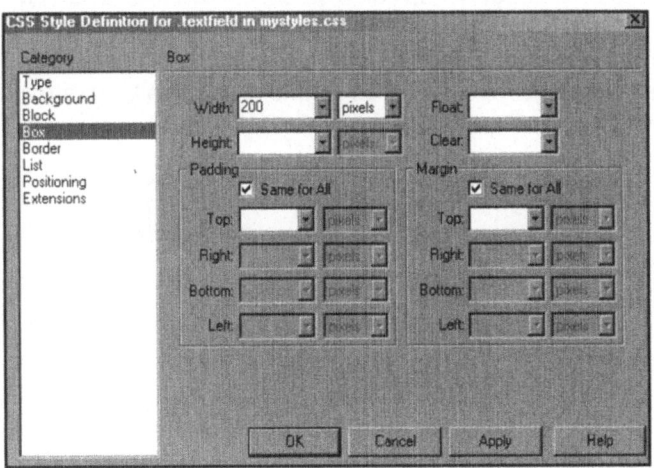

Click *OK*. To apply these styles to your text field, select the field in Dreamweaver. The *Properties* inspector changes to show the details of the field itself, but there is no option to apply the class there. So, right-click the *<input>* tag at the bottom of the document window and select *Set Class*. Then choose the class you created.

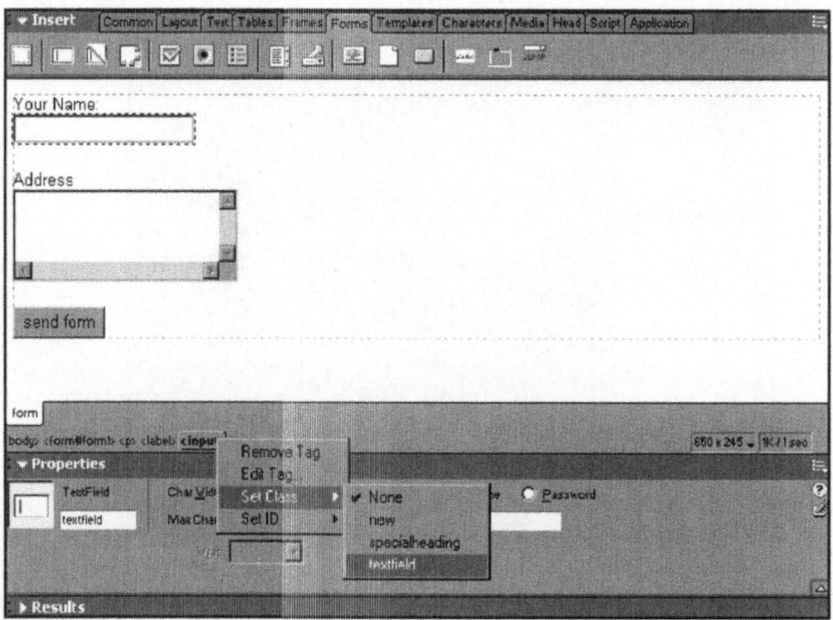

Many changes, in particular changes to form fields, do not show up in the Dreamweaver MX Design View, so you will need to preview your page in a browser to see the full effect.

You can style your other form objects in the same way. When styling your text area, you can add a height in the *Box* category. You can also experiment with padding on your submit button's class by changing the values in the *Box* category—once again you can set the padding all around the object by checking *Same for All* or change padding for *Top*, *Left*, *Bottom*, and *Right* individually. We used these simple style rules to create a form that looks like the next figure in Internet Explorer.

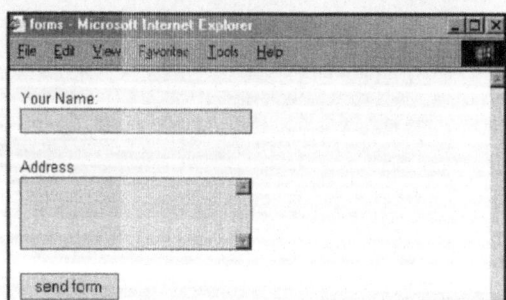

The CSS rules for this form within the stylesheet are as follows:

```
.textfield {
  background-color: #CCCCCC;
  border: 1px solid #333366;
  width: 200px;
}

.textarea{
  background-color: #CCCCCC;
  border: 1px solid #333366;
  width: 200px;
  height: 60px;
}

.submit {
  background-color: #CCCCCC;
  border: 1px solid #333366;
}
```

What about problems with CSS in older browsers?

CSS is generally very browser-friendly. If a browser does not support CSS at all, the user will just get your plain structured content. Some browsers support CSS badly or have their own proprietary implementation of CSS. Netscape 4 can have many problems, particularly where you have styled form fields with CSS. These may result in the browser crashing or the site being unusable. The number of people using Netscape 4 is small, but you probably don't want to crash someone's browser even if he or she is the only visitor who ever uses this browser.

Earlier, we covered two ways of attaching a stylesheet to your page: linking it or importing it. Netscape 4 does not recognize the @import directive. You can use this fact to your advantage by attaching two stylesheets to the page: one basic, Netscape 4–friendly stylesheet that you link to your page and another, more advanced stylesheet that you attach using @import. This latter stylesheet is invisible to Netscape 4.

To attach two stylesheets to your page in this way using Dreamweaver, you need to attach the basic Netscape 4–friendly stylesheet **first**, using the link method:

Then attach the second stylesheet, with the declarations for newer browsers, using `@import`:

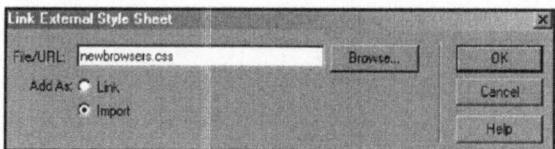

You have to specify the imported stylesheet after the linked stylesheet, so that the basic, Netscape 4–friendly CSS is overridden by the second stylesheet.

When creating your stylesheet, you need to remember to make sure that any redefined HTML tags or classes that you want to be different for newer browsers are included in the second, imported stylesheet. The browser will use the values in the linked stylesheet if no values are found in the imported one for that element. For instance, in your Netscape 4 stylesheet, you might include the following:

```
p, td, li {
      font: 12px Verdana, Geneva, Arial, Helvetica, sans-serif;
}
```

This would ensure that the text displayed a sensible size in Netscape 4. In you stylesheet for newer browsers, however, you would want the text slightly smaller and you would want to set the line height to give wider gaps between the lines of text (Netscape 4 can have problems with line height, so it is best to not have this in its stylesheet). For newer browsers you would use the following:

```
p, td, li {
      font: 11px/20px Verdana, Geneva, Arial, Helvetica, sans-serif;
}
```

The rules in the second stylesheet will override the rules in the first for newer browsers and, as Netscape 4 does not see the second stylesheet, it simply displays the one set of rules that it sees.

Resources

In this chapter we have taken a very brief look at CSS and how you can start to use CSS when working in Dreamweaver, yet we have only just touched on the power of this technology. To further your knowledge, here are some recommended web sites:

- **The Learning CSS section of the W3C web site** – *http://www.w3.org /Style/CSS/learning*

- **Cascading Style Sheets, level 1 Specification** – *http://www.w3.org/TR/REC-CSS1*

- **Cascading Style Sheets, level 2 Specification** – *http://www.w3.org/TR/REC-CSS2*

- **Mako 4 CSS (excellent web site with much information on CSS, including CSS in Dreamweaver, Netscape 4 issues, and more)** – *http://www.mako4css.com/*

- **W3Schools CSS Tutorials** – *http://www.w3schools.com/css/default.asp*

- **Macromedia Dreamweaver Designer and Developer Center, CSS** – *http://www.macromedia.com/desdev/topics/css.html*

and mailing lists:

- **TopStyle support forums** – *http://www.bradsoft.com/topstyle/forums/index.asp*

- **css-discuss mailing list** – *http://www.css-discuss.org/*

There are many excellent books available that can help you increase your knowledge of CSS, including *Cascading Stylesheets: Separating Content from Presentation* (Apress, ISBN 1-904151-04-3).

Summary

This chapter has provided a basic rundown of some of the things that you can do with CSS and why it is a way of working that you should embrace if you have not done so already. In this chapter, we covered the following topics:

- Why using CSS is a good thing
- CSS tools in Dreamweaver
- How to create stylesheets
- Common stylesheet tasks

One of the best ways to learn how to use CSS is to experiment with the different ways that you can influence the look of your documents by trying out different things from within Dreamweaver. We discuss CSS further in Chapter 12.

8

In this Chapter

- Templates in Dreamweaver MX

- Nested templates

- Repeating Regions

- Optional regions

Author: Nancy Gill

Templates

One of the greatest strengths of Dreamweaver MX is templates. If you have used templates in a previous version of Dreamweaver, then take note, because templates in Dreamweaver MX are a whole new ball game with four brand-new features that open up a world of possibilities: nested templates, repeating regions, optional regions, and editable attributes. In this chapter we cover how to use templates, the new template features in Dreamweaver MX, and the common problems you'll face when dealing with templates.

How Templates Work

Templates in Dreamweaver MX are a complex but very useful feature. You can create a template with the basic design of your web page and then create pages based on that template. If you need to change the design at a later date, then you can change the template and automatically update your whole site. Think of a template as a pattern for your site. The pattern provides basic structure and design, and allows changes to each child page to make it unique. The Dreamweaver MX template, in its simplest form, consists of two basic region types: **locked regions** and **editable regions**.

Templates in Dreamweaver MX are a complex but very useful feature.

Locked Regions

When you start to create a web site, chances are you begin with a program like Fireworks MX. In this program, you can draw the artistic elements of the page, create the navigation bar or buttons, and arrange items until you are satisfied with the look. Then you slice and export the document to Dreamweaver MX. You can create a template based on this design that contains elements that will be common to every page in your web site.

These elements are placed on the page and will be locked when child pages of the template are created. A locked region means that the region is editable in the template itself, but cannot be changed from the child page. In a child page, these locked regions are outlined in yellow (in the default Dreamweaver colors) in Design View and locked code is grayed out in Code View.

When you edit any locked regions in your template and save your template file, Dreamweaver will ask you if you want to update all pages created by the template. Answering *Yes* to this question will immediately apply the changes to all child pages created from that template.

Editable Regions

Editable regions are basically the rest of the page. In creation of the template, Dreamweaver MX creates two editable regions by default: the Page Title and an editable region in the `<head>` of the document. The Page Title is always editable so that the name of each page can quickly be made unique. The editable region in the head is for `<meta>` tags, JavaScript, and any dynamic page data that is typically written into the `<head>` of the document. If you create a child page from a template and attempt to save it with just these regions, Dreamweaver MX will prompt you that there are no editable regions in your document. You need to specify which parts of the document body are editable. We'll go into this in detail later on in the chapter.

Advantages and Disadvantages of Templates

The main advantage of templates is consistency. You can create dozens, even hundreds, of pages from one or a series of templates that will have a common look and feel. Another advantage is ease of updating: changing design elements in one template and updating a multitude of pages in just a few minutes is an amazing feature and can save lots of time.

The biggest disadvantage of templates is the learning curve. Templates are not an easy concept to grasp, particularly with the added features of Dreamweaver MX.

Creating a Basic Template Page

Templates in their simplest form are created for a basic HTML "static" site and contain locked content with at least one editable region in the body of the document. To create a basic template page, choose *File > New > General > Basic Page > HTML Template.*

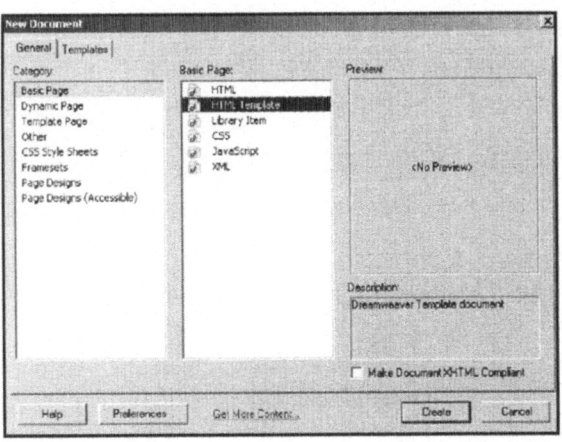

Click *Create* at the bottom right of the panel. Place the design elements imported from Fireworks MX or the art program of your choice or build the document from scratch in Dreamweaver MX. You can make use of ready-made *Page Designs* available in the preceding *New Document* dialog box or a host of snippets available in the *Snippets* panel.

Next, you need to arrange the design elements on the page until you are satisfied with the result. The design elements will be held in locked regions of the template. This means that those areas of the final page created by the template cannot be edited from the document based on the template. There are two main advantages of having locked regions. First, since the locked region cannot be edited in the child document, there is no chance that one of those elements will be inadvertently altered. Second, the locked regions of the document can be edited in the original template. This means that altering a locked template feature in the template allows you to update every document affected by that template all at once.

You can also create templates by taking an existing HTML page and saving it as a template using *File > Save As Template* when you are finished with the design. Dreamweaver will then prompt you to add an editable region.

Adding Template Features

There are a variety of ways to create template regions. One is from the *Insert* menu under the *Templates* tab. This contains, from left to right, *Make Template, Make Nested Template*, *Editable Region*, *Optional Region*, *Repeating Region*, *Editable Optional Region*, and *Repeating Table*. We will address each of these elements in depth.

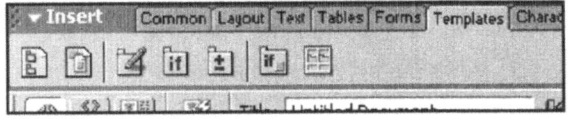

You can also use *Insert > Template Objects* from the main menu, which contains the options *Editable Region*, *Optional Region*, *Repeating Region*, *Editable Optional Region*, and *Repeating Table*.

Alternatively, you can right-click the page, bring up a context menu, and choose *Templates*:

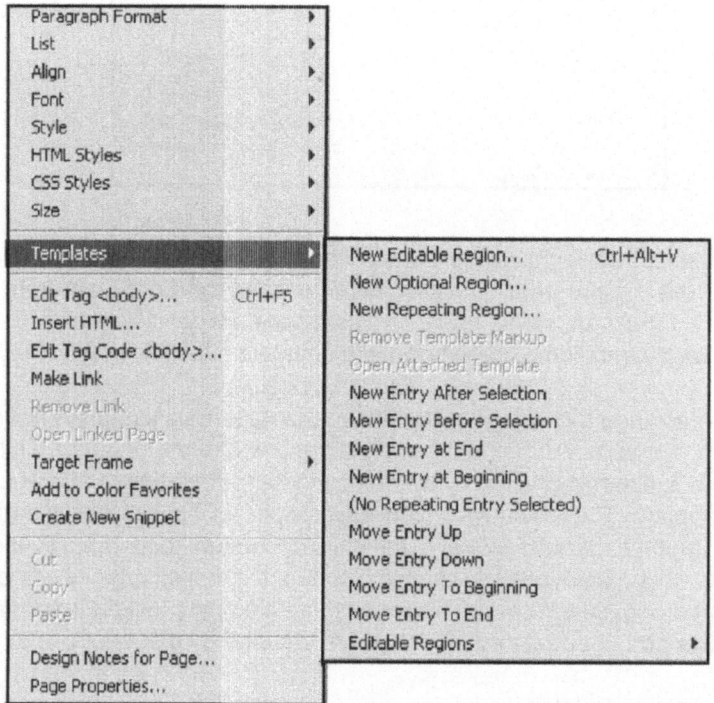

Editable Regions

You must create at least one editable region so that the child document will have somewhere you can place content.

You can create an editable region in one of several ways. Click the pencil icon in the *Insert* menu under the *Templates* tab, choose *Insert Menu > Template Objects > Editable Region*, or right-click the page, bring up the context menu, and choose *Templates > New Editable Region*.

 You must create at least one editable region so that the child document will have somewhere you can place content.

You'll use the first method, so click in the area of the template where you want the first editable region to appear and click the pencil icon (*Editable Region*) to apply the region. The dialog box will give you the option to give the editable region a name. This is a good idea because the name of the region will show up in the pages created from the template to remind you what content you wanted in that region

The editable region will look like this in Design View:

Once you have your editable regions in place and are satisfied with the way the template looks, you need to save it. You do not need to specify *Save As Template* unless you are creating a template from a normal document. When the template is saved, you will notice that the document is stored in a special `Templates` folder of your site, created by Dreamweaver for this purpose.

You can now create pages from your template by selecting *File > New > Templates.* The resulting window shows you a list of all your sites, and clicking the appropriate site will give you a list of the templates created for this site. Select the correct one and click *OK.*

You are now looking at a new page based on your template. Insert content into the editable region and save the document.

Now, should you wish to alter the look of your entire site, all you need to do is open the template and make the changes needed. When you save the template, you are asked if you want to update all the pages that use this template. Clicking *Yes* will result in Dreamweaver updating all of the pages based on that template. If not for templates, you would have had to create the new design, and copy and paste the content into it one page at a time.

You have now created a simple template for a basic HTML page. This is templates in their simplest form, but there's a lot more you can do with templates yet.

> *Now, should you wish to alter the look of your entire site, all you need to do is open the template and make the changes needed.*

Nested Templates

A **nested template** is just what its name implies: a template within a template. Nested templates allow for greater flexibility within a template-based site. Suppose that you have created the main template for your web site and you have established with that template a look for the company. Now you're ready to create a page, but the sales department has its own design elements that it wants incorporated into its pages of the site.

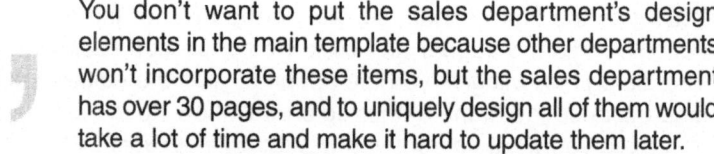

Nested templates allow for greater flexibility within a template-based site.

You don't want to put the sales department's design elements in the main template because other departments won't incorporate these items, but the sales department has over 30 pages, and to uniquely design all of them would take a lot of time and make it hard to update them later.

The solution is to create the first child page, incorporate the sales design items into that page, and use the *Save As Template* option to save that page as another template. This template will be used to create all the sales department pages. It will have all the features of the sales template available, but it will also inherit all the features of the original corporate template. Therefore, changing the corporate template will still update all the pages of the site, including the sales department nested template and all the pages created from it. You could have similar nested templates for the engineering department, the personnel department, and so on. All pages derived from these templates would have their own unique look, but they would also inherit the features of the main template.

You can create another level of nested template by creating a new page from the sales template and then making pages for U.S. sales and European sales. If you modified these pages so that each was different—for example, by having the U.S. and European Union flags on the respective pages—you can use *Save As Template* to create two more nested templates. Each template has the corporate branding and the branding of the sales department, plus the style of its own unique department.

Let's make a simple example and see how it works. Create the main template by selecting *New > HTML Template* and set up the design elements to form the locked regions. Create at least one editable region within the document (*Insert > Template Objects > Editable Region* or click the pencil icon from the *Template* tab of the *Insert* menu). Save the document as a template.

Now create a document from that template. This document is going to become the child template for the sales department. It will incorporate all the locked regions of the main template, but you will create some new areas in the editable region of the page that will be locked regions in the new template. Everything from the main template will be available in the sales template, but pages created from the sales template will contain their own locked and editable regions.

You will note something interesting with the editable regions here. The main template has editable regions outlined in green. They are labeled so content providers know just where to put the content.

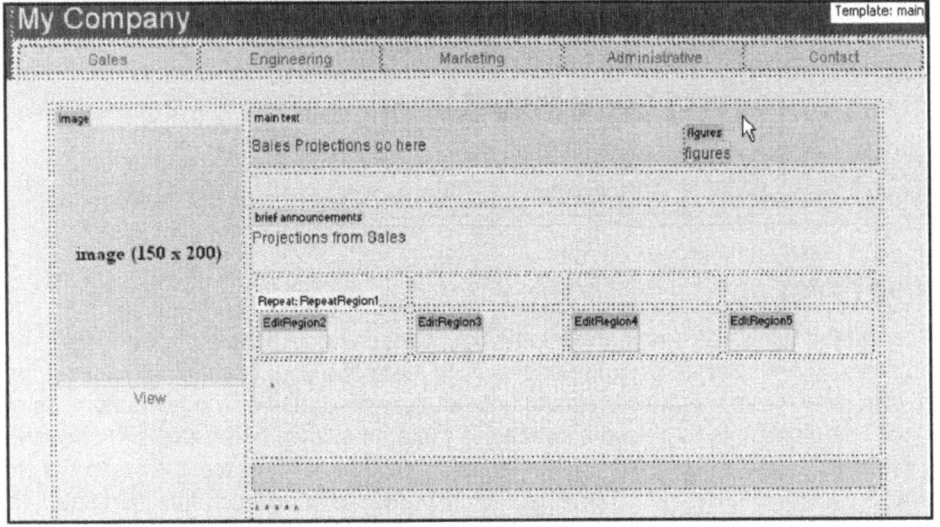

The editable regions of the sales department template are marked in green also, but now the editable regions of the main or parent template are marked in orange, so it's easy to see where the editable regions came from.

Repeating Regions

Repeating regions would be more aptly described as repeating content regions. They are basically locked regions that can be used to repeat a part of a page multiple times. However, when they contain an editable region, they are much more flexible. To add a repeating region, use *Insert > Template Objects > Repeating Region*. Dreamweaver will prompt you for the name of this repeating region. As before, if you assign a meaningful name, it will make it easier for you to remember what was supposed to go into this region when you're creating pages from the template.

For example, suppose that a given page will hold a series of news items in paragraph form. Each news item is an editable region, but the number of news items on the page will change. You can create a repeat region around it, so that people using the template merely have to click the plus sign (+) icon to add a new news item to the page. They can also reorder the items by clicking the arrow icons.

Repeating Tables

Repeating tables allow you to create a table that contains an editable region within each of the table cells. For example, in your company site, suppose your engineering department template is going to have a table containing figures, but you don't know how many rows will be needed. The solution is to set up a repeating table as follows. The table has two rows, but only the second row is repeating. In the pages created from this table, the first row holds the column headers, which won't be repeated in pages created from this template. The second will hold the data that may need to repeat a number of times. In each page created from the template, clicking the plus sign next to the repeat table header will add another repeat row. In the following example, we have added one extra repeat row to the template.

[Screenshot of template layout with "My Company" header and navigation: Sales, Engineering, Marketing, Administrative, Contact. Content shows "Engineering" main text, "brief announcements / The following are stats:", and Group 1-4 with EditRegion6-9.]

Optional Regions

Optional regions only appear on the page if certain conditions, specified by **template parameters** (see the next section), are met. They are useful for items that may appear regularly on pages but are not certain to be on every page. As an example, if you want to show a logo on your sales department pages when sales reach a certain figure, you can use an optional region. This is illustrated in the following screen shot. We have replaced our editable image field with an optional region that only appears when sales are $10,000. We do this by creating an optional region with the parameter if Sales == 10,000. Therefore, if sales are $5,000, for example, this "pat on the back" logo will not show. Once sales are equal to $10,000, it will.

> *They are useful for items that may appear regularly on pages but are not certain to be on every page.*

There are no editable regions in an optional region by default, but you can nest an editable region inside the optional region and, in most cases, you will want to do so. Therefore, when your logo shows up, you can create an editable region directly below it that will allow for input of the actual figures.

Template Parameters

Suppose that you want to show a region of the page only if a given condition exists. In the following example, we want to display some text saying *Welcome to Department 0* if the page in view is Department 0. We can set up a **template parameter** to achieve this:

The template parameter can be added to the template using the following code in the `<head>` of the document, which needs to be hand-coded:

```
<!-- #TemplateParam name="department" type="number" value="0" -->
```

Template parameters can have a type of `color`, `text`, `number`, or `Boolean`. `Boolean` parameters are `true` or `false`. If you plan to use parameters often, you may want to store the preceding code as a snippet.

If you use the preceding example, when a new page is created using the template, selecting *Modify > Template Properties* will bring up the following dialog box:

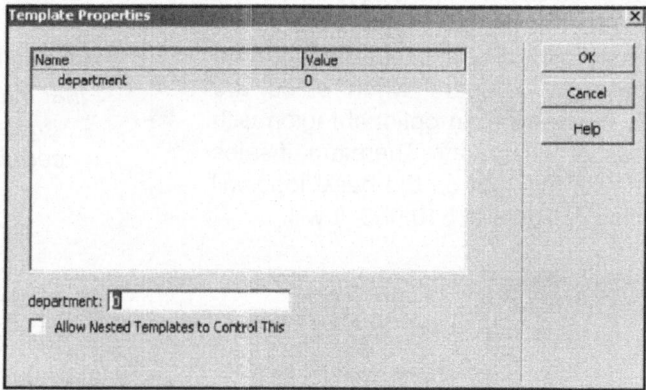

in which you can change the value of *department*. If you make it a value other than *0*, then Dreamweaver will know not to show your message.

Since you have the ability to put editable regions inside the optional regions, you can display alternative information depending on a condition. For example:

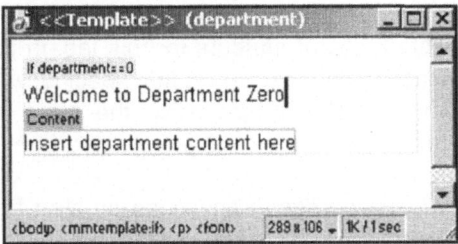

Editable Optional Region

There is another optional region object called the **editable optional region**. As with an optional region, you can set parameters or expressions that control whether or not the region shows on the page, but editable optional regions have an editable region inserted automatically. This allows you to insert content that is editable inside the region so that it can be changed from page to page.

Editable Tag Attributes

Suppose that you want to change something like the background color of the sales pages on your site based on the office location: head office pages shuld be white, New York office pages should be light blue, and Los Angeles office pages should be light green. You might think that you have to make a separate sales template for each location merely to change the background color attribute of the `<body>` tag. Actually, you can make the tag attribute editable in the template by selecting the tag and then selecting *Modify > Templates > Make Attribute Editable*. Open the template page and select the `<body>` tag. Choose *Modify > Templates > Make Attribute Editable*. The *Editable Tag Attributes* dialog box opens.

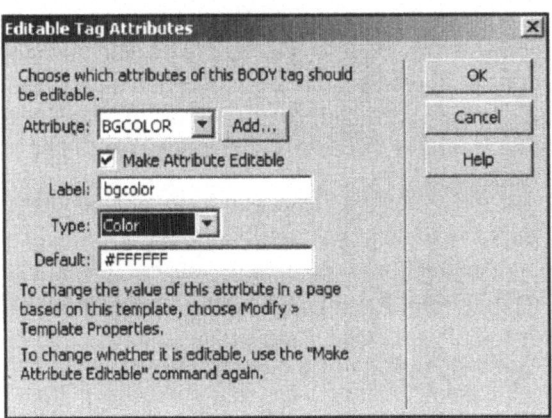

The attribute drop-down box will contain all the attributes of the tag you selected. For this example, find *BGCOLOR* on the list. Put a check in the box marked *Make Attribute Editable* and that will open the remainder of the options. The default name for your tag is already there as the value for the *Label* field. This can be changed if needed. The second drop-down contains the possible types of attribute for this tag. In this case, you need to select *Color*. The *Default* specified in the next field is that specified when the template was created. In this case, it's white. Click *OK* and save the main template page. Allow Dreamweaver to update the templates and any pages created from it.

If you go to *Modify > Template Properties* in any page created from this template, the *bgcolor* attribute is shown. You can select it and choose any color from the palette at the bottom of the box. You can do this on any one of the child pages or child templates. Changing this on the child template will change the template and thus affect any pages created with this template.

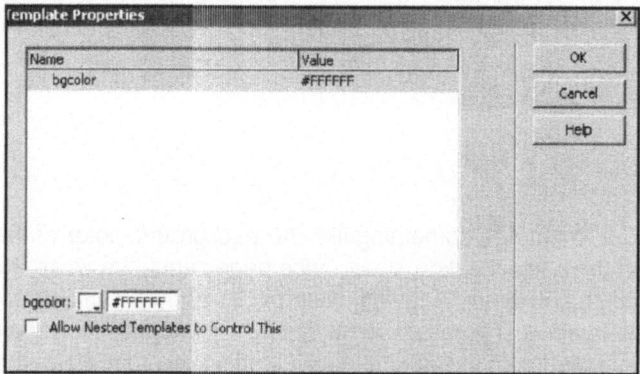

Creating a Template for Dynamic Pages

Creating a template for a dynamic page is much the same, but to start, you need to go to *File > New > General > Template Page* and specify the server model to match your site. For the sake of this example, assume it's an ASP/VBScript site. The barebones document looks the same from the Design View, but a quick look at the Code View shows you the ASP/VBScript declaration on the first line of the page. Your template will only create ASP/VBScript pages.

Now you can place the elements of your template in place and save it with a name that tells you which section the template was created to serve. Dreamweaver MX will save your page as `page.dwt.asp`. This means it is a Dreamweaver template for an ASP site.

Are templates necessary for a dynamic site? Consider the situation where you have a site for a company that has one look for the engineering department, another for sales, a third for administration, and yet another for features. If you create a template for the entire site and then create nested templates for each of those departments, you can create pages with both companywide branding and department branding on top of that. Any change you make to the main template will be picked up in the nested templates and any change you make to a departmental template will be picked up in the pages for that department with a couple of mouse clicks. Even if there are only two or three child pages because the rest of content comes from a database, it still makes sense to work this way. Why make changes three times if you can do it once?

Are templates necessary for a dynamic site?

Frequently Asked Questions

I am new to templates and I want to use them, but I have a lot of content on some of my pages and not much on others. How do I get my template to work with the long pages when it's a shorter page template?

When you build the template, you build it with editable regions. Your content then goes into these editable regions, not into the template itself. If you have a lot of content on the page, the editable region will be longer, but your template footer will still be there after the editable content is over and it will still look uniform.

Templates look like a good idea for someone with lots of static pages, but I'm primarily a developer of dynamic pages. My sites consist of three or four pages at the most, and everything is created on the fly from the database. Why would I need templates?

Of course, templates are of more importance for someone who has a multitude of pages, but even the dynamic developer can make use of them. Consistent changes to the look are still faster if you only have to update once and allow the template to update the other four or five pages than if you do them one at a time. Then the database will do the rest.

How do I modify content in the <head> section in my templates? I have <meta> tags and I want them to be carried from page to page, so it seems obvious to put them in the template, but the only editable region is in the <body> of the document.

If you are using Dreamweaver MX, there are two editable regions in the <head> section. The <title> tag is automatically made editable so that the page title can quickly be changed from page to page, but there is also another editable region in the head and that is for this purpose. Add your list of keywords and they will be put in this area, making them carry from page to page of the site.

How do I test if a template is valid?

You can easily check this by selecting *Modify > Templates > Check Template Syntax*. If an error is detected, an alert box will tell you what the problem is and what line of the template it was detected on. This makes finding errors very easy.

I'm having a hard time using DMX behaviors with templates. They aren't selected for me to use. Why is this? They work fine if I don't use templates.

When you use Dreamweaver behaviors, pay careful attention to the tag you need to apply the behavior to. If you are trying to apply a behavior that attaches to the <body> tag, and the <body> tag is not editable in the child page that you are working on (which is often the case because it would have been locked in the main template), you can't edit it in the page. To edit this attribute, you can either edit the main template or make the attribute editable and update the pages and templates affected by it.

How can I change the color of links in a locked area on just one page?

Give the links a class, and make that attribute editable from the template.

I've uploaded my template to the web site, but why hasn't it changed all the other pages?

The child pages of the template, not the template itself, need to be uploaded to the web site. Let Dreamweaver update the child pages on your local machine and then upload them.

My links aren't being updated any more. Why?

This usually happens if you move the template out of the `Templates` folder, or if you've put subfolders in there. It's also important to note that Dreamweaver can't update links that contain JavaScript.

Summary

In this chapter we've looked at the template features in Dreamweaver MX. Editable regions are areas that contain editable content in child pages created from the template. Optional regions give flexibility in design not seen in earlier versions. You can show areas of a page depending on whether or not a condition is met. Optional regions are not editable by default, but there is an optional editable region available that makes this possible. With a new feature called nested templates, you can design templates within templates and have the ability to customize every area of your web site, while still having one overall look and feel for the entire site.

There is no way we could cover the complete scope of templates in just this one chapter. For further information, here are some additional resources:

- *http://www.macromedia.com/desdev/topics/templates.html* – Macromedia's DevNet Resource area has an entire section devoted to templates. You can find a multitude of tech notes, articles, and examples.

- *http://www.macromedia.com/support/dreamweaver/ts/documents/newtemplate.htm* – Template features are discussed in depth here.

- *http://www.projectseven.com* – Excellent site containing tutorials, articles, and even ready-made templates to help you out.

- *http://web.mit.edu/is/help/dreamweaver/templates-mx.html* – This site discusses in depth many of the advanced template features of Dreamweaver MX and provides helpful examples.

9

In this Chapter

- Web standards
- Creating standards-compliant pages in Dreamweaver

Author: Rachel Andrew

Web Standards

When people use the term "web standards," they are talking about the rules that specify how languages such as HTML, XHTML, and CSS should be written. Most of the standards that are discussed under the term "web standards" are **open standards**. This means that they are freely available to be viewed, studied, and used by anyone.

The standards aren't there just for the education of web designers—browser and device manufacturers use these standards to develop new browsers and devices. They can be seen as a baseline for what their new products need to support. Device manufacturers can ensure that their device complies with those standards and can therefore be confident that it will display or read documents in the way that document authors intend. In theory, open standards also mean that web professionals can be sure that their pages, built to the standards, will display correctly in devices that support the standards.

Though this hopefully sounds like common sense, the reality is that today's Web is a mishmash of pages built using proprietary markup, invalid use of markup, and browsers that do not always display standards-compliant code correctly. This may be because they don't actually implement the standards correctly, or it may be that different browser manufacturers interpret the standards in slightly different ways, each of which may be regarded as "correct."

Who Sets the Standards?

Most of the "web standards" that are commonly discussed are developed by the W3C. The exception to this is JavaScript, which is based on the standard ECMAScript developed by ECMA (*http://www.ecma-international.org*). On the W3C web site at *http://www.w3.org* you can find the specifications to which we refer throughout this chapter.

They aren't always the easiest things to read since they have been written not as user manuals or tutorials, but as technical specifications. They do become easier to follow after you have worked with a language for a while, and there are also many tutorial and help sites online that can assist you in deciphering them.

Does It Take Longer to Work with the Standards?

Initially, yes. When you first begin validating your documents (testing whether they comply with the standards), you will need to learn what the validator messages mean (we will cover validating documents later in this chapter) and how to correct your markup in order that the page validates. When working with Dreamweaver MX, part of that initial difficulty is overcome because Dreamweaver automatically creates standards-compliant code for the most part, so you should have relatively few errors to find and fix. (We'll discuss validation through Dreamweaver and the W3C site in a later section of this chapter.)

Writing valid markup soon becomes second nature.

Once you have become accustomed to working in this way, however, you should find that it actually speeds up your working process. Writing valid markup soon becomes second nature, and compliant documents are far easier to debug when you do experience a problem in a certain browser, as browser bugs affecting valid documents are well documented and usually have fixes that you can find and use on your site.

Why Should I Work with the Standards?

A few years ago, checking that the site worked in the two main browsers (Netscape and Internet Explorer) was all that mattered; the validity of the markup was not deemed important. You will still hear people talking about "both browsers" as if nobody ever used anything other than Internet Explorer or Netscape, but this is a very outdated attitude. There are so many different devices now (such as PDAs, web phones, screen and Braille readers for the visually impaired, and a variety of alternative web browsers) that building a site for each of them would be impossibile. Even if you managed to cover all devices currently in use, something else will be released next week. Your best hope is to comply with the standards.

Future-Proofing

The latest generation of web browsers (Internet Explorer 6 and Netscape 7) are the most standards-compliant ever. Browser manufacturers have realized that standards are a good thing.

When Netscape released Netscape 6, they dropped backward-compatibility for many of the hacks and proprietary code that had been developed for their version 4 browsers, in favor of developing a browser that displayed code written to comply correctly with the W3C recommendations.

This phasing out of deprecated markup could easily happen again with mainstream browsers, as they continue down the path of compliance with the W3C recommendations. So if you write non-standards-compliant markup, it may not be readable in future browsers.

> *So if you write non-standards-compliant markup, it may not be readable in future browsers.*

Additionally, many of the presentational tricks in common use today are exploitations of browser behavior. There is nothing to say that a newer version of the browser will behave in the same way. Validating your document will give you peace of mind knowing that the latest and greatest version of Internet Explorer, Netscape, or another browser won't leave you with a broken web site.

Accessibility

Accessibility is becoming a legal requirement in many countries. Even in those where it is not, ensuring that everyone can use your site is an excellent aim. Should laws be applied to the organizations you are creating your sites for in the future, you will not need to begin rebuilding in order to comply with them.

> *Complying with web standards will assist you in ensuring that your web site is accessible to those with disabilities.*

Complying with web standards will assist you in ensuring that your web site is accessible to those with disabilities. Though you can still create an inaccessible site when adhering to the standards, compliance with the standards does, at the very least, offer a greater chance that devices such as screen readers and Braille readers can interpret the markup correctly and make your content understandable. With a solid base of valid markup, you will be on a good footing to ensure that your site is fully accessible to all web users.

Accessibility need not just apply to users with disabilities—those using limited devices such as PDAs and web phones will also benefit from clean, compliant code, as will search engine robots (which understand the standards and use them to help them spider and index the content of sites and decide where in the ranking a site should be placed).

Ease of Debugging

As we have already mentioned, standards-compliant code can be far quicker to debug. Often, by simply validating and fixing errors that are flagged up, you can isolate and correct a display issue. Even if the process does not correct the problem, you will be well placed to work out where the problem lies.

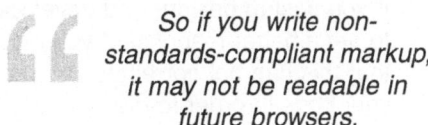

Web Standards

9

If you post to design- and development-related mailing lists with a problem, you are likely to get a better response if you can demonstrate that you have validated your markup and that this has not corrected the problem. It also makes it easier for someone to look over your code in order to give you some help and advice on the issue, so you are more likely to receive helpful replies to your queries.

Working As a Team

You'll also enhance your appearance as a professional who knows what he is doing—neat, valid markup looks far more impressive than a tangled mess of incorrectly nested tags and proprietary code.

Working to the standards also makes it easier for other people working on your project, or taking on the project after you, to pick up where you left off. Many designers create HTML pages that will be used as templates for a content management system or other dynamic site. By creating templates that conform to standards, you will make it far easier for those who then need to incorporate that design into server-side code. You'll also enhance your appearance as a professional who knows what he is doing—neat, valid markup looks far more impressive than a tangled mess of incorrectly nested tags and proprietary code.

Creating Standards-Compliant Documents in Dreamweaver MX

Your first decision is whether you are working in HTML or XHTML. In Dreamweaver MX you may choose to work in

- HTML 4.01 Transitional
- HTML 4.01 Frameset
- XHTML 1.0 Transitional
- XHTML 1.0 Frameset

The ability to work in XHTML is new in this version of Dreamweaver, and we cover this later in the chapter. This new feature is a reflection of the fact that HTML has come to its final version with HTML 4.01, and many developers are moving to XHTML.

HTML or XHTML?

HTML 4.01 is the last version of the HTML standard; the current recommended markup language for use on the web is XHTML. However, HTML is unlikely to make a sudden disappearance from the Web, and validating to any standard is better than validating to none.

That being said, moving to XHTML (particularly when you have Dreamweaver MX to assist you) is a simple process that just involves learning a few additional rules. If you are creating a brand-new site, you really have no reason not to use XHTML.

If you are creating a brand new-site, you really have no reason not to use XHTML.

So what is the difference? XHTML has been developed as a web language that reproduces all the features of HTML yet conforms to the stricter rules of XML. It is a logical progression from HTML 4.01 and certainly not something to be worried about, especially now that you can use your familiar visual development environment, Dreamweaver, to help you in making the transition. The main rules that make XHTML different to HTML are covered in the following sections.

XML Declaration

The XML declaration

```
<?xml version="1.0" encoding="iso-8859-1"?>
```

which Dreamweaver adds before the DOCTYPE at the top of a new XHTML document, is not strictly required. However, the W3C states that "XHTML document authors are strongly encouraged to use XML declarations in all their documents."

The XML declaration simply states that the document is an XML document and can also (as in the case of the declaration that Dreamweaver inserts) provide information on character encoding for the document.

DOCTYPE

An XHTML document must validate against one of the three XHTML DOCTYPEs: XHTML Strict, XHTML Transitional, or XHTML Frameset. An HTML document must validate against the relevant HTML DOCTYPE. To read more about DOCTYPEs, look to the section "What Is a DOCTYPE?"

Quote All Attribute Values

All attribute values must be enclosed in quotation marks. For example, in the following `<img>` tag, the `height` and `width` attributes are incorrectly defined:

```
<img height=100 width=300 alt="my logo" src="logo.gif" />
```

This is the correct way to do it:

```
<img height="100" width="300" alt="my logo" src="logo.gif" />
```

Whereas previous versions of Dreamweaver have tended to quote attributes correctly, you may find that code snippets that you (or other developers on your team) use may not be as careful. Selecting *Commands > Clean up XHTML* will quote any unquoted attributes within your document automatically.

Write Tags and Attributes in Lowercase

Element and attribute names must be in lowercase. Quoted attribute values can be in any case, although it is worth noting that CSS classes are case sensitive, so myclass is not the same as myClass.

For example, both of these lines are incorrect:

```
<IMG HEIGHT="100" WIDTH="300" ALT="my logo" SRC="logo.gif" />
<img HEIGHT="100" WIDTH="300" ALT="my logo" SRC="logo.gif" />
```

This is how it should be done in XHTML:

```
<img height="100" width="300" alt="my logo" src="logo.gif" />
```

JavaScript event handlers, such as `onclick` or `onmouseover`, must also be written in lowercase. The following JavaScript is incorrect:

```
onMouseOver="MM_swapImage('img1','','i/button01b.gif',1)"
```

And this is the correct way to do it:

```
onmouseover="MM_swapImage('img1','','i/button01b.gif',1)"
```

Dreamweaver MX, when working on an XHTML document, will generate lowercase code, including JavaScript. However, third-party extensions or code you copy and paste into the Code View may not allow for XHTML, so you may need to change the case by hand.

Nonempty Elements Must Have End Tags

By a "nonempty" element, we mean a tag that contains something between the start tag and the end tag. Some HTML elements can be written without the closing tag. For example, the end `</p>` tag of the paragraph element is optional and therefore omitted by many HTML authors. In XHTML, however, all elements must be closed.

The following, while valid in HTML, is incorrect in XHTML:

```
<p>This is some text formatted in a paragraph.
<p> This is the second paragraph.
```

This is the XHTML way of marking up the same text:

```
<p>This is some text formatted in a paragraph.</p>
<p> This is the second paragraph.</p>
```

Dreamweaver MX closes all nonempty elements, whether you are working in HTML or XHTML, and will add closing tags when you run the *Clean Up (X)HTML* command.

Close All Empty Elements

Empty elements are those tags that stand alone and do not include anything between a start and end tag, such as `<br>` and `<hr>`. In XHTML these need to be closed. This means that the HTML empty elements, such as `<br>` and `<hr>`, become `<br />` and `<hr />` in XHTML.

Note the space before the closing slash in the preceding examples. It is correct XML and therefore XHTML to leave out this space, however, for backward-compatibility with older browsers designed for HTML. Keeping this space ensures that those browsers render the tags correctly.

Dreamweaver MX uses the correct closing for empty tags such as `<br />` when generating markup in an XHTML document and also when cleaning up XHTML.

Documents Must Be Well-Formed

An XHTML document must be **well-formed**. This means that all tags must nest correctly—the first tag that you open should be the last to be closed.

This is an example of badly nested markup:

```
<p><strong>This is bold text.</p></strong>
```

This is the correct way of nesting the tags:

```
<p><strong>This is bold text.</strong></p>
```

Dreamweaver MX nests elements correctly and will also correct nesting of elements when cleaning up XHTML.

No Attribute Minimization

Attribute minimization refers to the practice of only writing an attribute name and not its value. In XHTML, all attributes should be written as name-value pairs, even where this means that the value is the same as the name.

9

This is incorrect in XHTML:

```
<input type="checkbox" name="checkbox" id="checkbox" value="True" checked
/>
```

This is the corrected version:

```
<input    type="checkbox"    name="checkbox"    id="checkbox"    value="True"
checked="checked" />
```

Dreamweaver MX will insert this correct markup when you work in Design View and it also will convert minimized attributes to name-value pairs if you convert an HTML document into XHTML or use *Clean Up XHTML*.

Use HTML Entities in Place of & < >

You will get an error when you attempt to validate your document if you have used & < or > in your markup instead of the HTML entities of `&amp; &lt; &gt;`. This applies even to & characters in URLs, but if you use `&amp;` in its place, the browser will convert it and your document will still validate. Dreamweaver will use HTML entities if you are working in Design View, but you will need to remember to deal with those in URLs or Code View yourself.

Give Images and Form Elements id Attributes

You commonly use `name` to give an image, form field, or other tag a `name` , so that you can refer to it with JavaScript. Name has been deprecated for images, other objects, and the form tag (although not for form fields where it is still an attribute). In Transitional XHTML, it is perfectly valid to give both a `name` and an `id` attribute, Dreamweaver will do this as it uses `name` to create JavaScript for browsers that do not support the W3C DOM and `id` for those that do.

```
<img src="myimage.gif" name="myImage" width="80" height="20" id="myImage"
alt="home" />
```

What Is a DOCTYPE?

In order to create a standards-compliant HTML or XHTML document, you must first include a **Document Type Definition** (DOCTYPE) at the very top of your document, before the `<html>` tag. This will tell the browser what standard this document adheres to. It must also be included for you to be able to validate your document, since it tells the validator which version of (X)HTML you are validating against. Therefore, you must select the correct `DOCTYPE` for your document.

Working in HTML

There are three current HTML DOCTYPEs available for you to use: Strict, Transitional, and Frameset. Unless you are using frames, Dreamweaver will presume that you are working to the Transitional DOCTYPE. This DOCTYPE allows the use of deprecated attributes; however, if you need to use frames, you will need to use the transitional DOCTYPE (as we cover shortly).

HTML 4.01 Transitional

```
<!DOCTYPE HTML PUBLIC "-//W3C//DTD HTML 4.01 Transitional//EN"
          "http://www.w3.org/TR/html4/loose.dtd">
```

By default, Dreamweaver MX will create HTML 4.01 Transitional code and therefore insert the preceding DOCTYPE. To create a new HTML 4.01 document, select *File > New* and ensure that the check box *Make document XHTML compliant* is unchecked. If you switch to Code View in the document that is created, you will see the DOCTYPE at the top of the document.

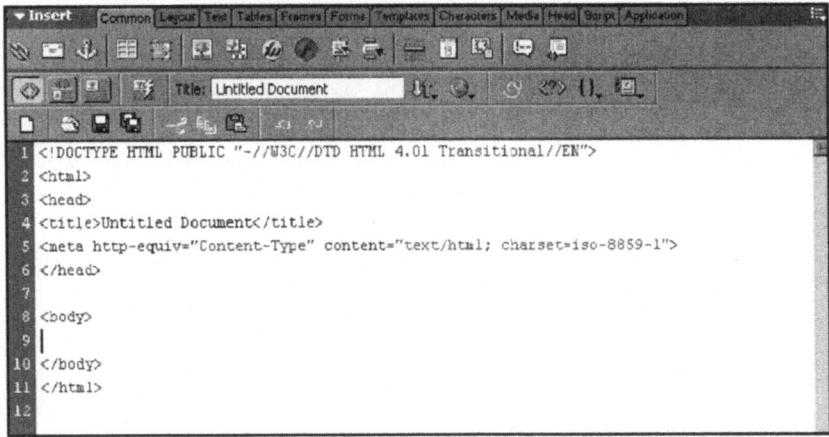

The markup that Dreamweaver generates when using this DOCTYPE will, for the most part, be valid HTML.

You may have noticed that the DOCTYPE inserted by Dreamweaver does not include the URL. For an explanation of this behavior see the section "Why Does My Page Look Different in Dreamweaver MX Than in the Browser?" at the end of this chapter.

HTML 4.01 Frameset

The full HTML 4.01 Frameset DOCTYPE looks like this:

```
<!DOCTYPE HTML PUBLIC "-//W3C//DTD HTML 4.01 Frameset//EN"
          "http://www.w3.org/TR/html4/frameset.dtd">
```

To create a document that contains frames, you need to use the HTML 4.01 Frameset DTD. Once again, Dreamweaver will insert this for you. You can create your framed document two ways. Select *File > New > Framesets* and choose the frames layout that you wish to use.

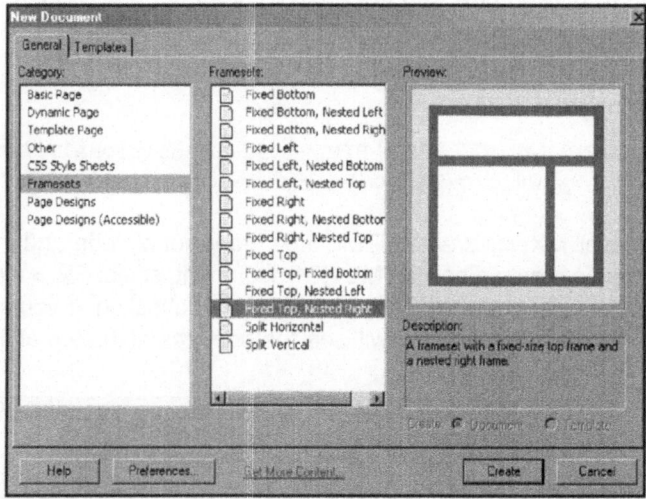

Clicking *Create* will create a document split into the component frames. The main document will contain the HTML 4.01 Frameset DOCTYPE.

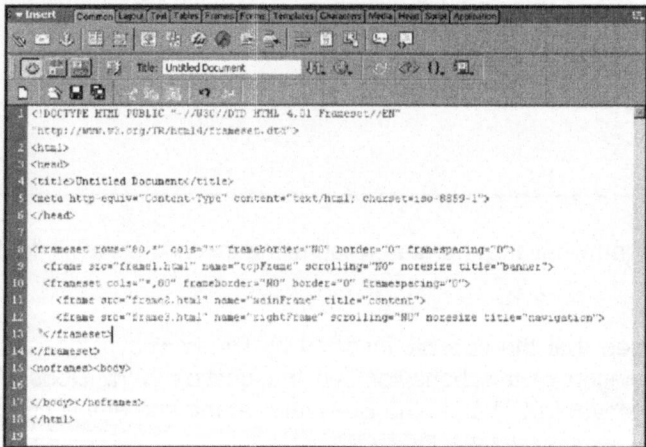

You can also add frames from the *Frames* panel of the *Insert* toolbar.

If you add a frame to a document with an HTML 4.01 Transitional DOCTYPE, Dreamweaver will automatically change the DOCTYPE of the containing frameset (your original document) to be the HTML 4.01 Frameset DOCTYPE.

HTML 4.01 Strict

```
<!DOCTYPE HTML PUBLIC "-//W3C//DTD HTML 4.01//EN"
          "http://www.w3.org/TR/html4/strict.dtd">
```

Dreamweaver MX does not write HTML that validates against the HTML 4.01 Strict DOCTYPE. This DOCTYPE does not allow the use of any deprecated elements—these elements include <font> tags and other presentational HTML tags that can be replaced by the use of CSS. It is possible to code to a Strict DOCTYPE from within Dreamweaver MX, but you will need to remember which elements are deprecated yourself and add the DOCTYPE manually.

Working in XHTML

As with HTML, there are three DOCTYPEs available when working in XHTML 1.0. Once again, Dreamweaver will presume that you are working to the Transitional DOCTYPE unless you have frames within your document. As with HTML 4.01 Transitional, the XHTML1.0 Transitional DOCTYPE allows the use of deprecated elements that are not allowable in the Strict XHTML DOCTYPE.

XHTML 1.0 Transitional

```
<!DOCTYPE html PUBLIC "-//W3C//DTD XHTML 1.0 Transitional//EN"
          "http://www.w3.org/TR/xhtml11/DTD/xhtml11-transitional.dtd">
```

To create a new XHTML document, select *File > New* and in the *New Document* dialog box, select the check box in the bottom-right corner that says *Make document XHTML compliant.*

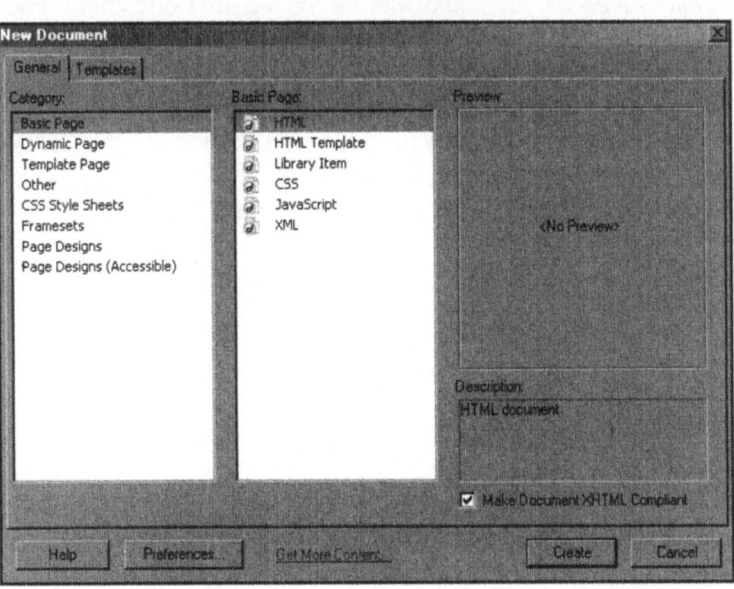

This will launch a new XHTML document in Dreamweaver. Switch into Code View and you will be able to see the DOCTYPE that Dreamweaver has added for this document:

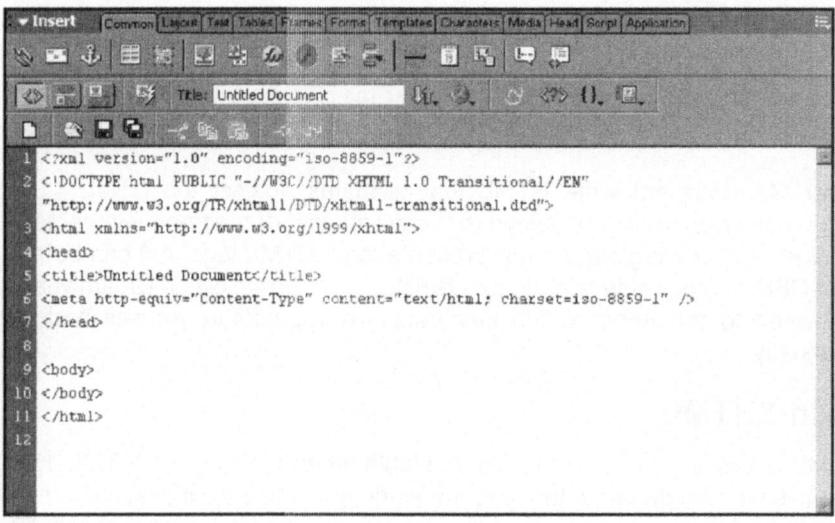

XHTML 1.0 Frameset

```
<!DOCTYPE html PUBLIC "-//W3C//DTD XHTML 1.0 Frameset//EN"
        "http://www.w3.org/TR/xhtml1/DTD/xhtml1-frameset.dtd">
```

If you are working with Frames and XHTML, you will not be able to create your document from *File > New* as you could with the HTML 4.01 document, because there is no *Make Document XHTML Compliant* check box for framesets. However, if you create a new XHTML document as you did previously, you can use the *Frames* panel of the *Insert* toolbar to insert your frames. Then Dreamweaver will change the DOCTYPE of the frameset to XHTML 1.0 Frameset. You may also notice in the following screen shot that Dreamweaver has automatically closed the `<frame>` tags and is not minimizing the attribute `noresize` as it does with the HTML 4.01 document.

```
<frame src="frame1.html" name="topFrame" scrolling="No"
noresize="noresize" id="topFrame" title="banner" />
```

```
1  <?xml version="1.0" encoding="iso-8859-1"?>
2  <!DOCTYPE html PUBLIC "-//W3C//DTD XHTML 1.0 Frameset//EN"
   "http://www.w3.org/TR/xhtml1/DTD/xhtml1-frameset.dtd">
3  <html xmlns="http://www.w3.org/1999/xhtml">
4  <head>
5  <title>Untitled Document</title>
6  <meta http-equiv="Content-Type" content="text/html; charset=iso-8859-1" />
7  </head>
8
9  <frameset rows="80,*" cols="*" frameborder="no" border="0" framespacing="0">
10   <frame src="frame1.html" name="topFrame" scrolling="No" noresize="noresize" id="topFrame"
   title="banner" />
11   <frameset cols="*,80" frameborder="no" border="0" framespacing="0">
12     <frame src="frame2.html" name="mainFrame" id="mainFrame" title="content" />
13     <frame src="frame3.html" name="rightFrame" scrolling="No" noresize="noresize" id="rightFrame"
   title="navigation" />
14   </frameset>
15  </frameset>
16  <noframes><body>
17  </body></noframes>
18  </html>
19
```

XHTML 1.0 Strict

```
<!DOCTYPE html PUBLIC "-//W3C//DTD XHTML 1.0 Strict//EN"
          "http://www.w3.org/TR/xhtml1/DTD/xhtml1-strict.dtd">
```

XHTML 1.0 Strict is comparable to the Strict HTML 4.01 DOCTYPE and once again means that you cannot use any deprecated elements. You will need to be very aware of these elements and avoid adding them in Dreamweaver if you wish to validate against the Strict DOCTYPE.

How Can I Convert an HTML Document to XHTML?

If you have existing HTML sites and would like to convert them to XHTML, you will not need to make these changes by hand. Dreamweaver MX ships with a *Convert to XHTML* feature that will assist you in this conversion.

To convert an existing document, select *File > Convert > XHTML*. (If your document contains frames, you will need to convert the frameset and each frame page individually.) The conversion utility will

● Replace the HTML DOCTYPE with the correct XHTML Transitional DOCTYPE (or add a DOCTYPE if none exists)

- Turn uppercase tags and attribute names into lowercase

- Make all JavaScript event handlers lowercase

- Add quotes to unquoted attributes

- Duplicate any name attributes of images, form fields, etc. with an `id` attribute

- Close all nonempty tags

- Close all empty tags with the correct /> closing

Converting an existing document or site to XHTML with Dreamweaver MX is a relatively painless process and is an excellent way to learn about the changes necessary for valid XHTML.

Converting an existing document or site to XHTML with Dreamweaver MX is a relatively painless process and is an excellent way to learn about the changes necessary for valid XHTML.

How Can I Check That My Document Is Standards-Compliant?

If you are working to create standards-compliant documents, then the best way to learn is to have a go at it. Validate your pages as you go along, so that you can pick up any problems quickly and fix them as you work, rather than getting your site "finished" and then finding loads of errors. Dreamweaver MX makes this way of working simple.

Validating Within Dreamweaver

If you have a static HTML or XHTML document that contains no server-side scripting, then you can validate the document using the Dreamweaver MX built-in validator.

Validator Preferences

Before using the validator, check that it is set to the version of HTML or XHTML that you wish to validate against—the version that is described in your DOCTYPE. Select *Edit > Preferences > Validator:*

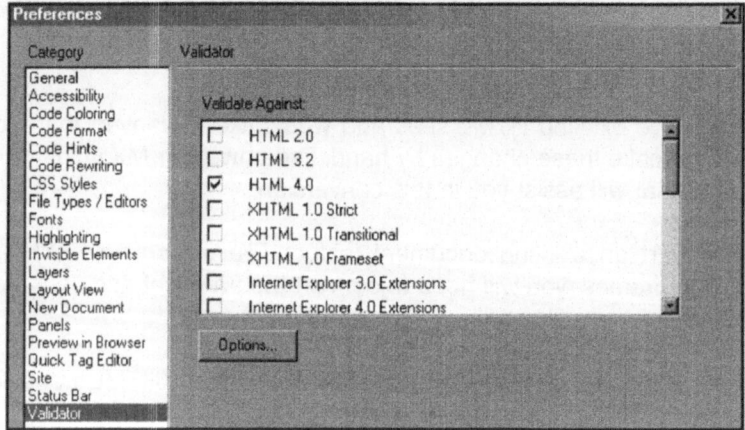

192

If you are validating for HTML, then check the HTML 4.0 check box; if you are validating for XHTML, then check the appropriate box that is correct for your DOCTYPE. Click *OK*.

To run the validator, open up the *Results* panel (*Window > Results > Validation*) and click the small green arrow:

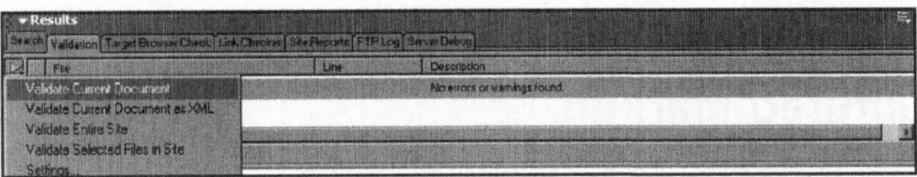

If you are validating an HTML document, then select *Validate Current Document*. If you are validating an XHTML document, then select *Validate Current Document as XML*.

You can also run the validator by selecting *File > Check Page > Validate Markup* for HTML or *File > Check Page > Validate as XML* for XHTML.

Validating at the W3C Web Site

Although the internal validator is a useful tool when working on your documents within Dreamweaver, validating at the W3C web site makes a good final check. The URL for the W3C HTML validator is *http://validator.w3.org/*. Dreamweaver MX has no validator for CSS, so you will need to visit the W3C web site to validate your CSS files, as we discussed in Chapter 7.

The W3C tool allows you to validate by entering the URI of the page that requires validation or by uploading the document. The easiest way to validate your pages is to upload them to your web server and then point the validator to the URL. If you are using the Dreamweaver validator as you work on your site, you will probably only need to make a check with the W3C validator as part of your final testing to ensure that all documents, including those that contain dynamic data, validate. If your pages do indeed validate at the W3C site, then you can place the W3C buttons on your web site to show that your pages are considered valid.

Validating Dynamic Pages

Dynamic pages should be validated with the online validator at the W3C site and, if they include conditional regions, each possible way that the page can be displayed should be validated if at all possible. Your server-side code will not cause you any validation problems at the validator because by the time that it has been parsed by the server, all that the validator is seeing is the (X)HTML that is returned to the browser.

Structured Markup

Although the validator can see and report on any errors in your HTML or XHTML, it cannot tell whether you are using the (X)HTML tags appropriately and structuring your document in a logical manner. This is something you will need to be aware of yourself.

The basic set of structural tags, including paragraph `<p>`, heading levels such as `<h1>` and `<h2>`, and lists `<li>`, were designed to mark up content in a manner that made it easy to read, and not particularly to force the way things "look." A screen reader, reading the content of a page to a visually impaired user, will read text between `<h1>` and `</h1>` tags with emphasis to demonstrate that this is a heading. Similarly, it will read text between `<blockquote>` and `</blockquote>` tags as a quote. As you can imagine, if these tags have been used simply because of the way they look in a regular browser—using `<h1>` for large text and `<blockquote>` for indentation—the experience of the visually impaired user is going to be quite confusing! Dreamweaver doesn't help in this regard as the button on the *Properties* inspector that creates a `<blockquote>` says *Text Indent*.

Ensuring you are using tags correctly is as simple as asking yourself "Is this a quote?" before you click the *Text Indent* button or checking that text that should be a heading uses a heading level that indicates its importance. You can then use CSS to get the visual display that you want without compromising the document's structure for those who do not have CSS support or who are having the page read out to them.

The following screen shot shows a use of `<blockquote>` to indent a paragraph that is not a quote.

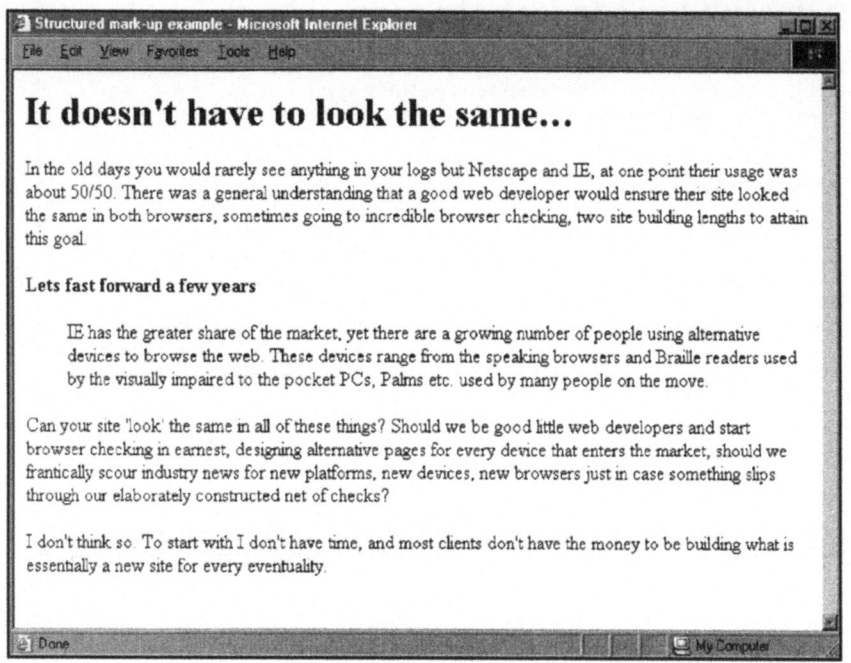

The indented paragraph has been wrapped in `<blockquote></blockquote>` tags:

```
<blockquote>
    <p>IE has the greater share of the market, yet there are a growing
number of
    people using alternative devices to browse the Web. These devices
range from
    the speaking browsers and Braille readers used by the visually
impaired to
    the pocket PCs, Palms etc. used by many people on the move.</p>
</blockquote>
```

A better way, from a document structure point of view, would be to create this effect using CSS. By creating a custom CSS class, either in the head of your document or in an external CSS file (see Chapter 7 for details of how to do this), you can create an effect that displays in exactly the same way, yet the text remains structurally a paragraph.

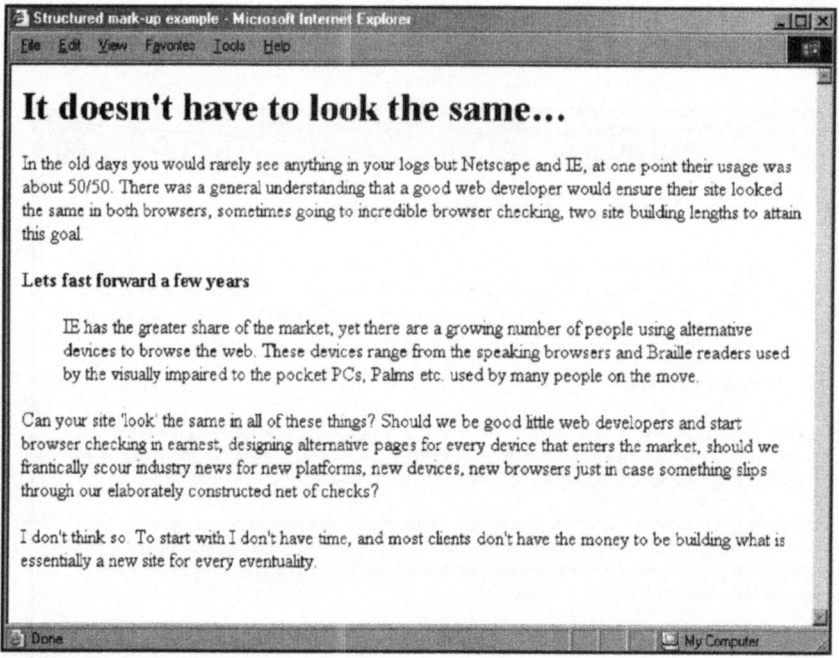

The CSS that creates this indentation looks like this:

```
.indent {
      padding-left: 35px;
}
```

and you simply need to apply this class to your `<p>` tag.

```
<p class="indent">IE has the greater share of the market, yet there are
a growing
   number of people using alternative devices to browse the Web. These
devices
   range from the speaking browsers and Braille readers used by the
visually impaired
   to the pocket PCs, Palms etc. used by many people on the move.</p>
```

Frequently Asked Questions

How do I deal with common validator errors?

There are a number of common validator errors that you should be aware of. We describe them in the next sections.

"there is no attribute leftmargin/topmargin/marginwidth /marginheight"

These attributes are inserted by Dreamweaver in the *Modify > Page Properties* dialog box and are in the body tag. For instance:

```
<body leftmargin="0" topmargin="0" marginwidth="0" marginheight="0">
```

These attributes are deprecated and should be replaced by the use of CSS.

"required attribute "alt" not specified"

All images need an `alt` attribute specifying what the image is. For images that are just for your layout, it is appropriate to insert an empty `alt` attribute `alt=""`. To do this in Dreamweaver, select your image, then in the box *Alt* either type your `alt` text or drop down the list to insert *<empty>*.

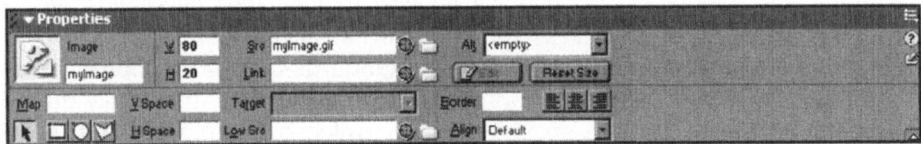

"character "&" is the first character of a delimiter but occurred as data"

This refers to the fact that we discussed earlier that `&` < and > must be replaced with HTML entities. Replace `&` with `&amp;` and this error will disappear.

Errors in JavaScript

The validator may take exception to some of the JavaScript in the head of your document. Often the simplest way around this is to place the JavaScript in an external file and link to it from your pages. The external JavaScript file should simply contain the JavaScript (no enclosing tags) and be saved with a `.js` extension.

On the document that needs this scripting, use the following markup:

```
<script language="javascript" src="yourfile.js"
type="text/javascript"></script>
```

to replace `yourfile.js` with the location of your JavaScript file. XHTML Strict does not allow the language attribute of the script tag; however, Dreamweaver inserts both type and language for backward-compatibility.

Why does my page look different in Dreamweaver MX than in the browser?

Dreamweaver MX applies an HTML 4.01 Transitional DOCTYPE to the document by default. You may also have noticed that the DOCTYPE it uses for HTML 4.01 is not the full DOCTYPE with a URL:

```
<!DOCTYPE HTML PUBLIC "-//W3C//DTD HTML 4.01 Transitional//EN"
"http://www.w3.org/TR/html4/loose.dtd">
```

but is just the first part of the DOCTYPE:

```
<!DOCTYPE HTML PUBLIC "-//W3C//DTD HTML 4.01 Transitional//EN">
```

This is still a valid DOCTYPE. However, using this DOCTYPE switches browsers into **quirks mode**, whereby they render pages in a similar way to the older generation of web browsers. If you use the full DOCTYPE, you will still be validating against HTML4.01 Transitional, but the browsers will be switched into **standards-compliant mode** and will render your pages far more closely to the way the standards dictate. Additionally, the use of the XML declaration on XHTML documents also switches Internet Explorer 6 and Opera 7 into quirks mode. Again, Dreamweaver inserts this by default.

Dreamweaver, for its internal rendering engine, uses the standards-compliant way of rendering regardless of the fact that it has added a DOCTYPE that will switch the browsers into quirks mode.

If you are a creating a brand-new web site, the simplest solution to the problem is to add the URL to the DOCTYPE that Dreamweaver inserts, or remove the XML declaration, thus ensuring that both Dreamweaver and the browsers will render the page in a similar way. You may also wish to create a snippet containing the correct pieces of code.

The Web Standards Project has some sample template pages that demonstrate the different DOCTYPES so you can simply copy and paste the one you wish to use: *http://www.webstandards.org/learn/templates/index.html*.

If you are working on an older site and it is rendering in this way within Dreamweaver, then you will probably just have to live with it; the differences tend to just involve small gaps appearing between images and can be safely ignored once you realize that your design will look fine in the web browsers.

For more information on the issue of standards-compliant versus quirks mode, see the excellent article on the Netscape DevEdge web site titled "Images, Tables, and Mysterious Gaps" (*http://devedge.netscape.com/viewsource/2002/img-table/*).

Summary

Complying with "web standards" has become less of a concern for geeks and more of a mainstream issue with the advent of browsers that are more compliant, accessibility regulations, and authoring environments that list their capability to code to web standards as a major selling point. This trend looks set to continue, and with the help of Dreamweaver MX it is not difficult for you to move in this direction.

For more information on web standards, how to use them, and why you should, the following web sites are a good starting point:

- *http://www.w3.org* – The W3C, where the standards are created.

- *http://www.webstandards.org* – The Web Standards Project. Check out the Learn section for lots of information.

- *http://www.w3schools.com/w3c/* – A section on W3Schools that explains the activities of the W3C. This web site also has excellent XHTML and CSS tutorials.

10

In this Chapter

- The problem
- Building a flexible layout

Author: Drew McLellan

Creating Flexible Layouts

We've all done it at some point. You lovingly craft the best web page you can create, using all the new tricks you've learned/pinched/borrowed from yesterday's cool-site-of-the-day. You're extremely proud and can't wait to show your friends. So, you upload your creation to the Web and dash around the corner to show your best buddy just how talented you are and have his jaw drop in the very presence of your masterly web prowess. He fires up his browser and… why doesn't it fit?

In this chapter, we're going to look at the common problem of making sure your page will look good no matter how big or small the viewing window is. Some people call this **liquid** design because a page will flow like water to fill the available space. Some call it **stretchable** or **flexible** design. Whatever you want to call it, it's essential to designing a high-quality web site, and that's what we're here for.

> *Some people call this **liquid** design because a page will flow like water to fill the available space.*

Sizing Up the Problem

To get started with learning how to master liquid design, you need to understand the issues at play. Why, exactly, is it that a page that fits on one person's screen will not be completely viewable on another person's, or will look tiny and tucked up in the corner on a third person's? The most obvious conclusion to reach is that it's a problem between the different monitors. As it happens, it's more of a problem with the page.

When designing for the Web, it's really difficult to be sure of anything to do with your visitors' computer setups. You can't guarantee what operating system or software they have installed, nor can you guarantee what physical pieces of hardware they use to make up their system. In fact, the only thing you can be sure of is that you can't be sure of anything!

Basically, this means that you have to be open-minded and consider common scenarios, trying your best to cope with everything and code for nothing specific.

Look at the two screen shots of the Yahoo! homepage presented next. The first is taken at 800x600, with all the content in view. The second shows the exact same page at 640x480. Much of the content is obscured and cannot be easily read without lots of scrolling back and forth. This layout is not stretchable—it's fixed for a particular screen size.

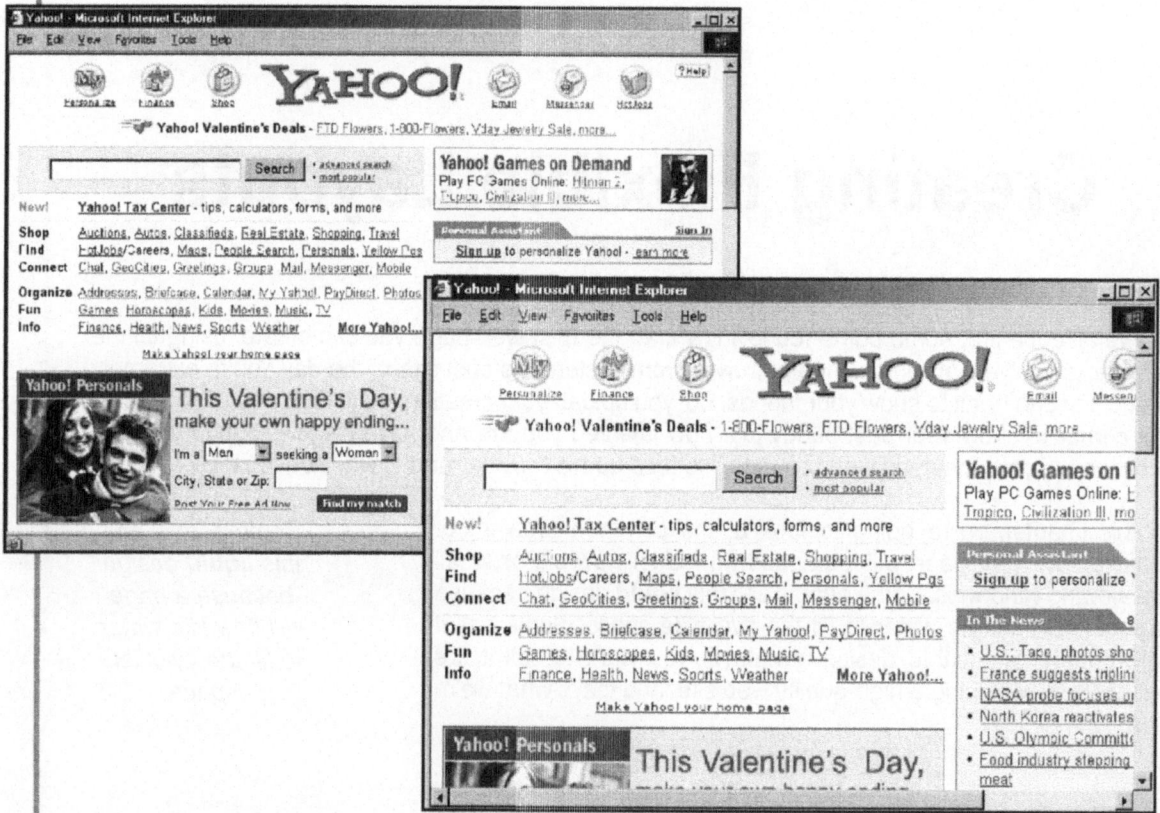

The Trouble with Resolution

You often hear people say that their page doesn't work on a 15" monitor, but it looked OK when they designed it on their 19" screen at home. The real problem here isn't the physical size of the glass, but the number of pixels it displays. Pixels are the individual "dots" that make up the picture. Allow us to explain...

Most 15" monitors can be set to display the image in a grid of 800 pixels wide and 600 pixels high. We call this the *resolution* of display. Some 15" monitors can also be switched to display a resolution of 1024x768 pixels. This has the effect of making everything look smaller, but with the benefit of enabling you to fit more on the screen at once. It's the same physical dimensions, but a different visual size.

The higher quality the monitor, the higher the resolution it can display. You can always configure a high-resolution monitor to display at a lower resolution if you desire, and this is particularly useful for testing web sites. The resolution anyone will be using will depend on a combination of the specification of their monitor, the type of work they normally carry out on the computer, and the size they feel is most comfortable for their eyes.

Not everyone views the Web at full screen on a desktop computer. Some browse using their TV, and it's increasingly common to see people using their mobile phones and PDAs to access vital information on the move. Those devices have really tiny screens.

Take a look at that same page from Yahoo! at 1024x768. You'll notice that there's a degree of underutilized page space for those viewing at the most common desktop computer resolution setting. One thing that Yahoo! has done well to combat some of the problem is to center the content on the page. This helps compensate for the otherwise large gaps that appear as the window gets larger.

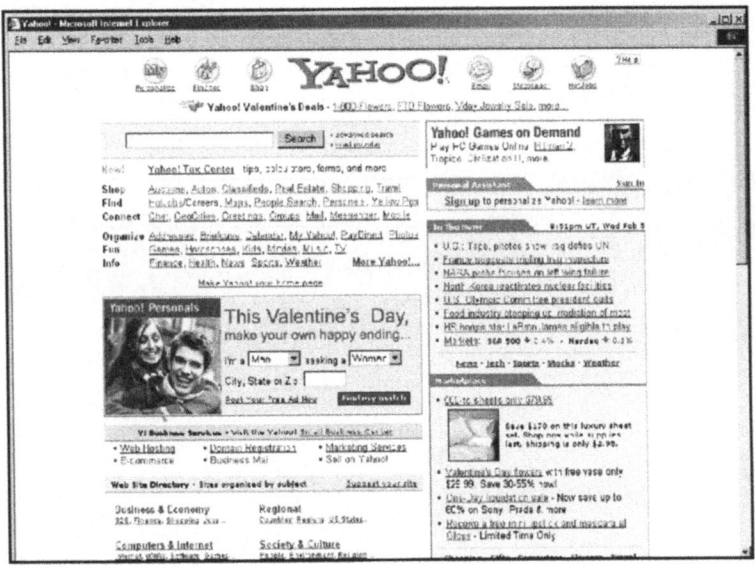

Why Should the Layout Stretch?

Many designers, even today, have trouble accepting that web pages need to flow to be usable in different-sized browser windows. They'll argue that it's impossible to construct a pleasant design that will work no matter how it's contorted … but mostly they'll be wrong.

Web design is vastly different from other sorts of design, despite sharing a lot of common principles. Print designers who make the transition to the Web often have to rethink the way they design, particularly with respect to spatial boundaries. When designing for a physical paper stock, you know where the edges are, you know how big your page is before you start, and you can work out how to fit the information you have into that space.

When designing for the Web, you know that your page is big, medium, and small all at once. You have to consider which areas will stay a fixed size and which might stretch and squash. You have to think very carefully about the images you use and how they will look if a page is very wide or very long.

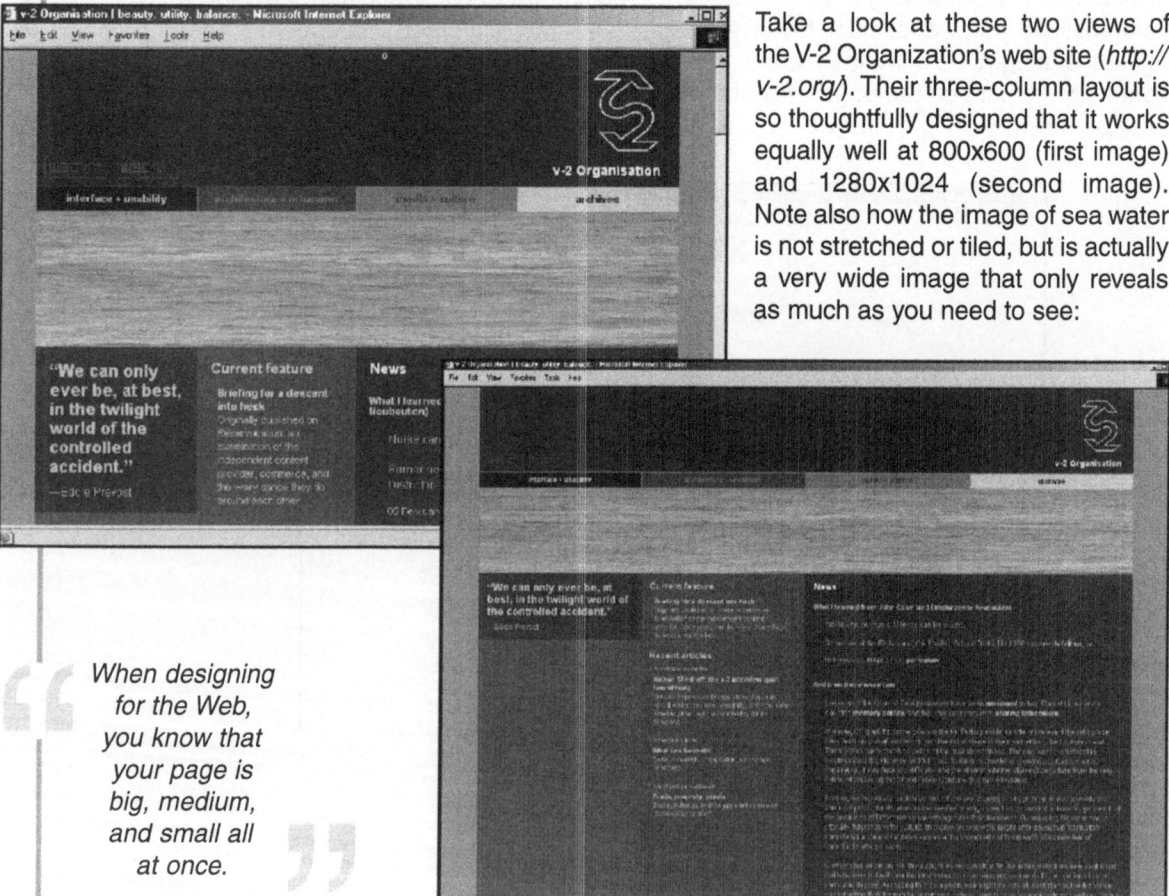

Take a look at these two views of the V-2 Organization's web site (*http://v-2.org/*). Their three-column layout is so thoughtfully designed that it works equally well at 800x600 (first image) and 1280x1024 (second image). Note also how the image of sea water is not stretched or tiled, but is actually a very wide image that only reveals as much as you need to see:

> *When designing for the Web, you know that your page is big, medium, and small all at once.*

Considerations

There are many things that must be considered when composing a stretchable web layout. You need to have a good understanding of how HTML elements interact and affect the flow of the document when put under stress. Most of these things can be adjusted for by following some simple rules of measurement. What's not so easily accounted for are some of the design considerations, which require a little more judgment and a good eye. Let's look at those design issues first.

Line Length

It is often said that to maximize ease and comfort of reading for your audience, you should try to keep lines of text to about ten words long. Some lines go over, some fall under, but ten words is a good average for a web layout. However, when it comes to laying out a page that could stretch or contract to almost any dimension, this obviously becomes more difficult to achieve.

One method of tackling the problem is demonstrated in the following screen shots. Tom Coates of Plasticbag.org has used a similar approach to Yahoo! in that his column of text is centered on the screen. However, this design differs from that of Yahoo! by using the graphical elements in the page to make the layout feel complete at higher resolutions. It's a subtle difference, but it helps the visual performance of the page at high resolution to no end.

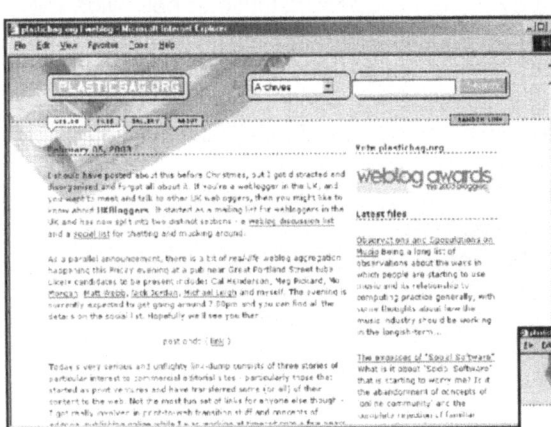

The first image is at 800x600, and the second is at 1280x1024:

Notice in the second image how much more of the blue bag image is revealed, extending beyond the edges of the text, to help soften the appearance of the white borders.

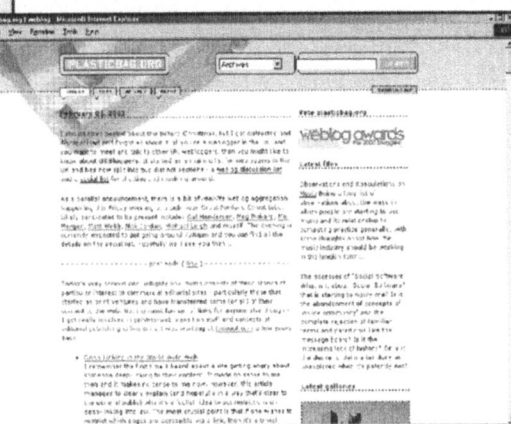

As the total focus of this site is the written content, it is important to the designer that the column width is maintained. This use of graphics to compensate, although not perfect, is a good step toward a stretchable layout and proves that a useful compromise can easily be met.

Graphics

Images are inherently dimensioned. If you create a new image in Photoshop or Fireworks, the first thing it asks you for are the dimensions of that image. This can pose a real big problem when it comes to making a page nice and stretchy—how do you make the graphics stretch?

While some images can be stretched without losing any quality, it has to be said that most cannot. This is where it takes quite a bit of design ingenuity to make sure that your images adjust their position to fit the layout of the document as it adjusts. Later in this chapter we will look at practical techniques for working with graphics in flexible layouts.

Measurements

The principles of building a stretchable layout fall into two categories: measurements and design. We have looked at some of the design issues and we are now going to look at measurements in close detail, to give you a better understanding of how you can practically compose your stretchable layout.

The first step in making any page stretch to fit its window is to specify some of your element dimensions as *relative* values rather than *absolute* values. The difference between the two is easy to grasp when you consider what you are trying to achieve. You want your page elements to stretch so that they fill up the space relative to how wide the browser window is. There are a few different units of measurement for defining relative values in CSS, but by far the most common in flexible designs is the percentage.

Let's look at a simple example. Take this really basic web page, `flow.html`:

```
<!DOCTYPE html PUBLIC "-//W3C//DTD XHTML 1.0 Strict//EN"
"http://www.w3.org/TR/xhtml1/DTD/xhtml1-strict.dtd">
<html xmlns="http://www.w3.org/1999/xhtml">
<head>
<title>A basic web page</title>
<style type="text/css">
p{
width : 75%;
}
</style>
</head>
<body>
<p>The following text consists of a mock Latin which has been
based upon
```

```
the average frequency of characters and word lengths of the
English
language in order to reproduce a reasonably accurate overall
visual
impression. Lorem ipsum dolor sit amet, consectetur adipscing
elit, sed
diam nonnumy eiusmod tempor incidunt ut labore et dolore magna
aliquam
erat volupat.</p>
<p>Et harumd dereud facilis est er expedit distinct. Nam liber a
tempor cum
soluta nobis eligend optio comque nihil quod a impedit anim id
quod
maxim placeat facer possim omnis es voluptas assumenda est,
omnis dolor
repellend. Temporem autem quinsud et aur office debit aut tum
rerum
necesit atib saepe eveniet ut er repudiand sint et molestia non
este
recusand.</p>
</body>
</html>
```

An HTML paragraph element will take up 100% of the available width by default unless a different width is specified. In this example we have specified that any paragraph should have a width of 75% of the available space. Here's how it looks in a narrow window.

You'll note the white gap down the right side. This is the 25% that's left over after the paragraph has taken its 75%.

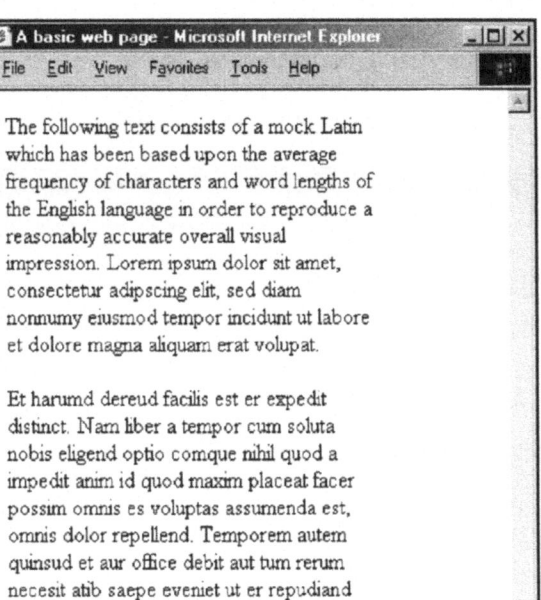

Now look at the exact same page when the window is stretched out:

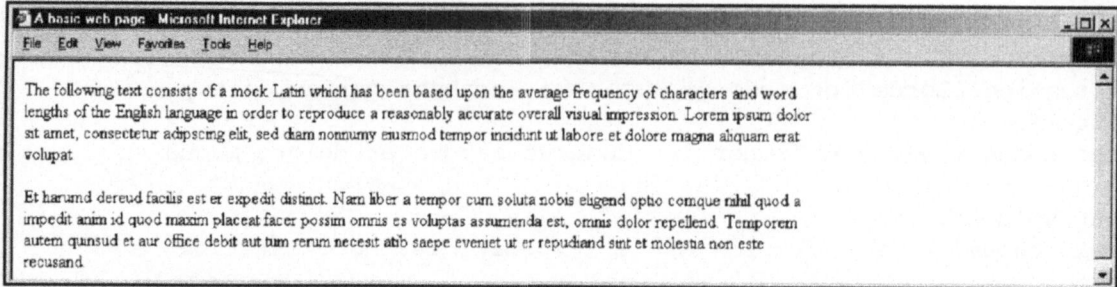

This clearly shows that the paragraphs are still taking up three quarters of the window, leaving one quarter empty.

Let's now change the page so that the paragraph width uses an absolute value. As many people have a screen resolution of 800x600, we'll set the width of the paragraph to be three quarters of this: 600 pixels wide. Replace the style block with the following code and save the page as static.html:

```
<style type="text/css">
p{
width : 600px;
}
</style>
```

Here's how this page looks in the same size window you've just tried for flow.html:

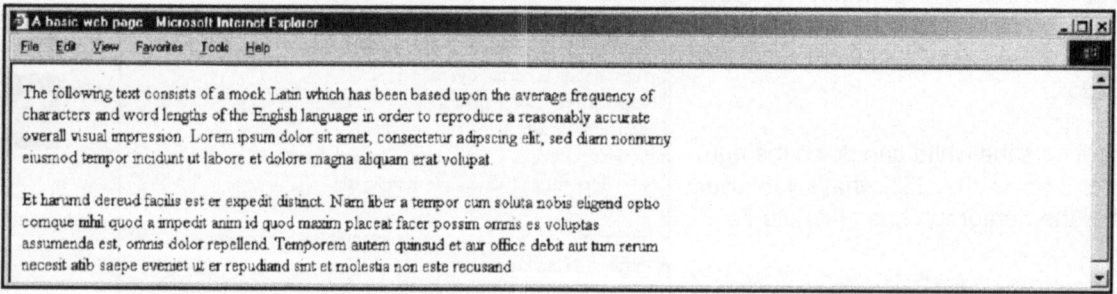

You'll notice that the paragraph takes up less width than before. The big question is what will happen if you make the window very small?

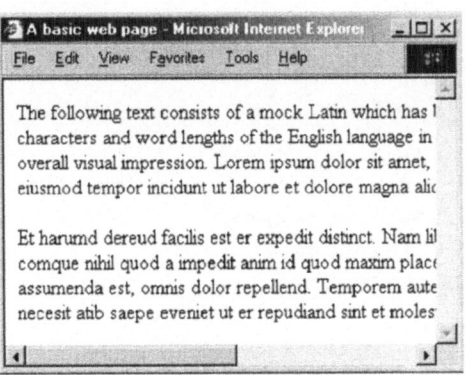

As you can see, we have a horizontal scroll bar at this size. The paragraph is set to be 600 pixels wide, so scroll bars have appeared because the window in less than those 600 pixels. This is what we try to avoid by using relative units of measurement.

Building a Stretchable Page

Without further ado, let's get on with constructing a simple page that will stretch or contract to fit the browser window. We have used XHTML and CSS for this example, along with the others in this chapter. For a discussion of why it's good to use XHTML and CSS, refer to Chapter 7 of this book.

First of all, we'll take this basic page with a banner, some navigation, and a few paragraphs of content. Let's call it `stretchable.html`:

```
<!DOCTYPE html PUBLIC "-//W3C//DTD XHTML 1.0 Strict//EN"
"http://www.w3.org/TR/xhtml1/DTD/xhtml1-strict.dtd">
<html xmlns="http://www.w3.org/1999/xhtml">
<head>
<title>XY UK</title>
<style type="text/css">
body{
margin: 0;
padding: 0;
font-family: Verdana, Geneva, Arial, Helvetica, sans-serif;
color: #000;
background-color: #fff;
}
</style>
</head>
<body>
```

10

```
<div id="banner">
<img src="logo.gif" alt="xy uk" width="177" height="100" />
</div>
<div id="navigation">
<a href="#" title="Lorum">Lorum</a>
<a href="#" title="Ipsum">Ipsum</a>
<a href="#" title="Dolor">Dolor</a>
<a href="#" title="Sit">Sit</a>
<a href="#" title="Amet">Amet</a>
</div>
<div id="content">
<p>The following text consists of a mock Latin which has been
based upon
the average frequency of characters and word lengths of the
English
language in order to reproduce a reasonably accurate overall
visual
impression. Lorem ipsum dolor sit amet, consectetur adipscing
elit, sed
diam nonnumy eiusmod tempor incidunt ut labore et dolore magna
aliquam
erat volupat.</p>
<p>Et harumd dereud facilis est er expedit distinct. Nam liber a
tempor cum
soluta nobis eligend optio comque nihil quod a impedit anim id
quod
maxim placeat facer possim omnis es voluptas assumenda est,
omnis dolor
repellend. Temporem autem quinsud et aur office debit aut tum
rerum
necesit atib saepe eveniet ut er repudiand sint et molestia non
este
recusand.</p>
</div>
</body>
</html>
```

As you can see, we've put a simple GIF image (*logo.gif*) in the banner, some dummy links in the navigation, and a couple of paragraphs of mock Latin as content. Each content area has been wrapped in a <div> tag with a sensible id.

Styling the Banner

Our mythical company XY UK has a logo that uses long horizontal stripes that we wish to continue across the top of the whole page. Here's how it looks:

We'll achieve this by using two images. The first is the textual part of the logo that includes both the text and the line endings. We'll align this to the top left. For the second image, we'll take a small cross-section of the stripes and tile them horizontally as a background image. This means that the appearance of a complete image will be maintained without the need for an enormously wide image.

Here's how our style definition for the banner looks now. Copy it into the CSS definitions in the head of `stretchable.html`:

```
#banner{
position: absolute;
top: 0;
left: 0;
background-image: url(background.gif);
background-repeat: repeat-x;
padding: 0;
margin: 0;
width: 100%;
}
```

Styling the Navigation

We're going to position the navigation to sit in the left column under the banner. We'd like that column to take up one-fifth of the width of the page, so we've set it to be 15% wide and 5% away from the left edge. We've also set all links to display as block-level elements, so that each link appears on a new line:

```
#navigation{
position: absolute;
top: 120px;
width: 15%;
left: 5%;
}
#navigation a{
display: block;
}
```

10

Styling the Content

This will also sit under the banner and to the right of the navigation column. It will fill the remainder of the width of the page, no matter how wide the browser is. We've allowed for a gap between the navigation and the content, and for a margin of 10% on the right side to stop the content running against the right edge:

```
#content{
margin-top: 120px;
margin-right: 10%;
margin-left: 24%;
}
```

With this CSS in place, our final page should look like the next screen shot. Note that Dreamweaver MX may not display the layout as accurately as modern browsers do:

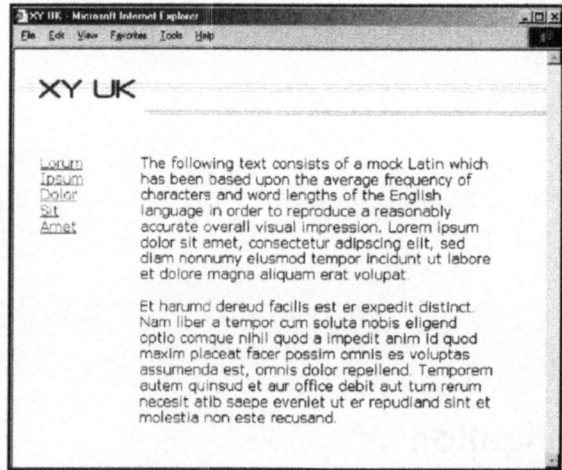

Try dragging the window edges around and seeing how the page responds to flowing into different sized spaces. Try experimenting with the dimensions and see if you can find how to make the page stretch in different ways.

Remember, different layouts will work differently at various sizes. It's always important to test and to keep modifying and retesting until you are happy with the way your page works when stretched or contracted.

Frequently Asked Questions

As with any more advanced topic, there are always questions that pop up time and time again. We'll look at some of them here.

I have to support Netscape 4 and my layout breaks when the window is resized. How can I prevent this?

Some very old browsers (notably Netscape Navigator 4) have trouble rerendering page layouts when the browser window is resized. This can cause your page layout to behave unexpectedly—in extreme cases, piling itself up in the top-left corner!

Fret not, though, there is an easy fix. From the *Commands* menu, select *Add/Remove Netscape Resize Fix*. This will add some JavaScript to your page that forces a reload each time the window is resized.

How do I center my page horizontally?

It's very easy to have a page centralize its content using CSS. There are two distinct methods for doing this and we'll examine both. Take this example page:

```
<!DOCTYPE html PUBLIC "-//W3C//DTD XHTML 1.0 Transitional//EN"
"http://www.w3.org/TR/xhtml1/DTD/xhtml1-transitional.dtd">
<html xmlns="http://www.w3.org/1999/xhtml">

<head>
<title>Centering a Page</title>
</head>

<body>
<div id="content">
The following text consists of a mock Latin which has been based
upon
the average frequency of characters and word lengths of the
English
language in order to reproduce a reasonably accurate overall
visual
impression. Lorem ipsum dolor sit amet, consectetur adipscing
elit, sed
diam nonnumy eiusmod tempor incidunt ut labore et dolore magna
aliquam
erat volupat.
</div>
</body>
</html>
```

The first method is to centralize the content in a fixed-width column, and the second is to use a column of varying width.

Fixed-width columns

In the example from Plasticbag.org earlier in this chapter, you saw how a flexible layout fixed the width of a column but centered it as part of the overall flexible effect. You can achieve this by setting the margins of your content area to auto. The browser takes this to mean "use as much space as you can," but it shares the greed equally between the two sides:

```
#content{
width : 400px;
margin-left : auto;
margin-right : auto;
}
```

Variable-width columns

The second method makes use of a flexible column that keeps its proportion relative to the window. This is achieved by setting the left and right margins to a relative value:

```
#content{
margin-left: 20%;
margin-right : 20%
}
```

By implication, the width of the content area will always be 60%. The equal margins make sure it will always be central.

Summary

To move forward and start designing flexible layouts of your own, there are a number of things that you should take away from this chapter. Let's look at the important topics we covered.

First, we tried to size up the problem. This included thinking about topics like a client browser's setup and the different resolutions browsers may be using. We then discussed measurements and showed how we can improve liquidity by using relative values for length rather than absolute values.

We then showed how to build a stretchable page. Specifically, we dealt with a banner, our navigation panel, and the page's content. Finally, we looked at some frequently asked questions, focusing on support for Netscape 4 and how to center pages horizontally.

11

In this Chapter

- Uploading files using PHP

- HTML e-mail in PHP

- Date and time problems

- Common PHP problems

Author: Gareth Downes-Powell

Top PHP Questions

In this chapter, we show working solutions for many of the PHP questions that are often asked. We look at dealing with session variables, file uploading, e-mail, date and time, common PHP errors, and other common queries.

For each question we show some basic working code that you can easily expand on for your own projects. For information on installing PHP and MySQL, see Chapters 5, 6, 7, and 8.

Why Don't Session Variables Work?

One of the main problems faced by users of PHP is that once they have installed it, they can't get session variables to work. The main cause of session variables not working on a new server installation is the default settings in the `php.ini` file. Information held in session variables is actually stored in files in a temporary directory on the server. PHP must be able to write to this directory successfully to use session variables. The setting that causes the problem is the default `session.save_path` in the `php.ini` file, which on a new installation is usually set to the following:

```
session.save_path = /tmp
```

On Windows systems, this directory doesn't exist, and it isn't created during the PHP installation, so PHP has nowhere to store session data. To fix this problem, create a directory somewhere on your server, such as `C:/temp`, and then edit the `php.ini` file and change the `session.save_path` setting to point to this new directory. For security reasons, make sure this directory is outside of the web folder, for example:

```
session.save_path = "C:/temp";
```

You'll then need to restart the web server so that the new setting takes effect, unless you're running PHP as a CGI module. On a Linux server running Apache, this situation doesn't occur so often, as most Linux servers do have a `/tmp` directory. However, it's a good idea not to use the `/tmp` directory and instead create a new directory exclusively for PHP temporary files. For example, you can create a directory at `/home/phptemp` using the command

```
mkdir /home/phptemp
```

Next, open the Apache configuration file, `httpd.conf`, and find which user the server runs under (usually nobody). Next, give PHP write permissions by using the command

```
chown nobody /home/phptemp
```

where the user that Apache runs under is `nobody`. Restart Apache, and session variables should now be working.

How Do I Check That Session Variables Are Working?

To check that session variables are working, you need to create two simple pages, one called `set_session.php` and one called `read_session.php`. The first page will set a session variable, and the second page will read it back.

`set_session.php` contains the following:

```php
<?php
// Code to place a value in a Session Variable
session_start();
session_register("testSession");
$HTTP_SESSION_VARS['testSession'] = "Sessions are working!"
?>
<html>
<head>
<title>Set Session</title>
<meta http-equiv="Content-Type" content="text/html; charset=iso-8859-1">
</head>
<body>
<a href="read_session.php">Read Session</a>
</body>
</html>
```

This page starts session support by using the `session_start` function. Next, you register a session variable with the name `testSession` using `session_register`. Finally, you assign it a value.

`read_session.php` includes the following code:

```php
<?php
session_start();
?>
<html>
<head>
<title>Read Session</title>
<meta http-equiv="Content-Type" content="text/html; charset=iso-8859-1">
</head>
<body>
<?php
echo $HTTP_SESSION_VARS['testSession'];
?>
</body>
</html>
```

This page uses `session_start` again to enable sessions, and then you print the value held in the `testSession` session variable to the screen.

Open a browser and request `set_session.php`. You can then click the *Read Session* link to go to the page `read_session.php`, and you should see the message *Sessions are working!*, which was stored in the session variable.

If the preceding code doesn't work, it could be because your browser is set not to allow cookies. PHP relies on cookies to store the ID of the users' sessions as they move between pages. If your browser does not allow cookies, then the session ID is lost. To check if this is the case, change the link in the `set_session.php` page from

```
<a href="read_session.php">Read Session</a>
```

to

```
<a href="read_session.php?<?php echo SID;?>">Read Session</a>
```

This uses the URL to send the session ID, and when you click the link to go to the `read_session.php` page, you'll see the URL is similar to the following:

http://linux/session_read.php?PHPSESSID=d00ac744017c1e782e10db9eb59a512e

The `read_session.php` page should now show the message *Sessions are working!*, as PHP can now identify the session.

You can set PHP to include the session ID in the URL automatically by setting the option `session.use_trans_sid` to 1 in your `php.ini` file. Be aware, though, that including the session ID in the URL is not entirely secure and is not recommended, because the session ID could be bookmarked or sent to another person.

When Do I Have to Use session_start?

The PHP `session_start` function needs to be on every single page that uses session variables, and it should be placed in the header of the page—in other words, above the `<html>` tag. Because `session_start` needs to be on every page that uses session variables, it's a good idea to add the following line of code to the top of your sites' template:

```php
<?php session_start(); ?>
```

How Do I Upload a File Through the Browser?

The first job is to create the HTML form through which the user selects the file to upload. This consists of the following HTML code:

```html
<form action="<?php echo $PHP_SELF; ?>" method="post"
enctype="multipart/form-data" name="form1">
<input name="filename" type="file" id="filename"><br>
<input name="Upload" type="submit" id="Upload" value="Upload">
<input name="MAX_FILE_SIZE" type="hidden" id="MAX_FILE_SIZE"
value="50000">
</form>
```

To create the form, insert a normal form onto your page (*Insert > Form*), and change the form `action` and `enctype` to the preceding values to allow file uploading. To create the file field, select *Insert > Form Objects > File Field*. This inserts a field for the filename and a button that the users can click to browse for a file on their computer. Set the name of the file field to `filename`. Next, add a submit button so the user can submit the form (*Insert > Form Objects > Button*), and change its label and value to `Upload`.

Finally, add a hidden field, and set its name to `MAX_FILE_SIZE` and its value to `50000`. This is the maximum size in bytes of the file that the user can upload for that particular form. This value cannot be higher than the `upload_max_filesize` setting in the server `php.ini` file.

The next step is to open the page in Code View and adding the following PHP code block to the top of the page, before the `<html>` tag:

```
<?
if($_POST['Upload'] == "Upload"){
$originalFileName = $_FILES['filename']['name'];
$tempFileName = $_FILES['filename']['tmp_name'];
$siteRoot = "c:/webserver/";
$newPath = $siteRoot . "/data/" . $originalFileName;
umask(0);
move_uploaded_file($tempFileName, $newPath);
system("chmod 755 $newPath"); //Linux only
}
?>
```

First, you check to see if the submit button named and labeled *Upload* was used to submit the form. If it was, then you run the block of code in the `if` statement. Next, you get the original name of the file and the temporary uploaded filename from the PHP `$_FILES` array. This array holds the following information:

- `$_FILES['filename_field']['name']` – The original filename of the file.
- `$_FILES['filename_field']['type']` – The MIME type of the file. For example, `image/jpg`.
- `$_FILES['filename_field']['size']` – The size in bytes of the uploaded file.
- `$_FILES['filename_field']['tmp_name']` – The temporary name of the uploaded file.
- `$_FILES['filename_field']['error']` – An error code if there was an error (PHP 4.2.0 >).

Next, you create a new path for the file, telling PHP where on the server the file is to be stored (in this case, in a directory called `data`, which is in the root directory of the web site). Finally, you use the PHP `move_uploaded_file` function, passing the temporary filename allocated when the file was uploaded, with the new name and path on the server. If there is already a file with the same name, it will be overwritten by the new file. If you want to avoid this, you can check to see if there is an existing file with the same name by using the PHP `file_exists` command, passing it the filename to check. If the `file_exists` command returns `true`, then you can change the name of the file before you move it with the `move_uploaded_file` command, so the original file is not overwritten.

Finally, you change permissions on the image, so everyone can read it. The PHP `umask(0)` command is used to temporarily remove any permissions mask that may exist, so the exact permissions you specify are set. Note that `$siteRoot` should be set to the path to your web site root directory, in terms of a server path rather than a web path. For example, if your server is IIS running locally at *http://localhost/*, then the path might be `c:/inetpub/wwwroot/`.

11

This completes all the code needed to actually upload the file. Note that it's important that PHP has write permissions on the directory in which the images will be stored. On Linux, you need to use the following command to set the correct permissions:

```
chmod 777 directoryname
```

Displaying an Uploaded Image

If the file upload is for images, then you can add the following code to your page, underneath the form, and this will display the image once it has been uploaded. Note that the dimensions of the image are read automatically using the PHP `getimagesize` function. We look at this function in more detail in the "Miscellaneous Questions" section at the end of this chapter.

```php
<?php
if($_POST['Upload'] == "Upload"){
$size = getimagesize($newPath);
echo "<img src=\"data/" . $originalFileName. "\" width=\"" . $size[0] .
"\" height=\""
$size[1]. "\">";
}
?>
```

The preceding code again only runs if the form has been submitted with the *Upload* button. Once it's run, the code prints out an HTML image tag to display the image.

How Do I Get a List of Files in a Directory?

To get a list of files in a certain directory, you use the PHP `readdir` function, as shown in the following example code, which you can add to the body of a PHP page:

```php
<?php
$mainDir = "c:/webserver/data/";
if (file_exists($mainDir)) {
$handle = opendir($mainDir);
while (false !== ($file = readdir($handle))) {
if($file !== "." && $file !== ".."){
echo $file . "<br>";
}
}
closedir($handle);
}
?>
```

First, you create the path to the directory you want to list in terms of a server path to the directory (rather than the web path). Before you carry on, you use the PHP `file_exists` function to check that the directory in the path does actually exist. If it does, you create a handle to the directory with the PHP `opendir` function. You then use a `while` loop to read in the files in the directory using the PHP `readdir` function, and display the filenames. When `readdir` has read to the end of the directory, it will return `false`, and the code stops. To check for this, you use the `while` loop, set to run when the output from `readdir` is not equal to `false`, which is done with the operator `!==` (which means "not equal to").

The filenames returned by the `readdir` command include the directory names "." and "..". You screen these out by checking that the filename isn't one of these two names before printing it to the screen.

This code comes in handy on web-based file manager pages, allowing users to manage their uploaded files.

This code comes in handy on web-based file manager pages, allowing users to manage their uploaded files.

E-mail

In this section, we are going to look at some of the frequently asked questions regarding e-mail and PHP. We will begin by looking at a more fundamental issue: how to actually send an e-mail as HTML.

How Do I Send an E-mail As HTML?

As the PHP `mail` function defaults to sending plain text e-mails unless otherwise specified, a frequent question is how to send HTML e-mails using the `mail` function. The format for the `mail` function is as follows:

```
mail($to, $subject, $message, $headers);
```

where `$to` is the e-mail address to send to, `$subject` is the subject line for the e-mail, `$message` contains the e-mail message, and `$headers` contains any optional headers you may wish to add.

To send an e-mail that's recognized and treated as HTML, you need to use two special headers:

```
MIME-Version: 1.0
Content-type: text/html; charset=iso-8859-1
```

11

These should be included in the `$headers` variable as shown in the following complete code:

```php
<?php
$to = "gareth@myemail.com";
$subject = "This is an HTML E-mail";
$message = " <span style=\"font-family: Arial, Helvetica, sans-serif;
font-size: 20px; font-weight: bold; color: #009900\">";
$message .= "This is an HTML e-mail message";
$message .= "</span>";
$headers  = "MIME-Version: 1.0\n";
$headers .= "Content-type: text/html; charset=iso-8859-1\n";
$headers .= "From: gareth<gareth@myemail.com>";
mail($to, $subject, $message, $headers);
?>
```

It's important to note that to run the code, you need to have an e-mail server set up, so it's easiest to test this code on your web host's server.

As the e-mail is being sent as HTML, you can include HTML tags in the message, as shown in the preceding code. When the e-mail is received, the e-mail will be rendered as an HTML page (assuming that the user's e-mail program has that facility).

How Do I Send a Newsletter with PHP?

If you wish to send a newsletter out to a number of users at once, hiding the e-mail addresses so the recipient can't see who else you sent the mail to, you can use the `bcc` header, which stands for "blind carbon copy." Any addresses in the `bcc` header will be sent a copy of the e-mail, but they can't see who else it was sent to. The following code shows a working example, which sends the e-mail to each address in the array provided:

```php
<?php
$addresses = array("fred@cemetry.com","george@another.com");
?>
<?
$to = "gareth@myemail.co.uk";
$subject = "PHP Newsletter";
$message = "This e-mail shows how to use a BCC Header to send a
newsletter";
$headers .= "From: gareth<gareth@myemail.co.uk>\n";
$headers .= "bcc: ";
$count = 0;
foreach($addresses as $address){
if($count == 0){
```

```
$headers .= $address;
}else{
$headers .= ", " . $address;
}$count ++;
}
$headers .= "\n";
mail($to, $subject, $message, $headers);
?>
```

In the preceding code, all the e-mail addresses are specified in the $addresses array. This could be changed to use a field from a recordset to get the e-mail addresses from a database table.

If you are sending the same e-mail to a large number of users, the previous method is the best way. This is because PHP contacts the mail server once, and then the mail server has the job of sending the e-mail to all the e-mail addresses specified, which means that the PHP script finishes quicker and uses fewer resources.

If, however, you're sending a personalized e-mail, each e-mail will have to be sent individually by PHP to add the individualized data.

How Do I Stop a Script from Timing Out When Sending Many E-mails?

If you're sending a personalized e-mail to a large number of users, you have to send each e-mail individually, and it may take a while for the script to send out all the e-mails. This creates a problem sometimes, as the script may time out before all the e-mails have been sent.

To avoid this, you need to increase the amount of time that the script can run for. The default setting is usually **30** seconds. You can increase the time limit for a script by adding the following code to the top of the page:

```
<?php set_time_limit(5*60); ?>
```

This will allow the script to run for up to 5 minutes (60 * 5 = 300 seconds) .

Date and Time Problems

In this section, we look at commonly asked questions regarding the date function in PHP.

How Do I Read the Date or Time from the Server?

To read the date or time from the server, you need to use the PHP date function. You pass the date function a string, with special tokens in place of the date parameters you require. When the code is run, the tokens will be replaced with the date or time section that they represent. For example:

```php
<?php echo date("d/m/Y"); ?> outputs 11/02/2003
<?php echo date("dS F, Y");?> outputs 11th February, 2003
<?php echo date("g:i a"); ?> outputs 9:10 pm
<?php echo date("H:i:s"); ?> outputs 21:10:48
<?php echo date("l, dS F, Y"); ?> outputs Monday, 21st January, 2003
```

Notice that you can put your own characters in the string that you pass to date, which can act as separators for the data, such as : or /. Using the tokens, you build up a date or time in any format you choose. It's worthwhile reading the manual page for the date function at the PHP online manual at *http://www.php.net/manual/en/function.date.php*.

How Do I Convert a Date to and from MySQL Format?

Another common question is how to work with dates and MySQL, as MySQL uses its own date format: yyyy-mm-dd. This means that if you want to display the date, you need to change the format to a more normal one, such as the U.S. date format: mm/dd/yyyy.

The easiest way to convert the date is to use the PHP explode function. The explode function takes a string and splits it by a common separator into an array. This is very useful for transforming dates, as dates have a common separator and so are easy to split into separate parts, which can then be rearranged into your desired format.

Note that you can also format the date in your SQL query using the MySQL DATE_FORMAT command, although this does make your SQL queries longer. Full details are available on the following page of the online MySQL manual: *http://www.mysql.com/doc/en/Date_and_time_functions.html*.

How Do I Convert a Date from U.S. Format to MySQL?

To convert a date from U.S. format to MySQL format, you can use the following function:

```php
<?php
function date2mysql($date){
$splitArray = explode("/",$date);
$newDate = $splitArray[2] . "-" . $splitArray[0] . "-" . $splitArray[1];
return $newDate;
}
?>
```

This function takes a date in U.S. format and converts it to the MySQL format. To call this function, you just pass it the date in U.S. format, as follows:

```php
<?php echo date2mysql("02/20/2003"); ?>
```

This will output the following:

```
2003-02-20
```

This can then be entered into a MySQL `Date` field. Note that to cater for other date formats, you can just rearrange the date parts into a different order.

How Do I Convert a Date from MySQL Format to U.S. Format?

To convert a date from MySQL format to U.S. date format, you can use the following function:

```php
<?php
function mysql2date($date){
$splitArray = explode("-",$date);
$newDate = $splitArray[1] . "/" . $splitArray[2] . "/" . $splitArray[0];
return $newDate;
}
?>
```

To use this function, you call it by passing the date in MySQL format as follows:

```php
<?php echo mysql2date("2003-02-20"); ?>
```

This will output the following:

```
02/20/2003
```

To use the function with a value from a recordset, simply use the field from the recordset as the parameter for the function, for example:

```php
<?php echo mysql2date($row_Recordset1['date']); ?>
```

This would convert a database field named date in the recordset named Recordset1 from MySQL format to the U.S. date format.

How Do I Find the Length of Time Between Two Dates?

In order to find the length of time between two dates, you need to convert both dates to a common format, and then you can take one date away from the other. The common format you use is the number of seconds since the Linux epoch date, which is **1/1/1970**. To convert a date to the common format, you use the PHP mktime function, which takes the following parameters and returns the number of seconds since 1/1/1970:

```php
mktime(hour, minute, second, month, day, year);
```

You use the mktime function to convert the start date and end date into seconds, take the start date away from the end date, and then divide by the number of seconds in a day. You can do this with the following code:

```php
<?php
$startDate = "02/20/2003"; $endDate = "02/28/2003";
$splitStart = explode("/",$startDate);
$splitEnd = explode("/", $endDate);
$start = mktime(0,0,0,$splitStart[0],$splitStart[1],$splitStart[2]);
$end = mktime(0,0,0,$splitEnd[0],$splitEnd[1], $splitEnd[2]);
$secondsInDay = 60 * 60 * 24;
$days = abs($end-$start)/$secondsInDay;
echo $days;
?>
```

When the preceding code is run, it will display 8, which is the number of days between $startDate and $endDate.

How Do I Find a Date, x Days/Months/Years in the Past or Future?

To find dates in the past or future, you can use a combination of the mktime and date functions, which allows you to easily add or subtract days, months, or years to/from the current date, as follows:

```php
<?php
$tomorrow  = mktime (0,0,0,date("m")  ,date("d")+1,date("Y"));
$lastmonth = mktime (0,0,0,date("m")-1,date("d"),  date("Y"));
$nextyear  = mktime (0,0,0,date("m"),  date("d"),  date("Y")+1);
echo date("m/d/Y", $tomorrow)  . "<br>";
echo date("m/d/Y", $lastmonth) . "<br>";
echo date("m/d/Y", $nextyear)  . "<br>";
?>
```

Any date can be found by simply adding or subtracting the desired period to/from one of the date parts, as shown in the preceding example code.

Common PHP Errors

In this section, we are going to look at some of the common PHP errors that occur and how to solve them.

Parse Errors

A parse error occurs when the format of your PHP code is incorrect. For example, the following code:

```php
<?php
for($i=1;$i<10;$i++){
$output = "Current Iteration: " . $i . "<br>"
echo $output;
}
?>
```

will return an error similar to the following:

Parse error: parse error, unexpected T_ECHO in c:\webserver\test2.php on line 4

This error message is shown because there is a missing semicolon at the end of the third line of the preceding example. The message tells you that PHP wasn't expecting the echo command on line 4. This is because it expected there to be a semicolon at the end of line 3. Most of the time when you get this error, the reason will be a problem with the previous line, such as the missing semicolon as in the previous example.

Most of the time when you get this error, the reason will be a problem with the previous line.

This error also occurs with braces, {}, for example with the following code:

```php
<?php
for($i=1;$i<10;$i++){
$output = "Current Iteration: " . $i . "<br>";
if($output==5){
echo "This is the fifth iteration";
}
}
}
?>
```

which will return the error message

Parse error: parse error, unexpected '}' in c:\webserver\test2.php on line 8

This is caused by an extra closing brace, }, on line 8. Although it's simple to see the problem in the preceding short block of code, it can be much harder with complicated code containing many nested loops or `if` statements, and it's hard to match the opening braces to the closing braces.

To quickly find the problem, you can use the Dreamweaver MX *Balance Braces* command, which is in the *Edit* menu. You can place the cursor at a line of code, select the *Balance Braces* command, and it will highlight all the lines of code for that block from the opening brace to the closing brace. By checking the layers of your code with the *Balance Braces* command, you can quickly find where there is a missing or extra brace.

Undefined Index or Variable

This section explains what to do if you receive a message on your web page like one of the following:

Warning: Undefined index: action in \home\www\login.php on line 25
Warning: Undefined variable: message in home\www\login.php on line 52

These messages frequently confuse people, as they look like error messages and can occur even with code that works perfectly. The messages aren't actually errors; instead, they are classed as "notices," which alert you to situations where there isn't actually an error that would stop the code from working. What the message tells you is that the variable mentioned hasn't been specifically defined using a PHP `var` statement.

As an example, look at the following two blocks of code:

```php
<?php
var $username;
$username = $HTTP_SESSION_VARS['username'];
?>
```

and:

```php
<?php
$username = $HTTP_SESSION_VARS['username'];
?>
```

Both blocks of code have identical results, but the second block of code will bring up a message similar to the ones shown previously, because we haven't specifically defined the variable $username. PHP works by defining your variables first, which means it can alert you if you misspell a variable in your code, as the variable will be new and not previously defined.

There are two solutions to this problem. The first is to go back through your code and make sure that every variable is specifically defined. The second option is to stop notices from being displayed, as they're often more trouble than they're worth. You can do this by adding the following code to the top of each page that has the error:

```php
<?php error_reporting (E_ALL &~ E_NOTICE); ?>
```

This tells PHP to show all error messages and warnings but not to show the notices. To do this permanently, change the error_reporting setting in your php.ini file to the preceding setting.

Headers Already Sent Errors

This is another error message that occurs frequently, especially when using cookies or sessions, and it is similar to the following message:

Cannot modify header information - headers already sent by (output started at /home/web/newtest.php:3) in /home/web/test.php on line 5

The following is a screen shot of the code that caused the error:

```php
1 <?php session_start; ?>
2
3 <?php
4 if($HTTP_SESSION_VARS['username'] == "fred"){
5   header("Location: test.php");
6 }
7 ?>
```

The problem is caused by the blank spaces before the `header` function. The PHP `header` function is used to redirect the user to another page, which it does by sending commands in the page header to the browser, telling it to go to the new page. However, once a header has been sent to the browser, you can no longer use functions that access the header, such as the `header` function. If anything is sent to the browser that isn't a special header function, the header is closed and everything else is assumed to be HTML for the web page. So why is this happening with the preceding code?

> If anything is sent to the browser that isn't a special header function, the header is closed and everything else is assumed to be HTML for the web page.

The problem occurs because there is a blank line (line 2) that is sent to the browser. This causes the header to be closed, so the `header` function fails, as it can no longer write to the header. However, even if you remove the blank line at line 2, you will get the same error message. This is because there are two spaces at the end of the `?>` tag on line 1. These must also be deleted, as again they will be sent to the browser and will close the header. These spaces at the end of lines can be hard to spot because they're invisible!

There is a method you can use, though, to make finding them easier. If you place your cursor at the end of each line and left-click and move the mouse right, any spaces at the end of the line will be highlighted, as shown in the previous screen shot. The spaces can then be removed, leaving the code looking like the following screen shot:

```
1  <?php session_start; ?>
2  <?php
3  if($HTTP_SESSION_VARS['username'] == "fred"){
4    header("Location: test.php");
5  }
6  ?>
```

If the code is now tested again, it should work correctly.

This error can also occur if there is output not enclosed in PHP tags in any include files for the page. So if your main page code looks fine and you're still getting the error, the next step will be to check through any include files the page uses. Often, the error is caused by a new line after the final PHP tag in the include file, which must be removed if present.

How Do I Force a File to Download Rather Than Open?

When a user clicks a link to download a file, and the browser recognizes the file type, it may open the file instead of downloading it. For example, if the user has Adobe Acrobat Reader installed, when the user clicks on a link to download a PDF file, the file will open in Adobe Acrobat instead of being downloaded and saved to a specified location.

Although this behavior is quite useful, there are times when you want to allow the user to download the file instead of opening it. To do this, create a new PHP page and remove all the default HTML so the page is blank. You can then add the following code:

```php
<?php
$filepath = "/home/www/webroot/downloads/manual.pdf";
$filename = "manual.pdf";
$size=filesize($filepath);
header("Content-Type: application/octet-stream");
header("Content-Length: " . $size);
header("Content-Disposition: attachment; filename=" . $filename);
header ("Content-Transfer-Encoding: binary");
$fh = fopen($filepath, "r");
fpassthru($fh);
?>
```

The preceding code is used to tell the user's browser to accept the file for downloading instead of opening. The user can now link to this page with a normal link, and once it's clicked, the file specified will be downloaded and the user will stay on the same page of your site.

How Do I Find the Dimensions of an Image?

When you're working with images whose paths are stored in a database, it's useful to be able to read the width and height straight from an image itself, rather than storing its dimensions in the database after asking the user for them.

To read the dimensions directly from an image (in any of the common web formats such as GIF, JPEG, PNG, and so on), you can use the PHP getimagesize function, to which you pass the path to your image. This function can read from all the common graphic file formats, and it returns an array where the first element (0) is the image's width and the second element (1) is the image's height. The following code shows an example of how to use the getimagesize function:

```php
<?php
$image = "images/image.gif";
$imagepath = $_SERVER{'DOCUMENT_ROOT'} . "/" . $image;
$size = getimagesize($imagepath);
echo "Width: " . $size[0] . "<br>";
echo "Height: " . $size[1] . "<br>";
echo "<img src='" . $image . "' width='" . $size[0] . "' height='" .
$size[1] . "'>";
?>
```

This code prints the width and height of the image, and it also inserts the width and height into an HTML <img> tag to display the image correctly.

How Do I Create a Random Password?

In some applications, it can be useful to generate a random password, such as setting the user's initial password and then letting the user change it if he or she wishes. The function shown in the following code generates a password with a number of random characters, and you can set the length of the password when you call the function:

```php
<?php
function randomPassword($length) {
    $possibleCharacters =
"abcdefghijklmnopqrstuvwxyz1234567890ABCDEFGHIJKLMNOPQRSTUVWXYZ";
$characterLength = strlen($possibleCharacters);
$seed = (double) microtime() * 1000000;
srand($seed);
$password = "";
for($i=1;$i<=$length;$i++){
$character = rand(1,$characterLength);
$character = substr($possibleCharacters,$character, 1);
$password .= $character;
}
return $password;
}
?>
```

To call the function, you can use the following code:

```php
<?php
$randomPassword = randomPassword(8);
echo $randomPassword;
?>
```

This would create a random eight-character password—for example, `VcF1TG65` or `BJuNj7ao`.

To create the password, first you set up a string containing characters that can be used for the password. You then find the number of characters in the string with the PHP `strlen` function.

Next, you seed the PHP random number generator and use it to create a random number between 1 and the number of characters that can be used. The seed is first created by using the PHP `microtime` function to return the number of seconds since the Linux epoch date, and you then multiply this by 1 million so that you have a whole number, which will be different each time the code is run. Next, you use this number as a seed for the random number generator using the PHP `srand` command, so that it generates truly random numbers. Note that with PHP version 4.2.0 and upward, you don't have to seed the random number generator as it's done automatically.

This random number is then used to extract a single character from the string of allowed characters by reading the character at the position in the string equal to the random number. This character is then added to the new password, until the number of characters in the password matches the number specified when the function was called.

Summary

In this chapter, we looked at numerous frequently asked PHP questions covering a range of subjects. For each question, we presented a solution that included working code to use as an example and as a base for your own PHP projects. Some of the main topics we covered included session variables, uploading files, date and time problems, and common PHP errors.

Top PHP Questions

11

12

In this Chapter

- Database connection strings

- E-mail in ASP

- Common ASP problems

Author: Drew McLellan

Top ASP Questions

ASP development holds many questions. In this chapter, we are going to look at some of the "aftermarket" questions that you may come across as you're building and deploying ASP applications with Dreamweaver MX. From dealing with hosting companies who don't let you work the way you're used to, through to web site visitors using language your grandmother isn't used to, we'll try to offer brief and practical solutions.

All the examples in this chapter make use of the most common scripting language used for ASP: VBScript. That said, there's absolutely no reason why the logic and principles of the techniques presented here can't be implemented in JScript or any other ASP-compatible language.

How Do I Connect to a Database Without a DSN?

Hosting companies can be real meanies! You've gone to all the time and trouble to build a cracking little ASP site using Dreamweaver MX. You've followed the tutorials and connected to your database using a system Data Source Name (DSN). You've come to upload your site, and your hosting company says, "Sorry, no DSNs."

Luckily, there's a fairly painless way around this problem that shouldn't involve any rewriting of your code. Because Dreamweaver is pretty clued up about how it uses its connections, all that data is stored in one place. You need to modify the connection to use what's called a "connection string" rather than a DSN. Once that's done, your pages will work just as they did *with* a DSN.

What's a Connection String?

A **connection string** is just a line of text that describes where your database is, what it's called, what type of database it is, and any security details needed to access it. The term "string" just means a bunch of ordinary text, so a "connection string" is a bunch of text that describes your database connection. The following sections contain some connection strings for common database types.

Microsoft Access

```
Driver={Microsoft Access Driver
(*.mdb)};Dbq=c:\mydatabase.mdb;Uid=admin;Pwd=pass;
```

As you can see, the connection string uses the following parameters:

- `Dbq` – The physical path to your database
- `Uid` – Your database users (can be blank)
- `Pwd` – Your database password (can be blank)

dBASE

```
Driver={Microsoft dBASE Driver
(*.dbf)};DriverID=277;Dbq=c:\mydatabase.dbf;
```

where `Dbq` is the physical path to your database.

Oracle

```
Driver={Microsoft ODBC for
Oracle};Server=OracleServer.world;Uid=admin;Pwd=pass;
```

where the parameters are as follows:

- `Server` – The name of your database server
- `Uid` – Your database users (can be blank)
- `Pwd` – Your database password (can be blank)

Microsoft SQL Server

```
Driver={SQL
Server};Server=servername;Database=mydatabase;Uid=sa;Pwd=pass;
```

This uses the following parameters:

- `Server` – The name of your database server
- `Database` – The name of your database
- `Uid` – Your database user name (can be blank)
- `Pwd` – Your database password (can be blank)

Microsoft Text Driver

```
Driver={Microsoft Text Driver (*.txt;
*.csv)};Dbq=c:\;Extensions=asc,csv,tab,txt;Persist Security Info=False;
```

where `Dbq` is the physical path to your database.

Microsoft Visual FoxPro

```
Driver={Microsoft Visual FoxPro
Driver};SourceType=DBC;SourceDB=c:\mydatabase.dbc;Exclusive=No;
```

where `SourceDB` is the physical path to your database.

MySQL

```
Driver={mysql};
database=mydatabase;server=servername;uid=admin;pwd=pass;option=16386;
```

MySQL uses the following parameters:

- `database` – The name of your database
- `server` – The name of the database server
- `uid` – Your database username (can be blank)
- `pwd` – Your database password (can be blank)

How Do I Modify My Connection?

The first thing to do before making any changes is to back up your site. This is really important if you're going to make any changes that can affect the whole site at once. Back it up, zip it up, and put it somewhere safe.

Dreamweaver stores its connection data in a file in the `Connections` folder of your site. It'll be called something like `myconnection.asp`. Make a copy of this file and call it `myconnection_live.asp`.

The first thing to do before making any changes is to back up your site.

Open up the new file. It will look something like this:

```
<%
Dim MM_myconnection_STRING
MM_myconnection_STRING = "dsn:myconnection;"
%>
```

All you need to do is change the last line to use your new connection string. In this case, you'll use an Access database:

```
<%
Dim MM_myconnection_STRING
MM_myconnection_STRING = "Driver={Microsoft Access Driver
(*.mdb)};Dbq=c:\data\mydb.mdb;Uid=;Pwd=;"
%>
```

Save the file. Now you have one file for making the connection via a DSN locally, and one for using a connection string on the hosting company's server. You need to upload `myconnection_live.asp` to the live site, rename it to `myconnection.asp`, and you're all set. Remember, you need to get the correct `Dbq` in order to locate your Access database succesfully.

How Do I Preserve Line Breaks from a Textarea?

The HTML textarea element is a multiline text box that allows users to enter large amounts of text. Of course, where there are large amounts of text, there are line breaks too. The first thing you'll notice about using a textarea in an ASP application is that when you come to display the data back to the page, all the line breaks get lost. So this:

turns out like this:

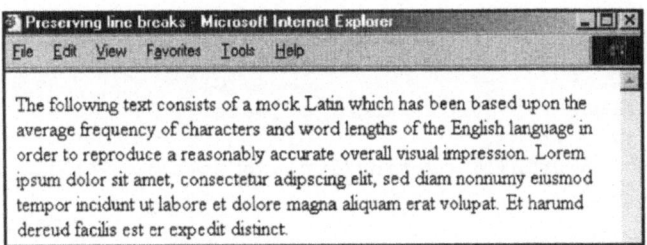

The reason for this is actually because of the way that HTML works rather than anything to do with your ASP. HTML recognizes any amount of whitespace, or line breaks, as being a single space. To combat this, you simply need to place the line breaks in the text in a way that HTML understands: the `<br />` element. This can be done with a simple replace statement as the data is being written back to the page. As a result, the following:

```
<%=(rs1.Fields.Item("comments").Value)%>
```

becomes

```
<%=replace(rs1.Fields.Item("comments").Value, Chr(13), "<br />")%>
```

What you're doing here is looking in the comments field of the recordset called rs1 for any instances of a line break (`Chr (13)`). Each line break found is replaced with a `<br />` tag.

Can I Prevent Offensive Language from Being Displayed?

There are lots of circumstances where you want your visitors to be able to post their comments on your site (discussion boards, guestbooks, and so on), but you need to make sure that nothing offensive is posted. One easy step toward this goal is to filter out any known offensive words.

The good news is that this is simple to do and uses the replace function you just learned about. The bad news is that you need to come up with a list of offensive words. Not a pleasant task!

 The good news is that this is simple to do and uses the replace function you just learned about. The bad news is that you need to come up with a list of offensive words.

First, you'll need to put this function in at the top of your page:

```
<%
function filter(txt)
dim aWords, i
aWords = Array("flour", "eggs", "sugar", "water")
for i = 0 to ubound(aWords)
txt = replace(txt, aWords(i), string(len(aWords(i)), "*"))
next
filter = txt
end function
%>
```

You'll want to replace our list of words with your own; otherwise, you'll unreasonably restrict site visitors from posting their cake recipes. Then in your page, replace this:

```
<%=(rs1.Fields.Item("comments").Value)%>
```

with this:

```
<%=filter(rs1.Fields.Item("comments").Value)%>
```

If your site is very busy or your page displays a lot of data that needs to be filtered, it would be wise to apply the substitution before the text goes into the database, as this would be more efficient than filtering each time the text is displayed. There's no reason that the same function could not be used at either stage.

How Can I Remember a Visitor's Name?

People like it if you remember their names. If your web site remembers your users' names, your users are not going to think they've gained a friend for life, but they may draw comfort from the fact that the site is intelligent enough to bother persisting data across sessions.

There are three basic steps to the process:

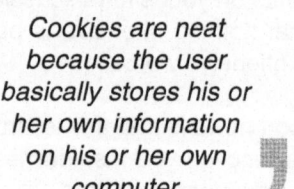

Cookies are neat because the user basically stores his or her own information on his or her own computer.

- Collecting a user's name
- Storing the user's name
- Retrieving and displaying the user's name

In this example, we'll store a user's name in a cookie. Cookies are neat because the user basically stores his or her own information on his or her own computer—you don't have to worry about keeping it in a database or anything.

As we're collectively as cool as cucumbers, we can do all three tasks on one page (`cookies.asp`):

```
<!DOCTYPE html PUBLIC "-//W3C//DTD XHTML 1.0 Transitional//EN"
"http://www.w3.org/TR/xhtml1/DTD/xhtml1-transitional.dtd">

<html xmlns="http://www.w3.org/1999/xhtml">

<head>
<title>Cookie cutter</title>
</head>

<body>
<%
if request.form("username") <> "" then
response.cookies("username").Expires = date+365
response.cookies("username") = request.form("username")
response.write("Thank you, " & request.form("username") & "!")
else
if request.cookies("username") <> "" then
response.write("Welcome back, " & request.cookies("username"))
else
%>
<form name="form1" action="cookies.asp" method="post">
What is your name? <input type="text" name="username" />
<input type="submit" name="submit" value="Go" />
</form>
<%
end if
end if
%>
</body>
</html>
```

The first time a user accesses the page, the user will see this:

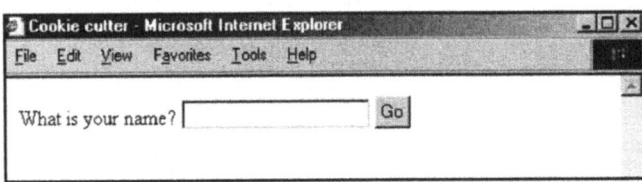

If the user enters his name as Bob, he gets this response:

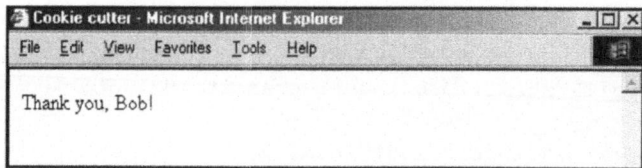

If Bob comes back to the page in a few days' time, he will see this:

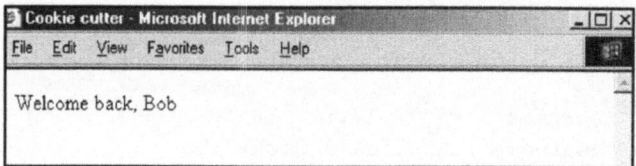

How Do I Create Tables with Striped Rows?

The standard Dreamweaver repeat region server behavior is very useful for pulling up big lists of data. The problem with big lists of data is that they can soon become unreadable and lines can become difficult to track from one side of the page to the other. For this reason, you often see data tables having alternatively colored striped backgrounds to their rows. This subtle trick makes it much easier for the eye to track from one side of the page to the other.

This subtle trick makes it much easier for the eye to track from one side of the page to the other.

It's very easy to adapt the repeat region code to offer striped rows. The first thing to do is to set up two new classes in your stylesheet, like so:

```
tr.odd{
color: #000;
background-color: #fff;
}

tr.even{
color: #000;
background-color: #ccf;
}
```

If you apply these classes to table row elements in your table, you can affect the colors in which they are displayed.

Create your table and apply a repeat region in the normal way. Looking at the source code, you should see a chunk like this:

```
<%
While ((Repeat1__numRows <> 0) AND (NOT rs.EOF))
%>
<tr>
<td><%=(rs.Fields.Item("pressHeadline").Value)%></td>
<td><%=(rs.Fields.Item("pressDate").Value)%></td>
</tr>
<%
Repeat1__index=Repeat1__index+1
Repeat1__numRows=Repeat1__numRows-1
rs.MoveNext()
Wend
%>
```

This is the repeat region loop, and it's the first `<tr>` element that you want to attack. You're going to use the modulus to work out if the row is odd or even. An even number will, of course, have no remainder, so you can use the following code to determine whether or not to stripe a row:

```
<%If (Repeat1__numRows Mod 2) Then%>
<tr class="even">
<%Else%>
<tr class="odd">
<%End If%>
```

So put together, the repeat region looks like this:

```
<%
While ((Repeat1__numRows <> 0) AND (NOT rs.EOF))
%>
<%If (Repeat1__numRows Mod 2) Then%>
<tr class="even">
<%Else%>
<tr class="odd">
<%End If%>
<td><%=(rs.Fields.Item("pressHeadline").Value)%></td>
<td><%=(rs.Fields.Item("pressDate").Value)%></td>
</tr>
<%
Repeat1__index=Repeat1__index+1
Repeat1__numRows=Repeat1__numRows-1
rs.MoveNext()
Wend
%>
```

How Do I Group Data by Its Headings?

While we are on the topic of aiding readability, imagine that you have a set of data coming from a database table that looks a little like this:

Appointment Date	Appointment Name
01-Feb-2003	Meeting with Jim
02-Feb-2003	Dinner at Rolly's
01-Feb-2003	Car in shop
05-Feb-2003	Meeting #2 with Jim
04-Feb-2003	Kid's school play
03-Feb-2003	Writing a big report
03-Feb-2003	Phone Mom
03-Feb-2003	Collect suit from cleaners
04-Feb-2003	Take dog to vet

If you were to pull this data out onto a page, you'd want to sort it by day so that it makes more sense. However, you would really only want to display each date once. So how do you group the data by its headings?

Sorting the Data

The most important thing is to pull the data out of the database in the correct order. Presorting like this will save you a lot of effort on the page. In your SQL statement, you want to sort the data first by the date and then alphabetically by the appointment name. Your SQL might look something like this:

```
SELECT appointmentDate, appointmentName
FROM appointments
ORDER BY appointmentDate ASC, appointmentName ASC
```

This would result in your data looking more like this:

Appointment Date	Appointment Name
01-Feb-2003	Car in shop
01-Feb-2003	Meeting with Jim
02-Feb-2003	Dinner at Rolly's
03-Feb-2003	Collect suit from cleaners
03-Feb-2003	Phone Mom
03-Feb-2003	Writing a big report
04-Feb-2003	Kid's school play
04-Feb-2003	Take dog to vet
05-Feb-2003	Meeting #2 with Jim

That's better, but it's still hard to tell where one day ends and the next begins. Let's look at that standard repeat region code, similar to the code you saw earlier in the chapter:

```
<%
While ((Repeat1__numRows <> 0) AND (NOT rs.EOF))
%>

<h2><%=(rs.Fields.Item("appointmentDate").Value)%></h2>
<p><%=(rs.Fields.Item("appointmentName").Value)%></p>

<%
Repeat1__index=Repeat1__index+1
Repeat1__numRows=Repeat1__numRows-1
rs.MoveNext()
Wend
%>
```

In order to decide whether or not to show the date, the technique is to compare the date to the previous iteration of the loop. As you no longer have the previous loop's data available, you need to store it each time you go around. We'll put it in a variable called previousDate, like this:

```
<h2><%=(rs.Fields.Item("appointmentDate").Value)%></h2>
<p><%=(rs.Fields.Item("appointmentName").Value)%></p>
<% previousDate = rs.Fields.Item("appointmentDate").Value %>
```

Next you need to enter a conditional statement around the line that writes the date, so that you only write it out if the date in this iteration is different from the last:

```
<% if rs.Fields.Item("appointmentDate").Value <> previousDate then %>
<h2><%=(rs.Fields.Item("appointmentDate").Value)%></h2>
<% end if %>
<p><%=(rs.Fields.Item("appointmentName").Value)%></p>
<% previousDate = rs.Fields.Item("appointmentDate").Value %>
```

The important thing to remember is that you should test against the variable first and set it to the current value second. If you get this the wrong way around, the code will never work!

Just to make sure, the final repeat region code should look like this (remember to declare `previousDate` before you use it):

```
<% dim previousDate %>
<%
While ((Repeat1__numRows <> 0) AND (NOT rs.EOF))
%>

<% if rs.Fields.Item("appointmentDate").Value <> previousDate then %>
<h2><%=(rs.Fields.Item("appointmentDate").Value)%></h2>
<% end if %>
<p><%=(rs.Fields.Item("appointmentName").Value)%></p>
<% previousDate = rs.Fields.Item("appointmentDate").Value %>

<%
   Repeat1__index=Repeat1__index+1
   Repeat1__numRows=Repeat1__numRows-1
   rs.MoveNext()
Wend
%>
```

How Do I E-mail the Results of My Form?

The main mechanism for gathering data from a visitor to your site is via a form. Once the data has been input, however, you need to be able to do something intelligent with it. There are all sorts of complex things that can be done with the data, involving database input and reporting, but if you're trying to keep it simple, the most straightforward thing to do is to send the results to someone via e-mail.

By default, Windows web servers come with a mailing tool called Collaboration Data Object for NT Server (CDONTS). You'll use this to send your e-mails direct from ASP. Some hosting companies use one of the handful of alternatives to CDONTS, but for sending simple e-mails, they're all about the same. Check with your hosting company and see what they've got; they should be able to point you to instructions similar to these for whatever mailing component they use.

Setting Up the Form

The following is a page with a simple contact form (`contact.asp`). As you discovered in Chapter 7, Dreamweaver doesn't always display every CSS property well, so be sure to preview the page in a browser.

```
<!DOCTYPE html PUBLIC "-//W3C//DTD XHTML 1.0 Transitional//EN"
"http://www.w3.org/TR/xhtml1/DTD/xhtml1-transitional.dtd">

<html xmlns="http://www.w3.org/1999/xhtml">
<head>
<title>Contact us</title>
<style type="text/css">
input, textarea{
display : block;
margin-bottom : 10px;
}
</style>
</head>

<body>
<form name="myForm" action="contact.asp" method="post">
<h1>Contact us</h1>
<label for="contact_name">Your name:</label>
<input type="text" name="contact_name" />

<label for="contact_email">Your e-mail address:</label>
<input type="text" name="contact_email" />

<label for="contact_phone">Your phone number:</label>
<input type="text" name="contact_phone" />

<label for="message">Your message:</label>
<textarea rows="6" cols="40" name="message">
</textarea>

<input type="submit" name="submit" value="Send" />
</form>
</body>
</html>
```

This is what you will see in the browser:

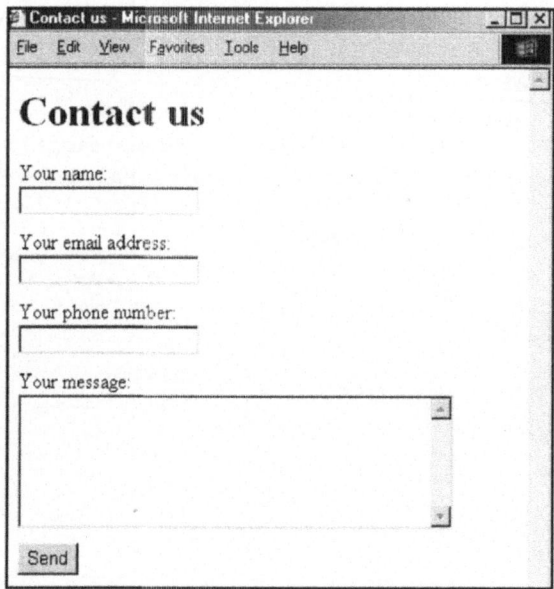

You need to place some ASP at the top of this page to check whether it is the first time the page is being displayed or the second time because the form has been posted. To do this, you'll just have a simple check to see if anything is in `request.form`:

```
<%
if len(request.form)>0 then
'our code goes here
end if
%>
```

All your "e-mail sending" code must go in the middle of this statement. Let's take a look at how you go about creating your e-mail sending code.

Creating the E-mail

Before you can state whom your e-mail is going to, or what it is to include, you need to create an instance of the mailing object. That sounds complicated, but it isn't really. This is how you do it:

```
dim objMail
set objMail = Server.CreateObject("CDONTS.NewMail")
```

This sets up an object called `objMail`, which is a new mail. It's just like opening a new e-mail window in your e-mail program—it's the empty shell of a new message.

You then need to specify who the e-mail will be sent to. This will generally be someone involved in running the web site, for example:

```
objMail.To = "bill.gates@microsoft.com"
```

You can also set the subject line:

```
objMail.Subject = "Contact from our web site!"
```

You'll make the e-mail come from the person submitting the form. To do this, you need to get the e-mail address from the form:

```
objMail.From = request.form("contact_email")
```

To make your code flexible for future changes to the form, include a loop to pick up all the information from the form and output it as the body of the e-mail:

```
dim strBody, formField
strBody = "Here are the results from our contact form." & vbcrlf &
vbcrlf
for each formField in request.form
if formField <> "submit" then
strBody = strBody & formField & ":" & vbtab &_
request.form(formField) & vbcrlf
end if
next
objMail.Body = strBody
```

All that's left to do is send the e-mail and kill off the object you're using in order to free up memory:

```
objMail.Send
set objMail = nothing
```

If you like, you can then redirect to a thank-you page, like so:

```
response.redirect "thankyou.asp"
```

Summary

In this chapter we have presented some of the common questions asked by ASP developers. There are a number of things you should take away with you from this chapter.

First, there are a number of different ways to connect to a database. If you can't use a DSN, you can use a connection string in its place. We looked at the connection strings of several databases to get a feel for them. We then covered how to replace line breaks with `<br />` tags that HTML understands to prevent multiline text input from losing its formatting.

Another topic we touched on involved how to use cookies to save, and later retrieve, a number of details about a user, including the user's name. Following this, we explained how to modify a repeat region to create tables with striped rows in order to aid readability. Since there are lots of ways of displaying data to make it easier to read, we also discussed grouping data by its headings rather than listing each heading multiple times. The repeat region code can be modified with just a few lines to make this possible.

Finally, we looked at one method of collecting form input by bundling it up in an e-mail. You can use CDONTS (or an alternative method if available) to send an e-mail with only a few lines of code.

In this Chapter

- Installing the ASP.NET Framework

- Server Controls

- Code Behind

- Page life cycle

Author: Kevin Marshall

Top ASP.NET Questions

To finish off our section on top questions, we are going to look at the most common issues that arise when using ASP.NET. More specifically, we will begin by looking at installing the .NET Framework followed by a look at server controls and a discussion on the technique of code-behind.

We also discuss the following topics:

- The web.config file
- Dreamweaver MX and Visual Studio .NET
- Events and a page's life cycle
- Various issues concerning ListBox and DropDownList controls

So, without any further delay, let's begin…

How Do I Install the .NET Framework?

Though installing the .NET Framework is relatively straightforward, there are a couple of questions raised on the subject:

- What version should I install?
- What are the system requirements?

Let's take a closer look at each of these points.

What Version Should I Install?

The .NET Framework is currently available in two flavors supplied free for download from *http://www.asp.net*:

.NET Framework Redistributable (`dotnetredist.exe`, 21 MB)
.NET Framework Software Development Kit (SDK) (`setup.exe`, 131 MB)

Although you can develop and run ASP.NET applications with any version, it is recommended that you install the Redistributable version on your production server where your site is publicly hosted and install the SDK version on your local development system. There is nothing to stop you from installing the SDK version on your production server, but under normal circumstances the production server is only required to provide the runtime environment for your ASP.NET applications, so it does not need the SDK's documentation or development tools. Some readers won't need to worry about the production server at all, as the company providing the hosting services will control this. By installing the SDK version on your development machine, you will gain the benefit from a vast wealth of documentation, compilers, development tools, and sample code.

What Are the System Requirements?

The .NET Framework can be installed and used by .NET applications with the following operating systems:

- Windows 98

- Windows NT 4.0 (SP6a)

- Windows Millennium (ME)

- Windows 2000

- Windows XP Professional

- Windows XP Home Edition

To build or run ASP.NET applications, the following additional requirements or constraints apply:

- Microsoft Internet Explorer 5.01 or later.

- Microsoft Data Access Components 2.7 (MDAC) is recommended. A free installer is available from *http://www.microsoft.com/data*. MDAC is used to allow programs and components such as the .NET Framework to access information in databases. It is worth noting that you can also obtain MDAC 2.7 as part of the Windows XP Service Pack 1 (SP1).

- Internet Information Services (IIS) version 5.0 or later (fully patched prior to installing the .NET Framework). You can determine if your system requires any patches (and also obtain them) at the Microsoft Windows Update web site: *http://windowsupdate.microsoft.com*. ASP.NET is only supported on the following operating systems: Windows 2000 and Windows XP Professional. Also, it will come preinstalled with Microsoft Windows .NET Server. Only these operating systems include a compatible web server to run ASP.NET.

Once you have verified that your system is ready to accept installation of the .NET Framework and you have downloaded the version of your choice, installing it is as simple as running the downloaded installer file and following the on-screen prompts.

How Can I Fix a Broken .NET Framework Installation?

A common cause of the .NET Framework breaking down occurs when you have to reinstall IIS for some reason not directly related to the .NET Framework. Doing so removes references to certain files and services that the .NET Framework configures within IIS during its initial setup. Once these references have been removed, IIS does not recognize the `.aspx` file extension used by ASP.NET pages, causing ASP.NET applications to fail. There are two options for resolving this issue:

- Use the `aspnet_regiis.exe` tool.
- Reinstall the .NET Framework.

You can use the first option if you have installed the SDK version of the .NET Framework or have Visual Studio .NET installed. Details on how to use this tool can be found at *http://support.microsoft.com/default.aspx?scid=kb;en-us;306005*.

If you only have the .NET Framework Redistributable version installed, the only option is to reinstall the .NET Framework.

What Does the Error "Access is Denied 'some.dll'" Mean?

At some stage you may start to randomly receive this error, where `some.dll` will be the name of a .NET assembly (DLL file) in the `bin` folder of your ASP.NET application. This is normally caused by the Index Server maintaining a lock on the assembly file in question. The best solution is to disable the Index Server.

To disable the Index Server, perform the following steps:

1. Go to *Windows > Control Panel > Administrative Tools*, and then click *Services*.

13

2. Locate *Indexing Service* in the list of services and double-click it to open the *Properties* dialog box.

3. On the *General* tab of the *Indexing Service Properties* dialog box, in the *Startup type* drop-down item list, click *Disabled*.

4. Click *OK* to exit.

If disabling the Index Server is not an option because you need to use it, you will have to exclude the `Temporary ASP.NET Files` folder from Index Server scans. To do so, perform the following steps:

1. Go to *Windows > Control Panel > Administrative Tools* and click *Computer Management*.

2. Expand the *Services and Applications* node, then expand the *Indexing Server* node, and then expand the *System* node.

3. Right-click the *Directories* folder, point to *New*, and then click *Directory* from the subform to open the *Add Directory* dialog box.

4. Click *Browse*, and then select the *Temporary ASP.NET Files* directory normally found in `c:\<WINDIR>\Microsoft.NET\Framework\v1.0.3705\Temporary ASP.NET Files`.

5. Under the *Include in Index? option* button, click *No*. Finally, click *OK* to close the dialog box.

6. Close the *Computer Management* dialog box, then stop the Indexing Services service by right-clicking the *Indexing Services* node and selecting *Stop* from the pop-up menu. Then restart it by selecting *Start* in the same pop-up menu.

Note: `<windir>` refers to the location of your Windows installation folder. This is normally found in `c:\winnt,` but if your Windows 2000/XP installation was installed as an upgrade to Windows 95/98/ME, then the Windows installation folder location could be `c:\windows`. The installation folder for the .NET Framework can also change depending on the installed version; yours may not be named `v1.0.3705`.

What Is a Server Control?

A **server control** is basically a tag you insert into an ASP.NET page that will output HTML into the page. When the page is run, the HTML output depends on the control being used. In the case of an `ASP:TextBox`, the resulting HTML equates to an HTML `<input>` or a `<textarea>` field.

The following `ASP:TextBox` tag:

```
<asp:textbox ID="TextBox1" runat="server" />
```

will produce the following HTML output in the client's browser:

```
<input name="TextBox1" type="text" id="TextBox1" />
```

Many server controls also contain complex logic that can perform common tasks relating to the HTML element they produce. For instance, `ASP:DropdownList` and `ASP:ListBox` render an HTML `<select>` to the client browser, `ASP:listBox` shows `multiple` items, and `ASP:DropdownList` shows a single item with other items in the list available as drop-down items. If `DropdownList` is bound to a data source such as a database table, the control will render all the `<select>` elements and `<option>` items automatically, saving you the trouble of doing so yourself.

Some server controls contain advanced internal logic that can output complex HTML structures. For example, the `DataGrid` control can be bound to a data source such as a database table, and it will render that data within an HTML table. It even has column sorting and paging capabilities built into it.

It's also worth mentioning that you can develop your own server controls or use those created by other developers in your projects. For details on custom server controls, refer to *http://samples.gotdotnet.com/quickstart/aspplus/doc/webformsintro.aspx#customctrls*.

What's the Difference Between Web Controls and HTML Controls?

A web control is just another name for a server control. An HTML control, on the other hand, differs from a server control in many ways, the most notable being that an HTML control does not contain any internal logic that affects the HTML output of the control. As they have no built-in logic, they have less of a performance overhead than true server controls. An HTML control can be defined as being any HTML element in your page that has an `id` and `runat="server"` attribute defined. Any HTML element can be an HTML control, and they are handy in situations where you wish certain HTML elements to be accessible to server-side code.

One such a situation might be where you want to determine whether certain elements of a page were included as part of the HTML sent to the client browser, depending on some condition defined within your code—for instance, removing a table row from an HTML table.

The following HTML table contains a row that is defined as an HTML control:

```
<table>
<tr id="MyRow" runat="server">
<td>this row is an HTML Control</td>
</tr>
<tr>
<td>this row is not</td>
</tr>
</table>
```

This row could be excluded from the HTML output using the simple instruction `MyRow.Visible = false`.

What Is a User Control?

The most basic definition of a user control is that it is an ASP.NET page that can be inserted into another ASP.NET page. User control pages are defined using an `.ascx` file extension and can't be browsed directly. They must not contain any `<html></html>` or `<body></body>` tags, and they also can't contain any `<form></form>` tags if the control is placed within an existing `<form></form>` tag of the host page. They can only be used within another ASP.NET page (a page with a `.aspx` file extension).

Normally, user controls are used for encapsulating common content, such as menu systems, into a single file that can be reused many times, thus allowing modifications to be made on a sitewide basis while only making changes to a single user control. You can think of them as being like a dynamic version of a Dreamweaver library item that can contain server-side code; you could also think of them as server-side includes.

Why Does Dreamweaver MX Sometimes Fail to Render Server Controls?

Sometimes when opening an ASP.NET page in Dreamweaver MX, server controls, such as an `ASP:TextBox`, don't get rendered. The problem lies in the method Dreamweaver uses to identify different types of pages (such as distinguishing an ASP page from an ASP.NET page). Dreamweaver looks for the `Page Directive` tag to decide if the page is an ASP.NET page or not. The problem is that it's a little too fussy about the format of the `Page Directive` tag. Take a look at the following two examples of `Page Directive` tags:

```
<%@ Page Language="VB" ContentType="text/html" ResponseEncoding="iso-
8859-1" %>
```

```
<%@ Page ContentType="text/html" Language="VB" ResponseEncoding="iso-
8859-1" %>
```

Although both tags are perfectly valid, as far as ASP.NET and the .NET Framework are concerned, Dreamweaver will only recognize the former as defining an ASP.NET page, because it only recognizes those tags that begin with the sequence <%@ Page Language. As you can see, the first tag does this, but the second doesn't. The simplest solution is to move the Language attribute to the front of the list of attributes in the Page Directive. Save, close, and reopen the page, and all should now be well.

How Do I Edit a Server Control's Tag After It Has Been Inserted?

After inserting an ASP.NET server control and setting some of the properties, you may wish to make changes to the tag. Unfortunately, the only way to edit the tag again is to find it in the Code View and right-click it. For instance, if you wish to edit an ASP:TextBox, the best method is to set Dreamweaver into split screen and select the TextBox in Design View. This will have the effect of automatically scrolling to and selecting the tag in Code View, as shown in the accompanying illustration:

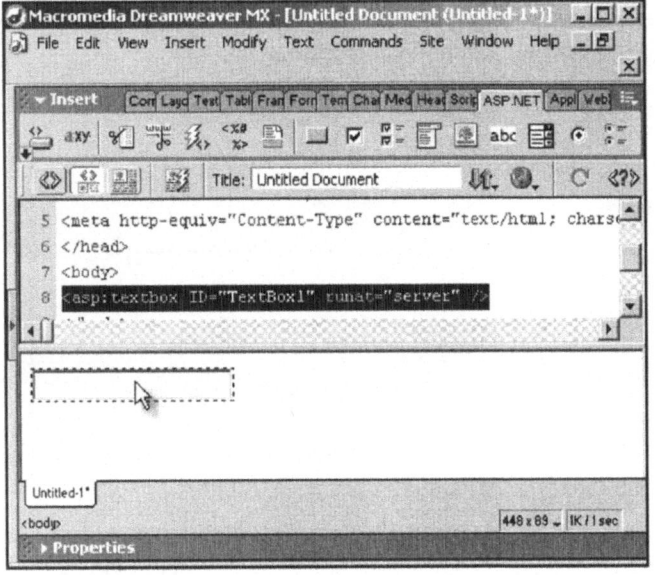

Next, right-clicking the `<asp:textbox` portion of the tag in Code View will result in the following pop-up menu:

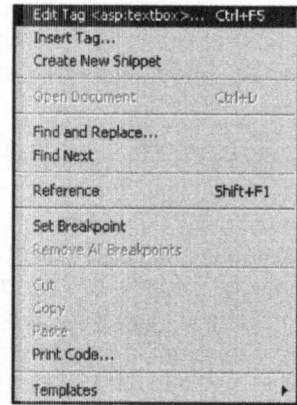

Select the first item on the pop-up menu: `Edit Tag <ASP:textbox>`. In the case of the `ASP:TextBox` shown in this example, the following tag editor dialog box defined for `ASP:TextBox` will pop up, allowing you to edit the tag:

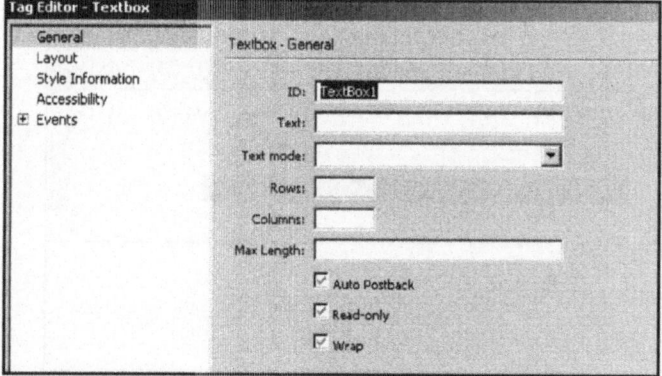

There are also free inspector extensions available for download at *http://www.webxel-dw.co.uk* to simplify this process. These extensions also simplify form validation by providing property inspectors for all the common ASP.NET server controls. This avoids the need to work in split screen mode all the time.

What Is Code-Behind?

Code-behind is a feature of ASP.NET that allows you to completely separate the server side code from the HTML portion of a page. It is implemented by holding the server-side code in a separate file from the HTML portion of the page. There are commonly two approaches you can take to implement code-behind:

- Using compiled assemblies
- Using a direct link to the code-behind file

Let's briefly look at each of these.

Compiled Assemblies

With compiled assemblies, the server-side code is compiled into an assembly file (DLL) that is stored in your site's `bin` folder. This is the default method employed by Visual Studio .NET.

Direct Link to the Code-Behind File

With a direct link to the code-behind file, the code gets compiled and cached for future use when the page is first loaded. The link to the code-behind file is defined using the `Src` attribute of the `Page Directive` tag. The `Src` attribute must be manually defined, as there is currently no direct support for `Page` directive attributes in Dreamweaver MX. This is shown in C# and VB .NET:

```
<%@ Page Language="C#" Src="yourfile.cs" ResponseEncoding="iso-8859-1"
%>

<%@ Page Language="VB" Src="yourfile.vb" ResponseEncoding="iso-8859-1"
%>
```

Naming Your Code-Behind File

A good habit is to name your code-behind file with the same name as the page that's using it, unless you have many pages with the same server code, which all share the same code-behind file. The file extension for the code-behind file should also be tied to the type of language used for the page: `.cs` for C# and `.vb` in the case of VB .NET files. This is useful in those cases where your ASP.NET application has some pages using C# and others using VB .NET.

What's web.config?

The `web.config` file is an XML-based configuration file for storing settings and other application-related information. A `web.config` file can be placed in any directory in your site. It can specify global settings when placed in the root directory of your site. You can also place other `web.config` files in any subdirectory of the site, so if a particular setting is defined within both files, then the setting in the subdirectory's `web.config` file will override the global setting for that subdirectory and any child directories that it contains.

The following is an example of how to store a retrievable key in the `web.config` file and how to retrieve the key's value for use in your code. This method can be used to store and retrieve any string value (for instance, a database connection string).

```
<?xml version="1.0" encoding="utf-8" ?>
<configuration>
<appSettings>
<add key="MyKey" value="this is the value of MyKey" />
</appSettings>
</configuration>
```

The line of code in C# used to retrieve the `MyKey` value is

```
string MyString;
MyString =
System.Configuration.ConfigurationSettings.AppSettings["MyKey"];
```

And in VB .NET it is

```
Dim MyString As String
MyString =
System.Configuration.ConfigurationSettings.AppSettings("MyKey")
```

In addition to the `appSettings` section shown in the example, many other sections are supported by `web.config`. For details on what they are and their uses and effects within your application, refer to *http://samples.gotdotnet.com/quickstart/aspplus/doc/configformat.aspx*.

How Do I Make My Site Use Its Own bin Folder?

There are a couple of good reasons to have your site use its own `bin` folder rather than the default location of `c:\inetpub\wwwroot\bin`. First, it keeps any assemblies being used by your site separate from those used in other sites. It also allows your site to be deployed to a production server, as a whole, using Dreamweaver MX's site publishing features. If your site uses the default `c:\inetpub\wwwroot\bin` folder, then any assemblies required would not be included when Dreamweaver publishes the site files.

Most developers building ASP.NET applications are working with Windows 2000 Professional or Windows XP Professional. When IIS runs on these systems, its default configuration is to use the folder `c:\inetpub\wwwroot` as the root web folder of the server. It does not allow separate dedicated web sites to be created, in the way that it does when running on Windows 2000 Server or Windows .NET Server. The reason for this is because Windows 2000 Professional and Windows XP Professional use a version of IIS not intended to be used as a live web server.

This means that most developers are using a system that really has only one true web site, `wwwroot`. As a result, many developers are resorting to storing their site's `bin` folder under `wwwroot`, rather than within a separate site folder. The secret to getting an individual `bin` folder for each of your sites is to define an IIS application.

Let's assume you have created a directory within `wwwroot` called `MyNewSite` and you want to make `c:\inetpub\wwwroot\MyNewSite` the root directory of the site, allowing it to host its own `bin` folder. First, select *Start > Run*. Then enter *inetmgr* into the dialog box and click *OK*.

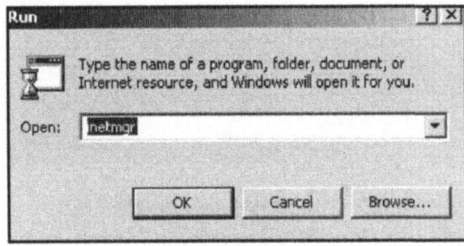

Next, in the IIS administration window that opens, expand the nodes in the left pane until you can see and select your `MyNewSite` directory, as shown in the following screen shot:

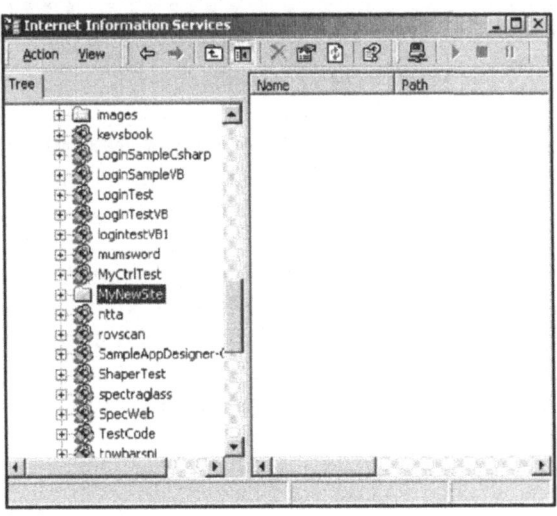

Now right-click the `MyNewSite` directory and select *Properties* from the bottom of the pop-up menu that appears. In the resulting dialog box, you should see a button marked *Create*, as shown in the following image. Click this button and then click *OK*. Your site directory will now be an IIS application.

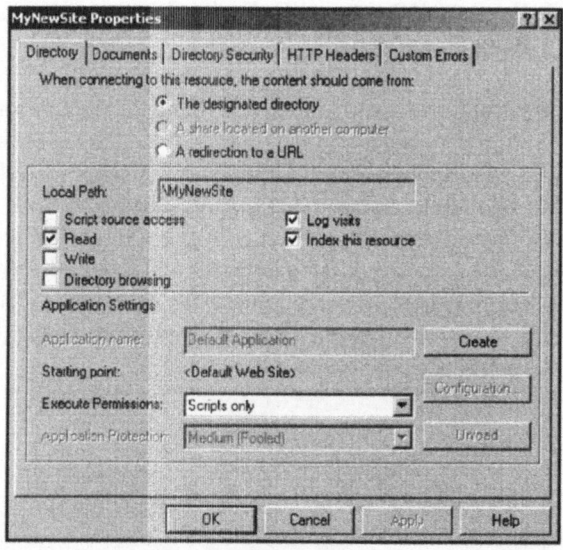

If you see a button marked *Remove* in place of the *Create* button, then your site directory is already defined as an IIS application. This could have been done by third-party applications such as Visual Studio .NET. Clicking *Remove* would turn it back into an ordinary directory.

Can I Use Dreamweaver MX and Visual Studio .NET Together?

A commonly asked question is how to use Dreamweaver MX and Visual Studio .NET simultaneously. The method we're going to suggest is our own preference and serves us well. You may decide to do some things differently, depending on your own requirements.

First, we should look at what each program is good at and what it's not so good at. Where manually writing code is concerned, Dreamweaver is as good as the next text-based code editor. Visual Studio .NET, however, excels in the code writing department and can't really be beaten for writing ASP.NET code. Visual Studio .NET is let down by its lack of flexibility and usability when it comes to visual HTML design, but Dreamweaver is the perfect tool when it comes to visual HTML design.

The approach we take is to do all our visual HTML design work and insert our server controls in Dreamweaver. We then write any server code we need in Visual Studio .NET. This way, we get the visual HTML design benefits of Dreamweaver and all the coding

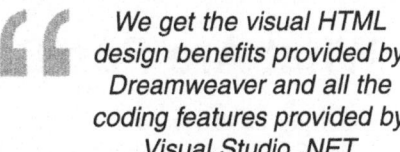

We get the visual HTML design benefits provided by Dreamweaver and all the coding features provided by Visual Studio .NET

features provided by Visual Studio .NET (which include automatic code-behind and compiled assemblies). Let's have a closer look at the process.

What Process Do I Use?

Begin by creating a new web project in Visual Studio .NET. This will create the appropriate directories and files, and set up the project as an IIS application. Then define a new site in Dreamweaver using the same directory that Visual Studio .NET created as the site's root when the Visual Studio .NET project was created. Now you can begin creating and editing pages.

There are a couple of things to point out when using these tools together. The first is that when you decide to include an ASP.NET page created with Dreamweaver into your Visual Studio .NET project, Visual Studio .NET will ask you if you want to create a code-behind file. If you select *Yes* in this dialog box, the page will not render correctly in Dreamweaver anymore. This is because of changes Visual Studio .NET makes to the page's `Page Directive` tag. This is easily cured by following the procedure outlined previously in this chapter, in the section entitled "Why Does Dreamweaver MX Sometimes Fail to Render Server Controls?"

The next thing to point out is that, when you insert a server control onto the design surface of a page with Visual Studio .NET, a declaration for the control is also added to the code-behind file. These declarations are required by Visual Studio .NET for compiling the application. If the page was created, or a server control is added using Dreamweaver, it will not add declarations to the code-behind file automatically. This means you have to add them manually or let Visual Studio .NET do it for you.

To make Visual Studio .NET add declarations to the code-behind file for those server controls not currently declared, ensure neither the page nor its code-behind file is open in Visual Studio .NET, and then open the page and close it again. Visual Studio .NET will prompt you to save the page (even though you did not change anything). This is because it automatically scans for server-side controls when a page is opened and updates the code-behind file declarations if required. Here is an example declaration for a `TextBox` server control in C#:

```
protected System.Web.UI.WebControls.TextBox TextBox1;
```

And here it is in VB .NET:

```
Protected WithEvents TextBox1 As System.Web.UI.WebControls.TextBox
```

13

What Are PostBack and ViewState?

You may have heard the term **PostBack**. This refers to the method employed by an ASP.NET page in which the HTML form on a page targets itself as the place to post its data when the form is submitted. ASP.NET pages have a Boolean property called **IsPostBack**. You can use this to determine if a particular request to the page was the result of a PostBack or a fresh request for the page. This can be used anywhere in your code, but it is typically used within the Page_Load method. The following examples of code show how this works. First, here it is in C#:

```
<script runat="server">
protected void Page_Load(Object Src, EventArgs E)
{
if(Page.IsPostBack)
{
//This page view is the result of a Post Back
}
else
{
//This page view is the result of a fresh request
}
}
</script>
```

And here it is in VB .NET:

```
<script runat="server">
Sub Page_Load(Src As Object, E As EventArgs)
If Page.IsPostBack Then
'This page view is the result of a Post Back
Else
'This page view is the result of a fresh request
End If
End Sub
</script>
```

As shown, ASP.NET makes it easy to detect if the page is the result of a PostBack or not. You may be asking yourself, "What's useful about making a form post to the same page?" This question brings us nicely to the next part of this section, the **ViewState**.

The ViewState is a mechanism employed by ASP.NET pages to persist user-specific data and the state of server controls on round-trips to the server. If you post an ASP.NET form with an ASP:TextBox control on the page, the TextBox control will automatically retain its value without your having to provide any of the logic required for this to happen.

This is useful when a user submits a form and is notified by the page that handles the form post data that he or she did not fill in some of the fields correctly. The user then goes back to the form only to find he or she needs to fill in all the fields again and not just the problem fields. ASP.NET's method of forms posting to the same page and maintaining control state using ViewState avoids this.

The way ASP.NET does this is by using a hidden field called __VIEWSTATE. This field is inserted into the form automatically on every page request. Its value stores all the captured values from all the server controls on the page at the point the form was last submitted. When the page is rebuilt after a PostBack, the values in the ViewState corresponding to each server control are extracted and applied to the respective control automatically. DropDownLists even remember which option was selected when the form was posted.

The following is an example of the ViewState field from a page containing an ASP:TextBox and an ASP:Button after the form was posted, as seen when viewing the source in the browser:

```
<input type="hidden" name="__VIEWSTATE"
value="dDwxNDg5OTk5MzM7Oz5DOQ91pKZrZi1cIT9g9ong/8hfcg==" />
```

As you can see, the value of the ViewState field is encrypted. In some cases, the ViewState field can get quite large (especially when you use lots of server controls on the page), and you may not want this in your page, or you may not require the functionality ViewState provides. In these cases, you can switch the ViewState off for the entire page or even for individual server controls with the EnableViewState property. This property can be applied to the page or to individual controls. The default value for EnableViewState is True, so to turn it off you need only add EnableViewState="False" to any control to switch its ViewState off. Alternatively, by applying EnableViewState="False" to the page directive, you can switch ViewState off for the whole page and all the server controls on it:

```
<%@ Page Language="C#" enableViewState="False" ContentType="text/html"
%>
```

Why Must Some Server Controls Be Placed Within a Form?

The ViewState, and how it tracks and persists server control values on round-trips to the server, is the reason many server controls such as ASP:TextBox must be placed inside an HTML <form> tag with a runat="server" attribute. ASP.NET needs to know where to place the hidden ViewState field. The field has to be inside a form. This is to ensure that it is included in the next form post, allowing its contents to be compared to the other control values and to determine if any of those values have changed. This is how ASP.NET knows when a control value was changed and that it must raise the appropriate events.

Events? A Page's Life Cycle? What's That About?

Events are among the most misunderstood features of ASP.NET, but they are also one of its most powerful. We need to briefly cover the execution life cycle of an ASP.NET page before we can explain events properly, though. When an ASP.NET page loads, there are many things going on behind the scenes of which you should have a basic understanding to get the most out of developing ASP.NET applications.

 When an ASP.NET page loads, there are many things going on behind the scenes of which you should have a basic understanding to get the most out of developing ASP.NET applications.

The Life Cycle of a Page

Here we will only cover the main stages in a page's execution life cycle. There are many more, but the stages we cover here and the order in which they occur are the basic information you should understand. For a more detailed description on the page life cycle, refer to *http://www.15seconds.com/issue/020102.htm*.

There is an example page highlighting the event flow included in the source files for this book (available from the apress site at *http://www.apress.com*). Look at the files `EventsCsharp.aspx` and `EventsVB.aspx`.

- `OnInit` – `OnInit` is the first notable event to be raised during the page's life cycle. At this point, all server controls on the page are initialized with their property values. Any changes to these as the result of a PostBack are not applied to the controls at this time.

- `OnLoad` – The `OnLoad` event is the next event to be raised and it is also the most important event of them all. A major part of your development work as an ASP.NET developer will involve this event. It is the most common place for the majority of your code. All server controls will have their PostBack values applied at this point.

- `PostBack Events` – This is where all your PostBack-related events such as `Button_Clicks` and `DropDownList_Change` events are raised. This stage is only performed if the page's IsPostBack check returns True.

- `OnPreRender` – The `OnPreRender` event is raised next. This is the last chance you will have to change any page or server control property values before the page's content gets sent to the client browser.

- `OnUnload` – The last event to be raised is `OnUnload`. This is where you should destroy any unmanaged object references and close any open databases. You can no longer affect the page's content at this point, because the response stream has already been sent to the client browser.

As each event of the page is processed, that particular event performs a hidden call to any relevant event of its server controls. For instance, server controls also have `OnLoad` and `OnPreRender` event methods. When the page's `OnLoad` method runs, it calls the `OnLoad` method of any of its child controls. If a child control has child controls of its own, then its `OnLoad` method calls the `OnLoad` method of its child controls, causing cascading calls to all `OnLoad` methods from the top of the control tree (the page) to the bottom. All `OnLoad` methods of all controls are called in this way before the top-level page execution moves to the next stage.

Events

Now you have a basic insight into what is happening behind the scenes when a page is loading, we can take a look at how events can be used. Understanding events is crucial to getting the most out of ASP.NET development. If you have any experience with ASP or similar server-side programming, you will have to disconnect your mind from the inflexible linear approach to execution flow taken by these technologies. Most server-side technologies execute your code line by line from the top down—ASP.NET is far more flexible in this respect.

Understanding events is crucial to getting the most out of ASP.NET development.

Imagine you needed to decide whether to run some of your own code depending on whether or not the user had changed the text value in an `ASP:TextBox`. ASP.NET gives you a built-in mechanism to catch this event and handle it any way you wish. When the page first loads, the current value of the `TextBox` gets stored in the page's ViewState. When the user has changed the value of the `TextBox` and posts the form, ASP.NET knows the value has changed because the posted value is different from the ViewState value.

Only once it has deduced that the value has changed will the page raise the `TextChanged` event of the `TextBox` control. If you have defined a method to be executed when this event is raised, the page execution will pause while that method is executed. Once this method has completed its execution, it passes control back to the page, which then continues its execution. This is a very powerful way of operating, and it is completely different from the linear execution flow employed in most other server-side technologies.

So you are probably wondering how you would go about defining a method within Dreamweaver MX to be executed for a specific event. That's a lot simpler than it sounds. First, you decide on a name for your method. In the case of your `TextBox`'s `TextChanged` event, call your method `TextBox1_TextChanged`, with `TextBox1` being the `id` of the `TextBox` and `TextChanged` being the event it handles. This naming convention will make it simpler to remind yourself what this method does when you're looking at the code months later.

13

On the `TextBox`'s tag, set the `OnTextChanged` property of the control to the chosen name for your method. This tells the page you want to execute the `TextBox1_TextChanged` method when the `TextBox`'s `TextChanged` event is raised, like so:

```
<asp:textbox ID="TextBox1" OnTextChanged="TextBox1_TextChanged"
runat="server" />
```

Then create the `TextBox1_TextChanged` method in the top of the page. Like this in C#:

```
<script runat="server">
void TextBox1_TextChanged(object sender, System.EventArgs e)
{
//your code here
}
</script>
```

and like this in VB .NET:

```
<script runat="server">
Sub TextBox1_TextChanged(ByVal sender As Object, ByVal e As
System.EventArgs)
'your code here
End Sub
</script>
```

And that's it. Any code you put in place inside the `TextBox1_TextChanged` method will be executed when the page raises the PostBack events during its execution life cycle.

When Do I Use <%# %> Instead of <%= %>?

There is often much confusion about what the `<%# %>` server tags are for and when to use them. These tags are **DataBinding** tags and they are only evaluated when the page or control containing the tag (container) has its `DataBind` method called. The `DataBind` method is normally called from the `Page_Load` event like this (in C#):

```
protected void Page_Load(Object Src, EventArgs E) {
DataBind();
}
```

and like this in VB .NET:

```
Protected Sub Page_Load(Src As Object, E As EventArgs)
DataBind()
End Sub
```

The following example tag is an `ASP:Label` with its `Text` property bound to the `Text` property of the selected item of a `DropDownList` called `DropDownList1`.

```
<asp:label ID="Label1" runat="server" Text="<%#
DropDownList1.SelectedItem.Text %>"></asp:label>
```

To see a complete working example of this, see the pages `DatabindingCsharp.aspx` or `DatabindingVB.aspx`.

When the `DataBind` method is called in a container such as a page or control, that container object calls the `DataBind` of any of its own child controls, and those controls do the same with any of their own child controls, propagating the `DataBind` calls down the control tree. When this is happening, any `<%# %>` type tags found are evaluated and replaced with the resulting value.

The `<%= %>` syntax is just shorthand for `Response.Write`, which is used to write text data to the response stream, so the alternatives `Response.Write("Hello World")` and `<%= "Hello World" %>` achieve identical results.

Why Does the Selected Item of a DropDownList or ListBox Get Lost on a PostBack?

This is a very common problem and is caused by how `Datasets` and data bindings are implemented within Dreamweaver MX. Dreamweaver uses its own `MM:PageBind` tag, which is implemented as a user control. The following is an example of the default `MM:PageBind` inserted when you define a `Dataset` in Dreamweaver:

```
<MM:PageBind runat="server" PostBackBind="True" />
```

This is what is responsible for initiating the data binding on all the controls on the page, including the `DropDownList`. What's happening is that the data binding routines are being called on every page request (even on a PostBack), so no matter what value you select, the list is being repopulated, losing the selected item. The cure is to set the `PostBackBind` property of this tag to `False`:

```
<MM:PageBind runat="server" PostBackBind="False" />
```

This will cure the problem of losing the selected item of `ListBox` and `DropDownList` controls. There is, however, a side effect: the `Dataset` will not be populated with data on a PostBack.

Unlike the `ListBox` and `DropDownList` controls, the `Dataset` will not persist its data on a PostBack since the `MM:PageBind` method of handling data binding is a bit crude and offers little control over whether a control gets data bound and when the binding occurs. The only solution is to remove the `MM:PageBind` tag completely and call the `DataBind` method from the `page_load` event.

It's best to avoid using `MM:PageBind` if you can. To avoid using the `MM:PageBind` tag, all you need to do is build your page using the built-in Dreamweaver MX behaviors as normal, and then manually remove any `MM:PageBind` tags. You can then manually control the data binding from your code as shown in the next example. This example assumes a page containing a `DataSet` with an `id` of `DataSet1`, an `ASP:DropDownList` with an `id` of `DropDownList1`, and an `ASP:Label` with an `id` of `Label1`. Here it is in C#:

```
<script runat="server">
protected void Page_Load(Object Src, EventArgs E)
{
this.DataSet1.DataBind();
if(!Page.IsPostBack)
{
this.DropDownList1.DataBind();
}
else
{
this.Label1.DataBind();
}
}
</script>
```

Here it is in VB .NET:

```
<script runat="server">
Sub Page_Load(Src As Object, E As EventArgs)
Me.DataSet1.DataBind()
If Not Page.IsPostBack Then
Me.DropDownList1.DataBind()
Else
Me.Label1.DataBind()
End If
End Sub
</script>
```

As you can see, the first line within the `Page_Load` method called the `DataBind` method of the `DataSet`. Then you check whether the page results from `IsPostBack` with this line (first in C#, then in VB .NET):

```
if(!Page.IsPostBack)
```

```
If Not Page.IsPostBack Then
```

If the page is not the result of a PostBack, meaning it's the user's first visit to the page, you call the DataBind method of the DropDownList to populate its items collection, like so:

```
this.Label1.DataBind();
```

```
Me.Label1.DataBind()
```

On the other hand, if the page is the result of PostBack, meaning the user has submitted the form, you don't fill the Items collection again but instead you call the DataBind method of the label Label to display the Text value of the selected item:

```
this.DropDownList1.DataBind();
```

```
Me.DropDownList1.DataBind()
```

How Can I Insert an Item into a Data-Bound DropDownList or ListBox?

We have seen many complaints about items manually defined in a ListBox or DropDownList control being lost when the control is bound to a data source. The reason is that, when the DataBind method is called and applied to these controls, the items collection is cleared prior to populating the list from the data source. The secret to inserting an item at the top of the list, such as *Please Select*, is to insert it after the DataBind method has been called and the Items collection has been filled. The best time to perform this task is when the ListBox or DropDownList control's PreRender event is raised. By the time this happens, the Items collection will have been filled. The following example has a DropDownList with an id of DropDownList1 with a method called DropDownList1_PreRender set to be called when the DropDownList raises its PreRender event. Please note that the properties used to define a data source of the DropDownList are not shown here for simplicity:

```
<asp:dropdownlist ID="DropDownList1"
OnPreRender="DropDownList1_PreRender" runat="server"></asp:dropdownlist>
```

Then add the DropDownList1_PreRender method to the page containing the necessary code to insert the new item into the list. This method will be called automatically when the PreRender event of the control is raised. Here it is in C#:

```
<script runat="server">
void DropDownList1_PreRender(Object Src, EventArgs E)
{
System.Web.UI.WebControls.ListItem MyListItem;
MyListItem = new System.Web.UI.WebControls.ListItem("Please Select",
"");
DropDownList1.Items.Insert(0, MyListItem);
}
</script>
```

And here it is in VB .NET:

```
<script runat="server">
Sub DropDownList1_PreRender(Src As Object, E As EventArgs)
Dim MyListItem As System.Web.UI.WebControls.ListItem
MyListItem = New System.Web.UI.WebControls.ListItem("Please Select", "")
DropDownList1.Items.Insert(0, MyListItem)
End Sub
</script>
```

In both versions of the code, the three lines within the `DropDownList1_PreRender` are responsible for creating a new `ListItem` and inserting it into the top of the control.

The first line declares an object variable that will represent the new `ListItem` (once again, presented in C# and then VB .NET):

```
System.Web.UI.WebControls.ListItem MyListItem;
```

```
Dim MyListItem As System.Web.UI.WebControls.ListItem
```

The second line actually creates the new `ListItem` and sets its `Text` and `Value` properties:

```
MyListItem = new System.Web.UI.WebControls.ListItem("Please Select", "");
```

```
MyListItem = New System.Web.UI.WebControls.ListItem("Please Select", "")
```

The third line inserts the new `ListItem` into the top of the control's `Items` collection by passing zero as the position to insert the item at and passing the item you created as the item to insert:

```
DropDownList1.Items.Insert(0, MyListItem);
```

```
DropDownList1.Items.Insert(0, MyListItem)
```

How Do I Programmatically Select an Item in a DropDownList or ListBox?

In some cases, you may want to force the selection of a particular item in a `DropDownList` or `ListBox`. There are two methods of the `Items` collection class you can use to achieve this task:

- `FindByValue`
- `FindByText`

The FindByValue method will find and return a reference to the first item that matches the value provided, and the FindByText method will find and return a reference to the first item that matches the text provided.

The following example uses the control's PreRender event, as shown in the previous example, "How Can I Insert an Item into a Data-Bound DropDownList or ListBox?" If you haven't already done so, you should read that example first, so you are not left confused while reading this one. Rather than inserting a new item, this example will look for an existing item with a value of 26 and select the first matching item. If no items match the search, then no items will be selected. Here it is in C#:

```
<script runat="server">
void DropDownList1_PreRender(Object Src, EventArgs E)
{
if(!Page.IsPostBack){
System.Web.UI.WebControls.ListItem MyListItem;
MyListItem = DropDownList1.Items.FindByValue("26");
if(MyListItem != null)
{
MyListItem.Selected = true;
}
}
}
</script>
```

Here it is in VB .NET:

```
<script runat="server">
Sub DropDownList1_PreRender(Src As Object, E As EventArgs)
If Not Page.IsPostBack Then
Dim MyListItem As System.Web.UI.WebControls.ListItem
MyListItem = DropDownList1.Items.FindByValue("26")
If Not MyListItem Is Nothing
MyListItem.Selected = True
End If
End If
End Sub
</script>
```

The first line checks whether the page is the result of a PostBack or not. Normally, you would not want to select your item if the user has already selected an item in the list and posted the form. If you do wish to force the selection, even on a PostBack, you can remove this check (code presented in C#, then VB .NET):

```
if(!Page.IsPostBack){
```

```
If Not Page.IsPostBack Then
```

13

The next line declares an object variable that will represent the `ListItem` returned by the `FindByValue` method:

```
System.Web.UI.WebControls.ListItem MyListItem;
```

```
Dim MyListItem As System.Web.UI.WebControls.ListItem
```

Next, you call the `Item`'s `FindByValue` method, passing the value of the item you want to find:

```
MyListItem = DropDownList1.Items.FindByValue("26");
```

```
MyListItem = DropDownList1.Items.FindByValue("26")
```

If no item is found, then `MyListItem` will not be a `ListItem` object; it will be `null` in C# or `Nothing` in VB .NET. You must check for this condition before you attempt to select the item, otherwise an error will result:

```
if(MyListItem != null)
```

```
If Not MyListItem Is Nothing
```

If the `MyListItem` object is not `null/Nothing`, then you have a valid object reference to an item in the list that has a value of 26. You can now select it by setting its `Selected` property to `True`:

```
MyListItem.Selected = true;
```

```
MyListItem.Selected = True
```

What's the Difference Between an MM:DataSet and a True DataSet?

The first thing to make clear is that the `MM:DataSet` (the tag used by Dreamweaver to define `DataSet`s) is not a `DataSet` at all. It really should have been called something else to avoid confusion. The `MM:DataSet` is actually a user control that returns a data table—nothing more, nothing less. A real .NET Framework `System.Data.DataSet` is an object that can contain multiple data tables and maintain relations between those data tables. It can even maintain data constraints for defined relationships and is more like an in-memory database. The .NET Framework SDK documentation is full of examples on how to work with `DataSet`s—providing examples of this is beyond the scope of this chapter. Just so long as you're aware that the vast majority of example code found on the Web can't be applied to an `MM:DataSet`.

Summary

In this chapter we covered how to choose which version of the .NET Framework to install and how to install it. We also covered how to repair a broken .NET Framework installation. Then we looked at what server controls, web controls, HTML controls, and user controls are and what they are used for.

We also looked at why Dreamweaver MX sometimes fails to render server controls and how to cure the problem as well as how to edit previously inserted tags using the tag editor. Following this, we looked at code-behind and the `web.config` file. We also covered virtual directories/IIS applications and how they affect the location of your site's `bin` folder.

We also looked at a method of using Dreamweaver MX and Visual Studio .NET together. Then we covered PostBack and ViewState and how they interact with controls on a page to maintain state. After this, we discussed the execution life cycle of an ASP.NET page and its events. Finally, we looked at some solutions to common problems associated with `DropDownList` and `ListBox` controls and briefly explained why an `MM:DataSet` is not really a `DataSet`.

13

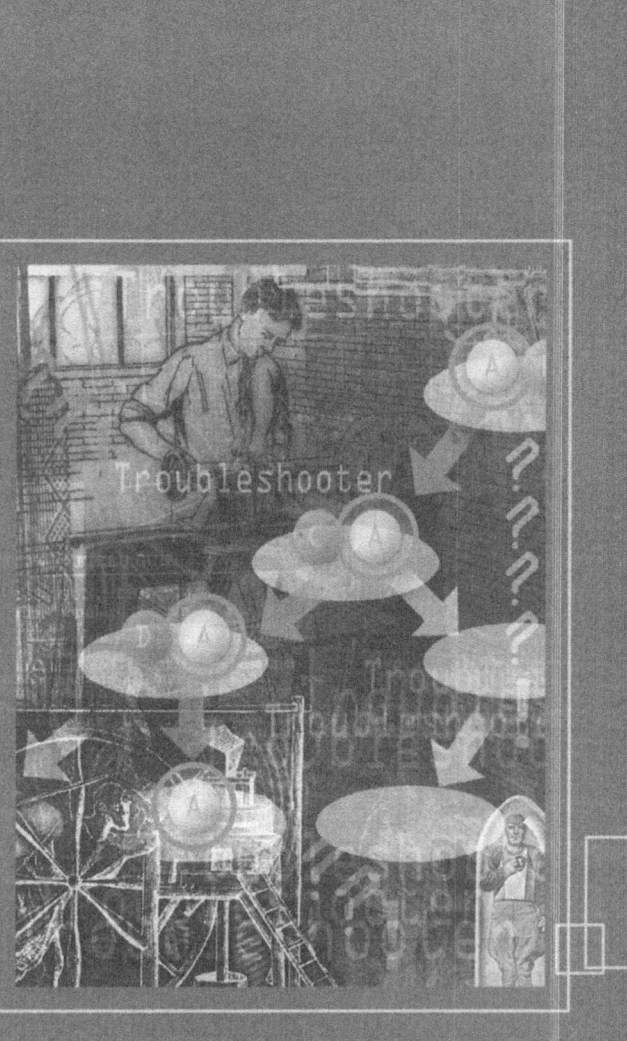

Index

A Guide to the Index

The index is arranged in word-by-word order (so that New York would precede Newark), with initial symbols ignored. Acronyms have been preferred to their expansions as main entries because they are easier to recall or to work out. Macromedia Dreamweaver MX has sometimes been shortened to DMX to save space in subentries.

sign, commenting out Apache modules, 72
15seconds.com site and page life cycle, 270

A

<a> tag restyling, 154
absolute sizing
  flow.html sample page, 208
  relative alternative to, 206
Access databases
  Access 2000 upgrade to SQL Server, 23
  candidate for supporting dynamic web sites, 22
  MySQL differences from, 109
  product catalog example database, 25
  using with ASP, 43
    sample connection string for, 238
access denied problem
  ASP.NET, 257
  MySQL using DMX, 133
Access Type setting, testing servers, 131
accessibility
  <blockquote> tags and, 194
  separating content from presentation and, 145
  web standards and, 181
Add/Edit Application Extension Mapping dialog box, IIS, 50
AddModule section, httpd.conf, 72
  troubleshooting the installation, 77

administering web sites using IIS and MMC, 40
administrative tools
  disabling the Index Server, 257
  MySQL databases, 136
ADO (ActiveX Data Objects) custom connection strings, 29
advanced site definition, 11-15
AllowOverride option, httpd.conf, 92
alt attribute not specified validator error, 197
ampersand character
  occurring as data, validator error, 197
  XHTML requires HTML entities in place of, 186
angle brackets, HTML entities in place of, 186
Apache online documentation
  Dynamic Shared Objects, 89
  list of available modules, 96
  online manual, 70
  running Apache as a service, 63
Apache web server
  configuration, 65
    checking using apachectl, 95
    checking without starting the server, 69
    compiling as an executable, 90
    configuring for PHP, 72, 100
    setting httpd.conf options, 91
  controlling using apachectl, 93
  downloading, 61, 85
  history and status, 59, 85

installing on Linux, 86
  DSO installation, 89
  testing the installation, 94
installing on Windows, 59, 61
  complete and custom installs, 63
  installing to run as a service, 63
  reinstallation, 70
  testing the installation, 68
installing PHP into, 70, 96
  testing, 76, 105
modules, 70, 96
  configuring, 72
restarting, 75, 104
static builds compared to DSO installation, 89
test page, 94
troubleshooting, 69, 95
versions, 60, 85
  downloading, 61
Apache.exe program file, 68
apachectl command, 93
  Apache troubleshooting, 95
  restarting Apache, 104
Application panel, DMX, 21
  connecting to MySQL, 131
  creating a connection using a DSN, 28
art programs
  see also Fireworks.
  creating templates, 165
ASP (Active Server Pages)
  checking page serving by IIS, 43
  connection from DMX for, 27
    custom connection strings, 29
  top questions, 237
    DSN-less connection to a database, 237
    e-mailing form contents, 248
    filtering out offensive postings, 241
    grouping table data, 246
    preserving text area line breaks, 240
    recalling visitor details, 242
    striping alternate table rows, 244
ASP.NET
  coding with Visual Studio .NET, 266
  connecting to from DMX, 30
  page life cycle, 270
  top questions, 255
    code-behind files, 263
    DMX fails to render server controls, 260
    editing a server control tag after insertion, 261
    events and page life cycles, 270
    inserting items into data-bound lists, 275
    installing the .NET Framework, 255
    loss of selected items on PostBack, 273
    making a site use its own bin folder, 264
    MM:DataSets and true DataSets, 278
    PostBack and ViewState, 268
    programmatically selecting items from lists, 276
    server controls explained, 258
    use of <%# %> instead of <%= %>, 272
    using Visual Studio .NET with DMX, 266
    web.config files, 264
  user controls, 260
aspnet_regiis.exe tool, 257
attribute minimalization prohibited by XHTML, 185
attribute values, quoting in XHTML, 183
attributes see editable tag attributes.
authorization failures, MySQL access from DMX, 133
auto margins setting, 214
AutoNumber fields, Access, 26

B

backing up
  MySQL databases, 135
  site definitions, 15
Balance Braces command, DMX, 230
banner styling, stretchable layouts, 211
basic site definition, 6-10
bcc headers, e-mail, 224
behaviors, DMX, selection failure when using templates, 176
bin folders, ASP.NET, 264
block level elements, stretchable.html navigation, 211
<blockquote> tags and accessibility, 194
<body> tag, editable tag attributes example, 173
Box category
  resizing fields using, 157
  resizing text areas using, 158

 element, replacing line breaks, 241
braces, parse errors caused by omitting, 230
browsers
  advantages of using CSS shorthand, 147
  CSS inheritance rule interpretation, 150
  CSS problems with older browsers, 159
  deprecated markup and future browsers, 180
  different appearance of pages in DMX and, 198
  forcing files to download, rather than open, 232
  quirks and standards-compliant modes, 198
  uploading files through, 220

C

case sensitivity
  Linux filenames, 114
  XHTML and CSS classes, 184

CDONTS (Collaborative Data Objects for NT Server), 248
centered content
  centering pages horizontally, 213
  Plasticbag.org example, 205
  Yahoo! site example, 203
CGI program option
  installing PHP for IIS, 46, 50
    troubleshooting PHP, 55
cgi.force_redirect option, php.ini file, 48, 55
check in/check out feature
  enabling during advanced site definition, 12
  enabling during dynamic site definition, 10
Check Template Syntax, 176
Clean Up XHTML command, 184, 185, 186
cloaking, 13
  by file type or by folder, 17
  file duplication and, 16
  new feature of Dreamweaver MX, 5
Cloaking category, Advanced Site Definition window, 13
Coates, Tom, Plasticbag.org designer, 205
code-behind files, ASP.NET, 263
  Visual Studio .NET and, 267
ColdFusion MX
  ColdFusion Administration panel doesn't appear, 35
  connections from DMX for, 31
  failing to restart the server, 34
color coding of editable regions in DMX templates, 164
  nested templates, 168, 169
columns, centering content in, 214
columns_priv table, MySQL, 123
command line operations
  see also DOS.
  installing Apache on Linux, 86

installing MySQL on Linux, 113

MySQL monitor, 119

Commands menu, Netscape Resize Fix, 213

commenting out

Apache modules, 72

php.ini files, 48, 54, 78, 101

compiled assemblies and code-behind files, 263

compression formats, 86

concurrent users, Access databases, 22

conditional statements and grouping table rows, 247

configtest argument, apachectl, 95

configure command, Linux, 90

connecting to databases, 21

Connection panel, DMX, and remote DSNs, 28

connection strings, 238

custom connection strings, 29

dwteam.com samples, 29

modifying DMX connection data, 239

OLE DB connection strings, 29

retrieving from web.config files, 264

using the Server.Mappath method, 30

connection timeout setting, IIS console, 41

consistency

advantages of templates, 164

separating content from presentation and, 145

content

see also centered content.

length and template use, 175

styling, in stretchable.html, 212

Contribute

Dreamweaver MX 6.1 new feature, 5

use of Design Notes by, 17

Contribute category, Advanced Site Definition window, 15

cookies

PHP session management and, 219

remembering visitors' names, 242

CREATE DATABASE command, SQL, 120, 136

CREATE TABLE command, SQL, 121

CSS (Cascading Style Sheets), 141

alternative stylesheets for Netscape 4, 159

alternative to using <blockquote> tags, 195

applying custom stylesheets, 148

centering pages horizontally, 213

custom classes, 150

Dreamweaver MX tools for, 146-148

editing stylesheets, 153

example stylesheet, 143

FAQ, 149-160

importing, 153

linking stylesheets to multiple pages, 152

problems with older browsers, 159

resources, 160

striped table rows and, 244

styling a banner, 211

styling forms, 156

styling links, 154

flexible layouts, 211

styling the content, 212

used for stretchable page example, 209

validating stylesheets, 153, 193

CSS Styles panel, DMX, 147

attaching stylesheets to multiple pages, 153

creating custom classes, 151

editing stylesheets, 153

CSV (Comma Separated Value) files and winmysqlprofessional tool, 137

custom classes, CSS, 150

Custom Connection String dialog box, 29

custom server controls, ASP.NET, 259

CustomLog setting, httpd.conf, 93

D

daemons
  see also Apache web server.
  xinetd program. 83
data binding
  problems from calling on PostBack, 273
  tags, use of <%# %> instead of <%= %>, 272
Data Bindings window, creating recordsets, 33
data corruption problems, Access databases, 22
Data Source not found and no Default Driver specified error, 34
data sources, adding new, ColdFusion, 32
data type setting in Access database Design View, 26
database connections, 21
  creating in DMX, 27
  DSN-less connection from ASP, 237
  FAQs, 34
databases
  accessing data from, 32
  choice of database to support dynamic web sites, 22
  components of relational databases, 21
  design, 25
Databases panel
  accessing the ColdFusion Administrator, 32
  connecting to ASP.NET, 30
  custom connection strings, 29
DataBind method alternative to MM:PageBind, 274
DataGrid control example of an ASP.NET server control, 259
datasets distinguished from MM:DataSet tag, DMX, 278
date and time problems
  finding dates in the past or future, 228
  subtracting dates, 228

date formats, MySQL and US, 226
date function, PHP, 228
  problems with, 226
DATE_FORMAT command, MySQL, 226
date2mysql function, PHP, 227
db table, MySQL, 123
DB2 databases, candidates for supporting dynamic web sites, 23
dBase databases, sample ASP connection string, 238
debugging and standards-compliance, 180, 181
decoration, removing underlining, 154
Default Web Site, IIS, 40
  changing web site properties, 41
    adding PHP, 48
DELETE command, SQL, deleting users, 129
deprecated markup
  HTML 4.01 Strict DOCTYPE and, 189
  standards-compliance and future browsers, 180
DESC command, SQL, 122
design changes and separating content from presentation, 145
design considerations
  basic template example, 165
  graphics, 206
  line length, 205
  measurements, 206
Design Note usefulness to single developers, 17
Design Notes category, Advanced Site Definition window, 13
Design Panel group, DMX, 147
Design View, form field changes not shown in, 158
development servers
  php.ini-dist file for, 47, 73, 102
  setting up Apache as, 65
  setting up IIS as, 37

transfer to production
    creating matching DSNs, 44
dimensions of elements, relative and absolute, 206
Directory setting and DocumentRoot setting, 92
directory structure
   see also folders.
   Directory Browsing Option, IIS, 41
   hosting additional IIS web sites, 40
   installing MySQL for Windows, 111
   listing files in, using PHP, 222
   PHP problems caused by spaces in names, 46, 71
   required for PHP, 97
   sapi subdirectory, 46, 71, 76
   setting paths for Apache, 86
     creating multiple directories, 88
     DocumentRoot option, httpd.conf file, 67
     installing PHP, 99
     ServerRoot option, httpd.conf, 66
   subdirectories required for PHP, 71
   symbolic links between, 87, 98, 100
disabilities *see* accessibility.
doc_root option, php.ini file, 47, 54, 74, 103
DOCTYPEs
   HTML DOCTYPEs, 187
   setting validator preferences, 192
   Web Standards Project and, 198
   XHTML differences from HTML, 183, 186
   XHTML DOCTYPEs, 189
documentation, using Design Notes for, 14
DocumentRoot option, httpd.conf file, 67, 92
Documents tab, Default Web Site properties, 42
DOS
   restarting IIS from, 51
   starting Apache from, 68
downloading files, forcing browsers to download, rather than open, 232
Dreamweaver 4 Site Definition window, 5, 11

Dreamweaver MX
  connecting to ASP from, 27
  connecting to ASP.NET, 30
  connecting to MySQL, 130, 131
    troubleshooting, 132
  connection data file, 27, 239
  converting HTML documents to XHTML, 191
  creating a new CSS stylesheet, 148
  creating recordsets, 32
  creating standards-compliant documents in, 182
  CSS tools, 146-148
  PHP version support, 97
  split screen operation, 261
  using DSNs in, 28
Dreamweaver MX new features
  cloaking, 5
  Contribute, new feature of DMX 6.1, 5
  new templating features, 163
  site definition choice, 5
DROP TABLE command, SQL, 122
dropdown lists
  inserting items into data bound dropdown lists, 275
  loss of selected items on PostBack, 273
  programmatically selecting items from, 276
DSN (Data Source Name)
  ASP database connections from DMX, 28
  DSN-less database connection from ASP, 30, 237
  using Access databases with ASP, 43
DSO (Dynamic Shared Objects)
  Apache installation using, 89
  Apache modules as, 72
  installing PHP as, 98
duplicating site definitions, 15
dwteam.com, connection string samples, 29
dynamic pages

accessing data from databases, 32

creating templates for, 174, 175

validating, 194

dynamic site definition, 8-10

server technology choice and, 9

E

ECMA (European Computer Manufacturers' Association), 179

Edit Sites window, 15

editable optional regions, DMX templates, 173

editable regions, DMX templates, 164

creating, 166

<head> section, 176

nesting inside optional regions, 171, 173

editable tag attributes, 173

changing link colors in locked regions, 176

DMX behaviors problem and, 176

editing files, dynamic site defintion window, 9

elements

closing empty elements in XHTML, 185

closing non-empty elements in XHTML, 184

HTML, as server-side controls, 259

relative and absolute sizing, 206

e-mail

multiple e-mails and script timeouts, 225

PHP and, 223

sending form input as, 248

sending newsletters using bcc haders, 224

empty elements, 185

EnableViewState property, Page directive, 269

encryption

MySQL passwords, 125, 127

ViewState field, ASP.NET, 269

entropy.ch site, Apache/PHP installation packages from, 109

error messages

2222 error, 134

access is denied 'some.dll', 257

Data Source not found and no Default Driver specified error, 34

HTTP error 410, 134

Microsoft Jet database engine cannot open the file message, 35

No Data Source or Driver Not Found error, 34

PHP make process, 100

error_reporting setting, php.ini, 74, 103, 231

ErrorLog setting, httpd.conf, 93

errors

common PHP errors, 229-232

headers already sent error, 231

parse errors, 229

undefined indexes or variables, 230

common validator errors, 197

unidentified errors, connecting to MySQL, 134

events, ASP.NET, 270

defining methods for, using DMX, 271

use in ASP.NET development, 271

explode function, PHP, 226

extension_dir option, php.ini file, 47, 54, 74, 103

F

FAQ (Frequently Asked Questions)

see also troubleshooting; top questions.

CSS, 148-160

database connections, 34

flexible layout, 213

MySQL databases, 130-137

Red Hat Apache Knowledgebase, 95

templates, 175

web standards, 197

field resizing using CSS, 157

15seconds.com site and page life cycle, 270

file extensions
   Apache recognition of PHP files, 101
   cloaking by file type, 13, 17
   defining new stylesheets in DMX, 149
   Linux text files lacking, 95
   user controls and ASP.NET pages, 260
file locations, MySQL installation on Linux, 117
file size and separating content from presentation, 145
file uploads *see* uploading files.
File View Columns category, Advanced Site Definition window, 14
file_exists command, PHP, 221, 223
file_uploads setting, php,ini, 74, 103
files
   editing, dynamic site definition, 9
   forcing to download, rather than open, using PHP, 232
   listing, from a directory, using PHP, 222
$_FILES array, 221
filtering offensive language from postings, 241
FindByText method, Items collection, 277
FindByValue method, Items collection, 277, 278
firewalls, protecting a web server with, 38, 60, 85
Fireworks MX
   artistic design of a site using, 6
   basing templates on designs from, 163
   use of Design Notes by, 13, 17
fixed-width columns, centering content, 214
Flash, use of Design Notes, 13, 17
flexible layouts, 201
   see also stretchable layouts.
   FAQs, 213
flow.html sample page
   absolute sizing, 208
   relative sizing, 206
FLUSH PRIVILEGES command, SQL, 128, 129
   troubleshooting MySQL, 135

folders
   see also directory structure.
   cloaking entire folders, 17
   making a site use its own bin folder, 264
   secondary folder use by remote servers, 16
   templates folder, 167
      link updating problem and, 177
font style, New CSS Style dialog box, 149
<font> tags and CSS advantages over, 141
footers, defining in Default Web Site properties, 42
form elements, XHTML naming, 186
<form> tags, placing ASP.NET server controls within, 269
forms
   DMX problems with forms information, 34
   e-mailing form data, 248
   PostBack and ViewState, 268
   styling, 156
   uploading PHP files through, 220
frames
   HTML 4.01 Frameset DOCTYPE, 187
   XHTML 1.0 Frameset DOCTYPE, 190
FTP (File Transfer Protocol)
   MySQL problems with Linux testing servers, 131
   problems caused by secondary folders, 16
   setting connections in site definition, 7
   testing connections in site definition, 8, 12
   troubleshooting DMX problems with MySQL, 132
future proofing and standards-compliance, 180

Get Database Path extension, 29
getimagesize function, PHP, 222, 233
Google Groups, 45, 70, 106

gotdotnet.com site
  custom server controls, 259
  web.config file settings, 264
GRANT command, SQL, 126
  MySQL online manual and, 127
graphics
  apache_pd.gif, 95
  stretchable layouts and, 206
  tiling, to produce stretchable layouts, 211
graphics programs, artistic design of a site, 6
grouping data in tables, 246

H

hash (#) sign, commenting out Apache modules, 72
<head> element
  editable region in DMX templates, 164
  modifying to carry <meta> tags, 176
  template parameters in, 172
headers already sent error, PHP, 231
hidden files, connecting to MySQL databases, 130, 132
  reading problems, 133
  upload problems, 132
Home Directory, IIS, 41
  adding PHP, 49
  setting under the IIS console, 41
host directory, setting in the site definition, 8
host table, MySQL, 123
.htaccess files
  HTTP error 410 and, 134
  overriding httpd.conf, 92
HTML
  ASP.NET server controls and, 258
  basic site definition, 7
  checking page serving by IIS, 42
  converting documents to XHTML, 191

creating static templates, 164
DOCTYPEs, 187
saving pages as templates, 165
sending e-mails as, 223
structured markup, 194
versions supported by DMX, 182
HTML 4.01 Frameset, 187
HTML 4.01 Strict DOCTYPE
  no DMX support for, 189
HTML 4.01 Transitional DOCTYPE
  DMX default, 187
HTML controls distinguished from ASP.NET server controls, 259
HTML entities, 186
HTTP addresses, Advanced Site Definition window, 11
HTTP Daemon, Apache precursor, 59
httpd.conf file
  Apache troubleshooting, 69, 95
  configuring Apache for PHP, 72, 100
  editing, 65
  troubleshooting PHP, 106
hyperlinks *see* links.

I

IBM Corporation, DB2 databases, 23
icons
  controlling an IIS web server, 40
  MySQL server traffic lights, 112
  pencil icon, Insert menu, 166
id attributes, required for XHTML images and form elements, 186
IE (Internet Explorer) version required for ASP.NET, 256
IIS (Internet Information Services)
  .NET Framework problems caused by, 257
  adding installed PHP to, 48

availability and versions, 37

defining an IIS Application, 265

installing, 38

  checking the installation, 39

  troubleshooting install problems, 44

installing PHP for, 45

  testing for correct working, 52

restarting after changing settings, 51

setting up as a development server, 37

web site administration, 40

  checking pages are served correctly, 42

Windows versions and, 265

IIS console

changing web site properties, 41

  adding PHP, 48

restarting IIS from, 52

IIS Knowledge Base, 45

IISFAQ.com site, 45

image location, Advanced Site Definition window, 11

images

  see also graphics; logos; icons.

  alt attribute not specified validator error, 197

  finding the dimensions of, 233

  uploading image files through a browser, 220

  XHTML requires naming with id attributes, 186

@import directive, Netscape 4 and alternative stylesheets, 159

importing, attaching stylesheets by, 153

include files, headers already sent error, PHP, 232

index server access denied problem, 257

inetd program, 83

inheritance rules, CSS, browser interpretation, 150

<input> tag, styling form fields, 158

install.txt file, 46

  for PHP, 71

internet daemon *see* xinetd.

IP address

  localhost equivalent, 43

  setting under the IIS console, 41

ipchains firewall, 85

ISAPI module option, installing PHP for IIS, 46, 50

  troubleshooting PHP, 55

Items collection, methods to force selection, 276

J

JavaScript

  link updating problem with DMX, 177

  validator errors, 197

  XHTML case sensitivity and, 184

JDBC (Java Database Connectivity), ColdFusion MX connections from DMX, 31

L

language attribute, <script> tag, 198

language attribute, Page Directive tag, 261

layers, value in design work, 6

layouts *see* flexible layouts; stretchable layouts.

libphp4.so file, 101

Library and Header Files package, MySQL, 115

line break character, text areas, preserving in ASP applications, 240

line height, Netscape 4 problems setting, 160

line length, design consideration, 205

linking, attaching stylesheets by, 152

links

  changing color in locked regions, 176

  styling, 154

    multiple link styles, 155

    tips for styling links, 156

  updating problem with templates, 177

Linux, 82
  administering remotely, 82
    connecting via Telnet, 84
    recommended software, 82
  configuring MySQL, 118
  distributions listed, 82
  installing MySQL on, 113-118
  MySQL inability to create sockets on, 134
  testing servers using, 131
Linux epoch date, 228
liquid design, 201
  see also stretchable layouts.
listboxes
  inserting items into data bound listboxes, 275
  loss of selected items on PostBack, 273
  programmatically selecting items from, 276
Liyanage, Marc, MySQL installation for Macs, 109
LoadModule directive, Apache web server, 72
  AddModule and, 72
  troubleshooting the installation, 77
Local Info category, Advanced Site Definition window, 11
LOCAL_ECHO option, Telnet, 84
localhost
  localhost equivalent, 43
  Network Domain equivalent, 62
locked regions, DMX templates, 163
locking down production servers, 47, 73, 102
  connecting to MySQL databases, 130
log files, Apache, locations, 93
logo.gif image, stretchable.html sample page, 210
logos
  see also graphics.
  using optional regions for, 171
looping and grouping table rows, 247

Macintosh, MySQL adminsitration for, 109
Macromedia Corporation *see* ColdFusion MX; Contribute; Dreamweaver; Fireworks MX; Flash; UltraDev.
macromedia.com site
  tech note on unidentified errors, 134
  templates and, 177
mail function, PHP, 223
mailing object, creating an instance of, 250
make and make install commands, Linux, 90, 99
Managed Data Provider, .NET Framework, 30
mappings, IIS application, 51
  troubleshooting PHP, 55
max_execution_time setting, php.ini, 102
McCool, Rob, HTTP Daemon developer, 59
MDAC (Microsoft Data Access Components)
  connecting to ASP.NET, 30
  DSNs and, 28
  version required for ASP.NET, 256
measurements, absolute and relative sizing of elements, 206
memory_limit setting, php.ini, 103
<meta> tags and templates, 164, 176
Microsoft Corporation
  see also Access databases; IIS; MMC; SQL Server databases; Windows.
  Technet site, 45
Microsoft Jet database engine cannot open the file message, 35
Microsoft Text Driver, sample connection string for ASP, 239
Microsoft Visual FoxPro, sample connection string for ASP, 239
microsoft.com
  aspnet_regiis.exe tool, 257
  MDAC download, 30

MSI installer downloadable, 61

Windows Update site, 257

mission-critical applications, MySQL suitability
for, 109

mit.edu site and templates, 177

mktime function, PHP, 228

MM:DataSet tag, DMX, distinguished from true
datasets, 278

MM:PageBind tag, DMX, problems caused by,
273

MMC (Microsoft Mangement Console),
administering web sites, 40

_mmServerScripts directory, 130, 134

modulus, detecting even numbered rows for
striping, 245

move_uploaded_file function, PHP, 221

MSI installer, 61

Muck, Tom, extension developer, 29

MySQL Control Center, 137

MySQL databases

backing up, 135

candidate for supporting dynamic web sites, 24

connecting to, from DMX, 130, 131

troubleshooting, 132

date format conversions, 226

FAQs, 130-137

administration alternatives, 136

backing up a database, 135

new user not working, 135

setting up a connection in DMX, 130

graphical administration tools, 136

online manual

GRANT command details, 127

restoring from a file, 136

sample connection string for ASP, 239

working with databases, 120

working with tables, 121

working with users, 123

MySQL monitor, 119

third-party alternatives, 136

USE command, SQL, 121

working with users, 123

MySQL server

administration, 119

downloading, 109

for Linux, 113

for Windows, 110

installing

for Windows, 110-113

library and header files, 115

on Linux, 114-118

mixing packages for different versions, 114

setup and configuration, 118-129

setting the root password, 119

starting on Linux, 116

starting on Windows, 112

version 4 status

for Windows, 110

mysql.com, third-party administrative tools, 136

mysql2date function, PHP, 227

mysqladmin command, setting the MySQL root
password, 119

mysqldump command, 135

N

names, remembering for repeat visitors, 242

naming conventions

see also symbolic links.

code-behind files, 263

CSS custom classes, 152

event handlers, 271

images and form elements in XHTML, 186

naming connections, 28

navigation, styling in stretchable.html, 211

nested templates, 167

nesting tags and XHTML well-formedness, 185

.NET Framework
installing, 255
    problems caused by IIS, 257
    Redistributable version and SDK compared, 256
    system requirements, 256
Netscape 4
    alternative stylesheets for, 159
    problems setting line height, 160
    resizing problems and their solution, 213
netscape.com site, on browser standards compliant and quirks modes, 199
Network Domains, installing Apache, 62
New CSS Style dialog box, 149
    creating custom classes, 151
New Document dialog box and XHTML compliance, 189
news items, template repeating regions example, 170
newsletters, e-mail, 224
No Data Source or Driver Not Found error, 34
notices distinguished from errors, 230

ODBC (Open Database Connectivity), ASP database connections from DMX, 27
    DSN-less connections, 30
offensive language, suppressing, 241
OLE DB connection strings, 29, 30
    connecting to ASP.NET, 31
OnInit event, ASP.NET, 270
online documentation, PHP, 77
OnLoad event, ASP.NET, 270
OnPreRender event, ASP.NET, 270
    inserting items into data bound lists, 275
    programmartic selection of a list item, 277
OnUnload event, ASP.NET, 271

opendir function, PHP, 223
operating systems
    see also Linux; Windows.
    supporting ASP.NET, 257
    supporting the .NET Framework, 256
optional regions, DMX templates, 171
    editable optional regions, 173
    nesting editable regions inside, 171, 173
Oracle databases
    candidate for supporting dynamic web sites, 23
    sample connection string for ASP, 238
overriding
    CSS stylesheets, 160
    httpd.conf settings, 92

<p> tag, example of styling, 150
Page Directive tag
    cause of DMX failure to render server controls, 260
    EnableViewState property, 269
    Language attribute, 261
    Src attribute and code-behind files, 263
page life cycle, ASP.NET, 270
page size and template use, 175
Page Title, editable region in DMX templates, 164
parse errors, PHP, 229
passwords
    automatic encryption in MySQL, 125, 127
    creating a random password with PHP, 234
    setting the MySQL root password, 119
Paths and Directives settings, php.ini, 74
pencil icon, Insert menu, creating editable regions, 166
percentages, relative sizing of elements using, 206
permissions see user privileges.

PHP
  adding to IIS, 48
    checking the application mapping, 51
  configuring Apache for, 72, 99
  configuring for Apache, 73, 99, 102
  configuring using a php.ini file, 47
  downloading, 45, 70, 96
  Dreamweaver support for PHP versions, 97
  installing for IIS, 45
    CGI and ISAPI alternatives, 46, 50
    checking correct working, 52
    installing extenstions, 53
  installing with Apache on Linux, 96, 97
    troubleshooting, 106
  installing with Apache on Windows, 71
  online documentation, 77, 106
    date function, PHP, 226
  top questions, 217
    common PHP errors, 229-232
    creating a random password, 234
    e-mail and PHP, 223-225, 226-229
    finding the dimensions of an image, 233
    forcing files to download rather than open, 232
    listing files in a directory, 222
    session variable problems, 217-220
    uploading a file through the browser, 220-223
  troubleshooting, 54, 77
PHP extenstions, 53
  consulting the online manual, 54, 77
php.ini files
  customizing the default file, 47, 73
  extensions section, 54
  location, 99
  session_save_path setting, 217
  troubleshooting the installation, 77, 106
  Windows Extensions listing, 78
php.ini-dist file, 47, 73, 102

php.ini-recommended file, 47, 73, 102
php4apache.dll file, 71
php4isapi.dll file, 46, 55
phpinfo() function, 53, 76, 105
PHPMyAdmin tool, 137
Pico text editor, 83
pixels and screen resolution, 202
Plasticbag.org site, 205, 214
Port option, httpd.conf file, 66, 92
ports
  for Telnet connections, 83
  list of normally used and free ports, 66
  TCP port setting under the IIS console, 41
PostBackBind property, MM:PageBind tag, 273
PostBacks, ASP.NET, 268
  loss of selected items on, 273
  PostBack related events, 270
PostgreSQL candidate for supporting dynamic web sites, 24
pound (#) sign, commenting out Apache modules with, 72
Preferences dialog box, DMX
  CSS Styles category, 146
  setting validator preferences, 192
presentation, separating content from, 141
  example stylesheet, 145
primary keys, setting in Access database Design View, 26
privileges see user privileges.
product catalog example database, 25
production servers
  locking down, 47
  php.ini-recommended file for, 47, 73, 102
  transfers from development servers
    creating matching DSNs, 44
projectseven.com site and templates, 177
Properties inspector, DMX
  applying classes to links, 155

applying custom CSS classes, 152

applying custom CSS stylesheets, 148

free extensions for server controls, 262

publishing, making a site use its own bin folder, 264

qslinux.org site, 85

quirks mode, browsers, 198

quoting attribute values

XHTML differences from HTML, 183

random characters, creating a password with, 234

RDS (Remote Development Service) connections, ColdFusion, 31

read_session.php file, 219

readability

grouping data in tables, 246

line length and, 205

preserving text area line breaks and, 240

SQL commands, 121

striped table rows and, 244

readdir function, PHP, 222

recordset creation in DMX, 32

Red Hat Apache Knowledgebase, 95

redirecting to a 'thankyou' page, 251

relative sizing

flexible layouts and, 206

margins, centering content and, 214

Remote Info category, Advanced Site Definition window, 11

remote servers

default DMX FTP destination, 15, 18

publishing to, 16

time determination problem, 18

use of secondary folders, 16

repeat region server behavior

grouping table data and, 247

striped table rows and, 244

repeating regions, DMX templates, 170

repeating tables, DMX templates, 170

Resource Limits settings, php.ini, 74

response.redirect method, 251

response.write method, <%= %> syntax as shorthand for, 273

restoring see backing up.

REVOKE command, SQL, 129

RPM (Redhat Package Manager), installing MySQL for Linux, 113

rpm command

MySQL file locations, 117

uninstalling MySQL, 118

upgrading MySQL, 115

Russell, Paul, on ipchains firewall, 85

Samba

administering Linux remotely, 84

testing servers using

problems with MySQL and DMX, 131

sapi subdirectory, 46, 71, 76

screen readers see accessibility.

screen resolution, 202

Plasticbag.org examples, 205

V-2 organization examples, 204

Yahoo! examples, 202

<script> tag, language and type attributes, 198

scripts, timing out when sending multiple e-mails, 225

scroll bars, avoiding, using relative sizing, 209

search engines
  accessibility and, 181
  separating content from presentation and, 145
security risks
  Directory Browsing Option, IIS, 41
  including session IDs in URLs, 220
  _mmServerScripts directory, 130
  protecting a web server with firewalls, 38, 60, 85
semicolons
  commenting out with, php.ini files, 48, 54, 78, 101
  MySQL command terminators, 119
  parse errors caused by omitting, 229
separating content from presentation, CSS, 141
  example stylesheet, 145
Server API settings, PHP configuration, 53, 71, 76
server controls, ASP.NET, 258
  declarations, Visual Studio .NET and, 267
  DMX failure to render, 260
  using DMX with Visual Studio .NET, 267
  editing a tag after it has been inserted, 261
  inserting items into data bound, 275
  PostBack and ViewState, 268
  programmatically selecting items from, 276
  requiring to be within <form> tags, 269
Server Model, specifying for dynamic page templates, 174
server tags, using <%# %> instead of <%= %>, 272
server technology, specifying, in dynamic site defintion window, 9
Server.CreateObject method, 250
Server.Mappath method, 30
ServerRoot option, httpd.conf file, 66, 91
servers
  see also ColdFusion; development servers; production servers; SQL Server.

dynamic site defintion and server technology choice, 9
dynamic site testing, 8
php.ini files for development and production, 47
protecting with firewalls, 38
protecting with firewalls, 60
runnig multiple servers, using different ports, 66
setting connections to, basic site definition, 7
specifying testing servers, 12
using Linux remotely, 82
server-side code, separating in code-behind files, 263
session_save_path setting, php.ini, 48, 75, 104
  PHP problems and, 217
session_start function, PHP, 218, 220
sessions
  checking the working of session variables, 218
  PHP top questions, 217
  problems caused by php.ini defaults, 75, 77
  troubleshooting PHP, 55
sessions settings, php.ini, 75
set_session.php file, 218
set_time_limit function, PHP, 225
shell prompts *see* command line operations.
shorthand, CSS, and browser accpetance, 146
SHOW DATABASES command, SQL, 120
SHOW TABLES command, SQL, 123
simultaneous users, Access databases, 22
site definitions, 5
  advanced site definition, 11-15
  backing up by exporting, 15
  basic site definition, 6-10
  duplicating, 15
  dynamic site definition, 8-10
  static site definition, 6
  top questions, 16

Site Map Layout category, Advanced Site Definition window, 14

sockets, MySQL inability to create on Linux, 134

sorting resultsets and grouping data in tables, 246

spaces
  avoiding in CSS custom class names, 152
  avoiding in database field names, 26
  avoiding in directory names, 46, 71
  blank lines and, header problems from, 232

special cases, CSS, 150

SQL (Structured Query Language)
  building SQL queries in DMX, 33
  sorting data for tabular display, 246

SQL Server databases
  ASP.NET Managed Data Provider, 30
  candidate for supporting dynamic web sites, 23
  sample connection string for ASP, 239

src attribute, Page Directive tag, and code-behind files, 263

standards bodies, 179

standards compliant mode, browsers, 198

standards-compliance
  checking a document for, 192
  creating compliant documents in DMX, 182
  effect on speed of working, 180
  reasons to embrace, 180-182

stretchable layouts
  building a stretchable page, 209
  design considerations, 205
  Plasticbag.org site, 205

stretchable.html sample page, 209
  styling the content, 212

striped table rows, 244

structured markup, 194

stylesheets see CSS.

swear words, 241

symbolic links between directories, 87, 98, 100

System Data Source Name see DSN.

tables
  grouping data in, 246
  MySQL databases, 121
  repeating tables, DMX templates, 170
  striping alternate rows, 244

tables_priv table, MySQL, 123

tag editor dialog boxes, 262

tar command, Linux, 87

TCP port see ports.

team working and standards-compliance, 182

Telnet, administering Linux remotely, 83

template parameters, DMX, 172
  optional regions and, 171

templates, 163
  additional resources, 177
  advantages and disadvantages of, 164
  ASP.NET connections from DMX, 31
  creating a basic template, 164
  creating for dynamic pages, 174, 175
  creating pages from, 167
  creating template regions, 165
  FAQs, 175
  including PHP session_start function, 220
  nested templates, 167
  uploading pages, not templates, 176
  validating, 176

Temporary ASP.NET File folder, excluding from Index Server scans, 258

Testing Server category, Advanced Site Definition window, 12

testing servers

  problems with checking off connections, 17

  problems with MySQL and DMX, 130, 133

  publishing to, 15, 18

  specifying the URL, dynamic site definition, 10

text areas

  preserving line breaks in ASP applications, 240

  styling using CSS, 158

text fields

  resizing using CSS, 157

  styling using CSS, 156

TextBox1_TextChanged method, example of creating methods in DMX, 272

textboxes, ASP.NET, editing in DMX, 261

tiling graphics, stretchable layouts from, 211

top questions

  see also FAQ; troubleshooting.

  ASP, 237

  ASP.NET, 255

  PHP, 217

  site definitions, 16

TopStyle editor, Bradbury Software, validating CSS, 153

traffic light icons, MySQL server, 112

troubleshooting

  Apache install problems, 69, 95

  DMX connections to MySQL, 132

  IIS install problems, 44

  PHP, 54, 106

avoiding spaces in database field names, 26

unidentified errors, connecting to MySQL databases, 134

UNIX *see* Linux.

unmask command, PHP, 221

updating, advantages of templates, 164

upload_max_filesize option, php.ini file, 75, 104, 220

upload_tmp_dir option, php.ini file, 48, 75, 104

uploading files

  file uploads seettings, php.ini, 74

  through the browser, 220

  troubleshooting PHP, 56

  uploading pages, not templates, 176

URL prefix settings

  problems with MySQL and DMX, 130, 133

URL prefix, ColdFusion, 31

URLs

  testing site, dynamic site definition, 10

USE command, SQL, 121

Usenet newsgroups, 45, 70

user controls, ASP.NET, 260

user privileges

  granting, 126, 127

  MySQL databases, 123

  removing, 129

user table, MySQL, 123, 124

users

  deleting, using SQL, 129

  remembering names and personal details, 242

U

UltraDev 4 Site Definition window, 5, 11

undefined indexes or variable errors, 230

underlines, removing from links, 154

underscores

  avoiding in CSS custom class names, 152

V

V-2 organization web site, example of thoughtful design, 204

validating documents

  common validator errors, 197

  DOCTYPEs and, 186

W3C validator, 193
  within Dreamweaver, 192
validating stylesheets, 153
validating templates, 176
variables, defining for SQL queries in DMX, 33
variable-width columns, centering content, 214
ViewState, ASP.NET, 268
visitors, remembering names and personal
  details, 242
Visual Studio .NET, using with DMX, 266

W3C (World Wide Web Consortium)
  CSS developers, 141
  CSS Validator, 153, 193
  web standards from, 179
warnings, notices distinguished from errors, 230
web controls *see* server controls.
web design characteristics, 204
web pages, different appearance in browsers
  and DMX, 198
web sites
  administering with IIS and MMC, 40
    checking pages are served correctly, 42
  defining default pages to be served, 42
  IIS one web site rule, 40
web standards, 179
  see also standards-compliance.
  FAQ, 197
  resources, 199
  standards bodies, 179
Web Standards Project, 198
web.config files, 264
webxel-dw.co.uk site, free extensions for server
  controls, 262
welcome messages, personalizing, 244
well-formedness, XHTML, 185

Windows Components Wizard, installing IIS, 38
Windows operating system
  configuring MySQL, 118
  installing Apache web server, 59
  installing MySQL, 110-113
  installing PHP with Apache, 70
  single root folders, 265
  testing servers using
    problems with MySQL and DMX, 131
Windows Server Operating System
  installing IIS, 37
winmysqladmin.exe file, 112
winmysqlprofessional tool, 137
WS_FTP program, 16

XHTML
  converting HTML documents to, 191
  differences from HTML, 182-186
  DOCTYPEs, 189
  naming images and form elements, 186
  structured markup, 194
  used for stretchable page example, 209
  versions supported by DMX, 182
XHTML 1.0 Frameset DOCTYPE, 190
XHTML 1.0 Strict DOCTYPE, 191
XHTML 1.0 Transitional DOCTYPE, 189
xinetd program, 83
XML declaration
  browser quirks mode and, 198
  XHTML differences from HTML, 183

Yahoo! screenshots, showing resolution effects,
  202